M & E HA

M & E Handbooks are examination syllabuses all over the world. Because each Handbook covers its subject clearly and concisely books in the series form a vital part of many college, university, school and home study courses.

Handbooks contain detailed information stripped of unncessary padding, making each title a comprehensive self-tuition course. They are amplified with numerous self-testing questions in the form of Progress Tests at the end of each chapter, each text-referenced for easy checking. Every Handbook closes with an appendix which advises on examination technique. For all these reasons, Handbooks are ideal for pre-examination revision.

The handy pocket-book size and competitive price make Handbooks the perfect choice for anyone who wants to grasp the essentials of a subject quickly and easily.

NOTICE TO LECTURERS

Many lecturers are now using HANDBOOKS as working texts to save time otherwise wasted by students in protracted note-taking. The purpose of the series is to meet practical teaching requirements as far as possible, and lecturers are cordially invited to forward comments or criticisms to the Publishers for consideration.

P. W. D. Redmond
General Editor

THE M. & E. HANDBOOK SERIES

MODERN COMMERCIAL KNOWLEDGE

L. W. T. STAFFORD,
B.Sc.(Econ.), M.Phil.,
Principal Lecturer in Economics at the City of London Polytechnic

FOURTH EDITION

MACDONALD AND EVANS

Macdonald and Evans Ltd.
Estover, Plymouth PL6 7PZ

First published 1966
Reprinted 1967
Reprinted (twice) 1968
Second Edition 1969
Reprinted 1969
Reprinted 1971
Third Edition 1973
Reprinted 1975
Fourth Edition 1977

7121 1399 1

Printed in Great Britain by
Butler & Tanner Ltd
Frome and London

PREFACE TO THE FOURTH EDITION

THE last few years have not been ones of great prosperity or economic success for this country but its real future depends on the ability and industry of those who are still young. One of the brighter signs, therefore, has been that a great number of young people are choosing to study Commerce, Economics and related subjects. Some of these students are taking the examinations of institutions such as the Royal Society of Arts and the professional bodies, others are studying at colleges of further or higher education, taking National Certificate or National Diploma Courses in Business Studies, while some are still at school studying Commerce as a G.C.E. subject. The emergence of the Council for National Academic Awards as a major degree-awarding body has added many more students who need to acquire a knowledge of the business world as part of their first year courses. It seems reasonable to surmise that courses in Commerce and Business Studies are popular because they are concerned with aspects of modern life that can be seen to be of direct and immediate importance. Few other subject areas are so closely related both to economic events which affect us all and to the ways in which millions of people earn their living. In this HANDBOOK an attempt has been made to reflect this relevance to modern life and to present the complex pattern of commercial activity in a logical way, so that the student can see how the various topics are related to each other. This fourth edition of *Modern Commercial Knowledge* also reflects continuing social, political and institutional change. While some of these changes are purely technical or organisational, others are a consequence of the increasing polarisation of political life. Thus, the passing of new legislation on industrial relations is recorded. Other revisions are the consequence of social trends which are largely independent of political movements. Greater emphasis on consumer protection is a case in point. A commercial trend which is evident is of a tightening up of procedures and an increasingly efficient and technically competent approach. Such a steady tendency towards modernisation is discernible in the commodity markets and exchanges. In other fields, there has been technical change but only a partially successful solution to very urgent problems. This edition of *Modern Commercial Knowledge* contains many references to changes in the field of inland transport, but a really effective and socially acceptable transport policy remains elusive. Problems in this area, as in that of banking and monetary control, are of especial difficulty, but in following the attempts to deal with them we can at least be aware that we are studying and analysing matters of real concern.

Keeping up to date. Any attempt to present a view of the current scene is bound to be inadequate to some extent. Events which appear to be of importance prove to be less significant with the passage of time, others which were thought to be minor changes turn out to have the most profound effects. No book can tell the student all he needs to know or wholly replace his own judgment. To keep abreast of events in the business world it is necessary to read a good newspaper and be aware of current developments. Gradually, the student will not only accumulate a fund of up-to-date knowledge, but will also begin to get the "feel" of commercial life. For a more extensive treatment than the daily press can give, he should read *The Economist*. Like other subjects concerned with the activities of human beings, commerce is as complex and various as people are themselves, so that in addition to wide and careful reading, the student will also need to be observant as he goes about his everyday affairs. As consumers, we are all involved in commercial activities at some time almost every day and there is much to be seen, noted and learnt.

Syllabuses. Because of the wide field covered, syllabuses tend to vary a good deal, as does the emphasis placed on the different topics by the various examining bodies. Students must familiarise themselves with the syllabus with which they are concerned and must make sure that their studies have covered all the necessary aspects of the subject.

Further reading. In addition to this HANDBOOK, there are a number of general works on commerce, such as: *The Structure of Modern Commerce* (Macdonald & Evans), and *Modern Commerce* (Pitman). It is also advisable to study some topics in greater depth. Those chosen will depend on the student's syllabus and his personal inclinations, but he may find the following books helpful:

Business in Britain. Graham Turner (Pelican).
Capital City: London as a Financial Centre. Hamish McRae and Frances Cairncross (Eyre Methuen).
The City in the World Economy. W. M. Clarke (IEA/Pelican).
Competition for Consumers. C. Fulop (Allen & Unwin).
Modern Merchant Banking. C. J. J. Clay and B. S. Wheble (Woodhead-Faulkner).
Money. R. F. Harrod (Macmillan).
The Stock Exchange and Investment Analysis. R. J. Briston (Allen & Unwin).
Hobart Papers (Institute of Economic Affairs).

Acknowledgments. My thanks are due to the following examining bodies for permission to use questions from the examinations shown:

The Chartered Insurance Institute: Commercial Practice (C.I.I.).
The London Chamber of Commerce and Industry: Commerce & Finance (L.C.C.I.).
The Royal Society of Arts: Commerce Stage II (R.S.A. II), Commerce Stage III (Finance) (R.S.A. III, F), Commerce Stage III (Marketing) (R.S.A. III, M).
City of London Polytechnic: Higher National Diploma in Business Studies, Higher National Certificate in Business Studies (C.L.C.).
Cambridgeshire College of Arts and Technology: Ordinary National Diploma in Business Studies, Ordinary National Certificate in Business Studies (C.C.A.T.).

I should also like to thank *International Computers Ltd.* for permission to reproduce material and *Barclays Bank Ltd.* for permission to use their balance sheet and other material. Once again, I must thank my wife for her help in preparing the manuscript of this book for publication and for her patience at my total neglect of domestic duties during the preparation of this new edition.

August 1977 L. W. T. STAFFORD

CONTENTS

PART ONE

THE ECONOMIC BACKGROUND

CHAPTER I

COMMERCE AND INDUSTRY

SPECIALISATION

1. Development of specialisation. In primitive societies people provide for nearly all their own wants. Agriculture is simple, but provides a family with its food. Rough clothing is made at home. There is little specialisation and little trade; each family is almost self-sufficient although the standard of life is poor.

Such societies must have represented man's first attempts at settlement after he ceased to be a nomadic hunter (and a few such societies still exist). Even in these early settlements there must have been some specialisation by unusually skilled individuals. The community would have been willing to support these people so that everyone could enjoy the benefit of their gifts.

The number and variety of special skills must have increased as settlements became more secure. Trade would have developed, money have come into use and elementary codes of laws have become necessary to govern the rights of parties to exchanges and to provide for the settlement of disputes. Archaeological and anthropological research has confirmed that an evolution of this sort did take place in early societies in the Eastern Mediterranean lands long before the birth of Christ.

2. The division of labour. The commonsense arrangement by which each person concentrates on the work he can do best is known as the *division of labour*. Even if no special gifts are apparent in an individual, concentration on a given task soon develops skills in excess of those of the non-specialist. The simple division of labour begins when individuals specialise in particular trades or crafts, as carpenters, shoemakers or silversmiths, for example. The advantages of specialisation can be increased if individuals concentrate on particular tasks within a trade. In a carpenter's shop, one man might be wholly engaged on turning chair legs while another made the seats and others assembled the complete chairs from parts already made. The productivity of the shop would be increased, but there would be some loss of *general* woodworking skill and the extra productivity would be wasted unless there was sufficient demand for the larger output.

This subdivision of tasks can be seen at its most striking on the production line of a modern factory, where each worker carries out some very small task usually with the help of specialised machinery.

3. Specialised services. Specialisation not only permits the more efficient production of goods but also makes it possible for the members of a community to have various *services* performed for them. The provision of an increasing variety of services is one of the marks of an advanced society. Such services include those provided by doctors, teachers, lawyers and entertainers, among many others.

4. Interdependence in modern life. Life without specialisation is meagre and hard. Specialisation increases productivity and provides a greater variety of goods and services, but this is achieved only by a loss of independence. This is very apparent in a modern society, where the pattern of life can only be maintained if everyone makes his or her specialised contribution. This interdependence is brought home to us forcefully when a key group of workers decides to strike or some vital service is interrupted by accident or natural disaster.

5. Geographical and international specialisation. Just as individuals have different talents and abilities, geographical areas have advantages which make them suitable for particular industries. These advantages may be purely physical, the existence of mineral deposits for example, or they may be historical in that people of special skill or industry have settled there. Britain's textile, shipbuilding or iron and steel industries are examples of such specialisation.

The international specialisation which is made possible by situation, natural advantages or climate, tends to make life richer and enables people everywhere to enjoy a wider and more plentiful range of goods than would otherwise be possible, but like individual specialisation, it leads to greater interdependence. From time to time this interdependence has led to dispute, as in the oil crisis of 1973–4.

Partly as a result of efforts to attain national self-sufficiency and partly because of the inevitable spread of technology, many of the emerging nations have developed quite advanced manufacturing industries which compete strongly with those of the more established countries.

EXCHANGE

In order to reap the benefits of specialisation it is necessary for each person to exchange the products of his own specialisation for those of other people.

6. Barter. One way of doing this is to arrange the direct exchange of one commodity for another or of goods for services performed. Barter requires that the person having goods to offer should find another person who not only requires his goods but has some desirable commodity to offer in return. This *double co-incidence of wants* is unlikely and barter is so clumsy that it soon breaks down in any but the most primitive societies.

7. The use of money. Exchange in a modern society, therefore, implies first, an exchange of goods or services for money and second, an exchange of the money received for commodities and services needed in the ordinary course of life. The characteristics of money and the problems arising from its use are fully discussed below (*see* XI).

8. Exchange in a modern society. In a modern society, such as present-day Britain, the network of specialisation and exchange is complex and widespread. Its effective working requires the existence of well-developed trading institutions, excellent communications and a great deal of expert knowledge. Much of this book will be concerned with the specialised institutions and techniques which make the system of exchanges possible.

PRODUCTION

It is possible to think of the economic life of a nation as a system of flows (*see* Fig. 1). Goods and services flow in one direction, the money paid for them flows in the other. These economic flows cannot be maintained without the system of exchanges discussed in the previous section. At the receiving end of the flow of goods and services is the consumer. The purpose of production is the satisfaction of consumers' wants. All activities that lead to such satisfaction are productive.

9. Industry. Industry is concerned with the actual production of goods and the provision of services. It is customary to divide industry into:

(*a*) *Primary industry*, concerned with winning the fruits of nature from the soil, taking fish from the sea or minerals from the earth.

(*b*) *Secondary industry*, concerned with the processing of primary products.

Naturally, any such division must be somewhat arbitrary and artificial. A more descriptive categorisation would be into *extractive industry* (agriculture, fishing, forestry, mining and quarrying), *manufacturing industry* and *construction*.

Industries that are concerned with the provision of services of various kinds are sometimes known as *tertiary industries*, although this term covers a rather wider field than the *direct services* provided by teachers, lawyers, entertainers and others.

10. The chain of distribution. Production is not complete until the goods reach the final consumer. The process of distribution includes all the activities necessary to get the goods from the factory to the consumer. The physical transfer of goods involves *transport* and *warehousing*. Distribution may be regarded as a series of exchanges which culminates in final purchases by customers in retail shops. Both *wholesale* and *retail trade* are therefore concerned.

11. Aids to trade. For trade to be carried on smoothly and effectively, various auxiliary services such as *banking*, *finance* and *insurance* are necessary. If consumers' satisfactions are to be maximised, and that is the purpose of production, it is important that the range of goods and services should be as great as possible. *Market research* helps to ensure that the goods produced are saleable and *advertising* and *selling* have a part to play in telling the

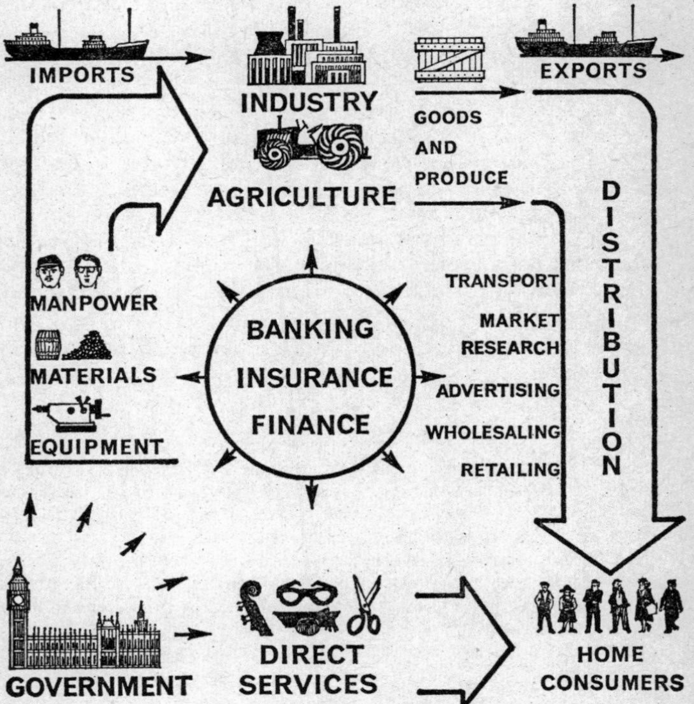

Fig. 1. The pattern of commerce.

public what is available, in developing public taste and in maintaining demand.

THE NATURE OF COMMERCE

12. Definition of commerce. Previous paragraphs of this chapter have shown how the production and distribution of goods and the provision of services depend on exchange. This exchange of goods and services we call *commerce.* The word "commerce," however, means more than this. It implies an interchange or communication between the people concerned. In commercial life there are a great many techniques, practices and conventions without which the system of exchanges would not be possible.

A study of commerce, therefore, must include an examination of:

(*a*) *All aspects of trade* from the purchase of raw materials to the eventual sale of finished consumer goods.

(*b*) *The auxiliary services* which help trade, and make it possible, i.e. transport, warehousing, banking, finance, advertising and selling.

(*c*) The more important *detailed procedures* involved in both trade and the auxiliary services including those concerned with the flow of information.

A full understanding of commerce also requires some knowledge of the economic "climate" in which trade takes place.

PROGRESS TEST 1

1. What do you understand by the term "division of labour"? What part does the division of labour play (*a*) in an industry where most jobs are carried out by hand, and (*b*) in an industry where most of the processes are mechanised? **(1, 2)**

2. "The advantages of specialisation are achieved only at the cost of an almost complete loss of independence." Explain this statement. What is the importance of good labour relations in a modern economy? **(4, 5)**

3. Write brief notes on each of the following topics:

(*a*) Production.
(*b*) Exchange.
(*c*) Barter. **(6–11)**

4. Distinguish between "industry" and "commerce" and outline the activities which fall under the latter heading. To what extent do these two categories overlap or interrelate? (9–12)

CHAPTER II

THE UNITED KINGDOM ECONOMY IN OUTLINE

A study of commerce is concerned with the way in which men conduct their business affairs. Business does not take place in a vacuum and cannot be considered separately from the economy as a whole. This chapter outlines the more important aspects of the British economy and attempts to clarify some current problems by putting them into a longer-term perspective. The economic difficulties which make headlines did not spring up overnight; they are a consequence of the long-term changes which the economy is undergoing.

THE BIRTH OF MODERN BRITAIN

Between about 1750 and 1850 changes took place in Britain that altered the whole life of her people and, ultimately, of people in most other countries. These changes are generally known as "the Industrial Revolution."

1. Britain before the Industrial Revolution. Britain in 1750 was an agricultural country; large numbers of her people lived by farming and only a minority of the population lived in towns. The population was about eight million and growing. There was already a considerable overseas trade with the colonies and banking and commerce were well developed. There had already been a number of improvements in agriculture such as better crop rotation, the use of root crops and improved cattle breeding. There was a growing interest in science. The stage was set for the more rapid changes of the next hundred years.

2. Population. The first census of population was taken in 1801 and showed that about 10 million people lived in

Great Britain. By 1850, the population had doubled and by 1900, it had risen to over 35 million. The pressure of an expanding population was a spur to agricultural reform and provided a labour force for growing industries.

3. Industrial change. During the second half of the eighteenth century, inventions were made that radically altered textile production in Britain. The new machines were too big to be used in workers' homes and were power-driven. There was consequently a change from handicraft production to machine production and from cottage industry to factory industry. These changes were typical of others, and the movement of large bodies of people into the factories, where work was for set hours under firm discipline, was a most profound change in social conditions.

The first power source was moving water, but this was displaced by steam. Large quantities of fuel were needed and this, with the wider markets for the greater production, made improved transport a necessity. A boom in canal building met this need, but by the 1830s and 1840s intensive railway building was taking place.

Power-driven machinery, steam engines to provide the power and steam locomotives for the railways stimulated heavy engineering. The need for coal stimulated mining. By the mid-nineteenth century Britain had become "the workshop of the world" and was exporting cotton cloth, coal and machines. She was also importing quantities of food and materials, particularly raw cotton.

DEVELOPMENTS BEFORE 1939

4. 1850-1914. When Britain was the world's leading industrial power, her export industries earned a large surplus over what had to be paid for imports. This surplus was invested overseas, so that Britain acquired substantial foreign investments. During the latter part of the nineteenth century, however, foreign competitors' industrialisation caught up with Britain's. Britain lost some of her markets and met fierce competition in others. New industries such as the manufacture of chemicals, motor cars and heavy electrical equipment were growing up in the years before the First World War. In these industries, Britain had no outstanding advantages.

5. The inter-war years. The years from 1919 to 1939 saw a considerable decline in older industries such as cotton, coal and shipbuilding, but many of the newer industries flourished. The older industries had been concentrated in the areas where coal was to be found and so these areas experienced high unemployment as their basic industries declined. Competition from other countries had already reduced the export markets of the older industries and they suffered further blows when international trade declined in the "Great Depression" of the thirties.

By this time, Britain's export surplus had disappeared and her balance of payments was favourable only because of her invisible exports and foreign earnings (*see* XVIII). In spite of the depressed state of trade, the inter-war years saw a great deal of improvement in industrial efficiency. This was often accompanied by increased concentration of ownership and control and the disappearance of the less efficient, high cost firms.

The newer industries, manufacturing motor cars, radios, electrical appliances and so on, were not dependent on coal as a source of power. Electrical power was becoming more important and could be transmitted easily and cheaply. New industries using electrical power chose to be near to their markets and to sources of labour. The magnet for industry was now London and the South East, while the old northern industrial areas lapsed into chronic unemployment and stagnation.

THE ECONOMY TODAY

6. Industry. Inter-war trends continued in the post-war years so that consumer goods industries and the service trades flourished, but continued to congregate in the South East and the Midlands, close to their markets and their labour force. The Second World War revived the shipbuilding, heavy engineering, coal, textile and iron and steel industries but the changed conditions of the post-war world clearly indicated that their size and their importance in the economy must be reduced. The effort to ensure that this contraction was a controlled and orderly one has been only partially successful and the recent experience of the older industries has been painful for both management and workers. In the process of contraction, however, much has been done to make these industries more modern and so better able to compete in a more ruthless and competitive international trading world.

A new generation of fast-growing, science-based industries has appeared since the war. This group includes the electronics, petro-chemicals, plastics and synthetic fibres industries. Another significant post-war trend has been the increased use of motor transport for both goods and passengers. This has led to a notable growth in the car industry. A further result of the greater use of road transport has been the construction of a number of large oil refineries in the United Kingdom.

7. Nationalisation. In the early post-war years several industries were nationalised. The reasons for this were mixed, some being political, some economic. The major nationalised industries are coal, steel, railways, electricity, gas, civil aviation (in part), ship-building, aircraft construction and some sections of the road transport and freight industry. The Atomic Energy Authority was set up as a state concern from the start. Although the tendency is to think of the nationalised industries as unprofitable and bureaucratic, they have many special problems and have made considerable achievements. Because they are financed with loan capital (*see* IX, **13**) it is difficult to make direct comparisons with private industry, but if their profits and losses are calculated before interest payments are deducted the position is by no means one of unrelieved inefficiency and waste.

8. The service industries. Some 49% of the total working population of the United Kingdom is employed in the provision of services of one kind or another. It is a mark of economic development that people become more interdependent, requiring more services to be performed for them instead of carrying them out for themselves. In the twenty years since the end of the war there has been a steady increase in the numbers employed in the professions, in insurance, banking, the distributive trades and catering and hotel services. While this growth in service employment was to be expected, it was far greater in the early seventies than was justified by the expansion of the economy and, as well, greater than comparable increases in other European countries. There was an even larger growth in the numbers employed by central and local government, so that by the mid-seventies there was concern that the non-industrial part of the economy had become too large.

9. Growth. Over the last fifteen years the total output of the United Kingdom has been growing at about 2½% per annum. Even this modest growth rate has proved difficult to sustain in recent years and the failure of the UK economy to keep pace with those of other Western European countries has caused great concern. It had been hoped that entry to the European Economic Community (*see* XVIII, **10**) would offer opportunities for more rapid growth, but since the United Kingdom joined the Community at a time when the economy was in an uncompetitive and inefficient state, these hopes were disappointed.

10. Demand, employment and prices. For twenty-five years after the end of the Second World War, the level of employment was consistently high, but the inability to sustain a high level of industrial activity without increasing the volume of imported goods has endangered this position. The working population now numbers almost 26 million, of whom one-third are women. During most of the post-war years, there has been an acute shortage of labour and until the mid-60s unemployment seldom reached 500,000 and was below 2% of the labour force. Since that time unemployment has risen steadily and by early 1972 had reached one million workers. In conditions of full employment, workers had been able to look forward to rising wages and to constantly higher material standards. The continuation of these attitudes, reasonable in themselves, in periods of economic stagnation has tended to intensify the unemployment problem. With incomes rising so much faster than production it is not surprising that prices have tended to rise at an ever increasing rate and, in a climate of trade union militancy, this has led to even greater wage claims among the more highly organised workers.

The long period of full employment referred to above owed much to the control of the economy by manipulation of government expenditure and taxation. These policies, influenced by the work of the economist Lord Keynes (1883–1946), tended to lead to high levels of public expenditure and to uncertainty among business men, since control of the economy led to frequent variations in taxation. The result was that by the mid-70s there was less confidence in "Keynesian" policies, much more emphasis on regulating the money supply (*see* XIV), and more reliance on securing the co-operation of the trade unions, and frequently the employers, in carrying out agreed policies.

11. Planning and the role of government. Over the years governments have accepted increasing responsibility for prosperity and for the general performance of the economy. In the last year or two, all the major political parties have made it clear that economic growth is an important part of their programmes. They are also committed to the maintenance of full employment. It is unfortunate that a rapid growth rate and full employment seem to involve balance of payments difficulties.

The way out of this dilemma seems to demand both a high level of exports and a firm control of prices and incomes. In order to influence the economy towards growth the *National Economic Development Council* was set up under the Conservative administration in 1962 and continues in being.

Ambitious plans by the Labour Government which came into power in 1964 were frustrated by the international monetary problems with which it was faced and such ventures as the National Plan, aiming at a 25% increase in gross domestic production over the period 1965–70, failed disastrously. After these disappointments, it was obvious that a great deal more than drive and optimism was required in order to return to a pattern of economic growth and that it was necessary to "restructure" the economy, rationalising the older industries and encouraging investment and innovation in the technically more advanced industries. To promote larger and more efficient groupings of firms, which would be able to compete with their international rivals, an *Industrial Reorganisation Corporation* was formed and in order to co-ordinate price and wage changes with the rate of growth of the economy a *National Board for Prices and Incomes* was set up. In a number of industries *Economic Development Committees* under the *National Economic Development Office* (NEDO) were established to coordinate economic performance and to ensure co-operation in securing a higher growth rate.

This attempt at direct intervention in the economy to promote growth and industrial efficiency undoubtedly had some good effects. Several important regroupings of firms resulted from the work of the IRC and the "Prices and Incomes Board" had some limited success in its difficult task. Perhaps the results were not sufficient to justify the massive expenditures of effort, however, and most of the apparatus of intervention was swept away when the Conservatives returned to power in the summer of 1970.

The new administration's economic policy was to interfere with industry as little as possible and to give much more freedom to the play of economic forces in eliminating inefficient firms and in bringing about industrial change. High unemployment and crises in key organisations such as Rolls-Royce forced the government to intervene much more directly than they had intended.

The policy of intervention was extended by the Labour Government which followed. A *National Enterprise Board* (NEB) was set up to promote industrial efficiency by providing funds for re-organisation or for the extension of public ownership. This development was partly a response to the persistent failure of companies to invest in new plant and machinery and partly an aspect of a new industrial strategy, intended to tackle the economic problems of the United Kingdom in a more practical and detailed way.

12. Regional problems. For long-term, historical reasons already outlined, the areas dependent on the old staple industries have not shared fully in the country's prosperity. From time to time measures have been taken to improve conditions in these regions, but it has been realised in the last few years that regional development should have a more important place in government planning. Shortage of skilled labour and pressure on resources in the South East and the Midlands are as much a problem as unemployment and under-utilised resources in the North. In each region of the country, therefore, a Regional Economic Planning Board and a Regional Economic Planning Council have been set up.

In order to help specific areas where unemployment was unusually high or which merited special attention in the light of the government's regional policies, the *Industry Act*, 1972 designated a number of *Special Development Areas*, in which the problems were seen as specially urgent, *Development Areas* and *Intermediate Areas*. In these areas, now collectively known as *Assisted Areas*, not only were a variety of investment incentives, including *investment grants* over and above the normal depreciation allowances, offered to firms, but selective financial assistance was made available for large projects likely to provide employment. Other assistance such as the provision of government-built factories and assistance for workers forced to change their employment was also made available. The regional problems of the United Kingdom have been brought into sharper focus by two additional factors in recent years. One of these is the emergence of North Sea oil as a significant influence in regional and national development and the other is the growth of pressures for the devolution of political power.

13. Overseas trade and the balance of payments. The UK's dependence on overseas trade has been mentioned earlier and the current level of imports is running at about £20,000 million per annum. Without these imports Britain would not be able to feed her people adequately nor to keep her industry supplied with necessary raw materials. If the prices of British goods are high, however, it is difficult to export enough to pay for these imports. Often the services which British business carries out for foreigners are sufficient to bridge the gap between the goods she exports and the cost of her imports, but she cannot rely on this remaining so.

When Britain's economy is buoyant and production is increasing, industry requires more imported materials, people are well-off and buy more imported foodstuffs and consumer goods. On the other hand, prices and wages tend to rise fastest in times of prosperity. The result has been that imports have risen faster than exports in periods of rapid growth. At these times, therefore, it is found that Britain owes more to foreigners than they owe to her. The inevitable consequence of this is a fall in the value of the pound sterling as compared with other currencies and a reduction in the UK's reserves of gold and foreign currency.

14. North Sea oil and the balance of payments. It was expected that the discovery of oil under the North Sea, and the possibility of similar discoveries under the Celtic Sea, would revolutionise the British economy. While the eventual effects of these discoveries and their exploitation may be considerable, the impact on the balance of payments was unfavourable until 1976. Before that year the changes associated with importing or hiring drilling and exploration equipment outweighed the savings due to the reduction of oil imports. It is expected that the eventual net favourable effect on the balance of payments will be as much as £6,000 million per annum at 1976 prices, but the debts accumulated during successive payments crises have been so large that much of this gain may be lost in repayments of borrowing and interest.

15. Sterling and the foreign exchanges. In 1967, the pound sterling was devalued to $2.40. The effect of such a change in the rate of exchange is to give exporters more £s to the dollar and consequently to offer the opportunity either of reducing their dollar prices or of making greater export profits, which could be expected to act as an incentive to export. This effect is the same with respect to other currencies which have not followed the UK's devaluation. Imports, conversely, tend to be dearer, but the tendency for the import bill to rise should be offset by the reduced *quantities* of imported goods purchased at the higher prices.

The rate of $2.40 to the pound sterling continued until the

summer of 1971 when there was a general re-alignment of currencies, but this proved to be short-lived and later in the year the pound was allowed to "float," that is to take whatever value market dealings might determine.

Largely because of underlying weaknesses in the British competitive position, the pound sterling experienced continuing difficulties and the crises of 1976 saw the pound fall firstly to below $2.00 and then to levels below $1.60.

Britain's problem of overseas finance is complicated by the fact that a number of countries, mostly members of the Commonwealth, use the pound sterling as the unit in which to hold their reserves. Britain has acted as "banker" to these sterling area countries and has held gold and convertible currencies for the area as a whole.

Following the devaluation of 1967, there was some concern that countries holding sterling balances might withdraw a large part of their holdings, with consequent further damage to the value of the pound sterling. Eventually, in the summer of 1968, this possibility was safeguarded against by guaranteeing the value of sterling balances to foreign holders, and providing for their replacement by a dollar debt in the event of withdrawal.

The whole position was made more difficult by the practice of raising interest rates during balance of payments crises in order to attract an inflow of capital. This naturally tended to attract the more volatile funds and to make the sterling balances even more susceptible to large and sudden withdrawals. This unfortunate situation played a part in the collapse of the pound during 1976.

16. The Common Market, EFTA and the Commonwealth. The Commonwealth still forms Britain's largest single group of customers. More of Britain's imports come from Commonwealth countries than from other parts of the world and more of her exports go to the Commonwealth than to any other group. In recent years, however, Commonwealth trade has been growing less fast than trade with other parts of the world.

Britain, like other European countries, has been conscious of the need for wider economic groupings. In 1957, Belgium, France, West Germany, Italy, Luxembourg and the Netherlands signed the Treaty of Rome to form the *European Economic Community*, usually known as the *Common Market* or "the six." In 1972, amid bitter debate, the Treaty of Accession to the European Communities, which came into force on 1st January, 1973, was signed. The nature of the E.E.C. and the position of the United Kingdom within it is discussed in Chapter XVIII.

Earlier, Britain had taken a leading part in the formation of the *European Free Trade Association.* Under the EFTA agreements, the United Kingdom, Norway, Sweden, Denmark, Austria, Switzerland and Portugal (the "outer seven") agreed to take steps towards the abolition of tariffs and quotas between them and to set up a free trade area. Originally, EFTA was intended as a step towards a more comprehensive free trade area that would eventually include both the "outer seven" countries and "the six." On the whole, the smaller EFTA market, formed mainly of countries scattered around the edge of the European continent, has not proved a particularly satisfactory alternative to membership of the E.E.C. Fulfilment of Britain's economic plans demanded larger exports and while these might have been possible within the existing market groupings, they seemed much more feasible within the larger and richer European market. However, the United Kingdom entered the Community at a most difficult time and it is by no means clear that earlier hopes will be fulfilled.

MEASURING THE UK ECONOMY

The nature of the UK economy cannot be appreciated fully without some idea of the scale of the economic effort involved. In addition to discussing the issues which are important for Britain today, we should *measure* the factors involved whenever possible.

17. The national income. For the people living in a country, the important thing is the total of goods and services available for their consumption in a given period of time. The only way to measure this flow of goods and services is in terms of money and this money total is known

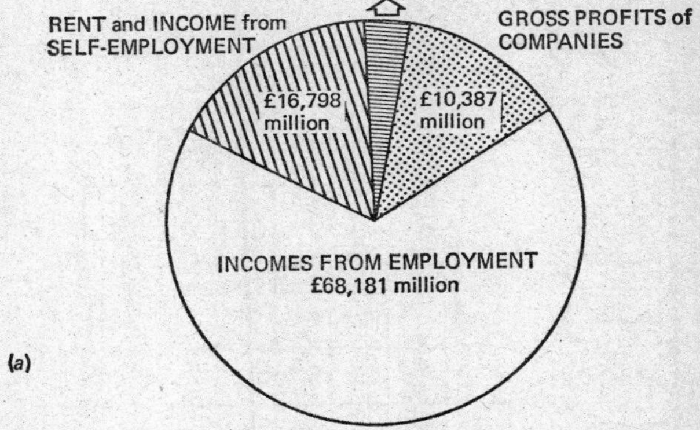

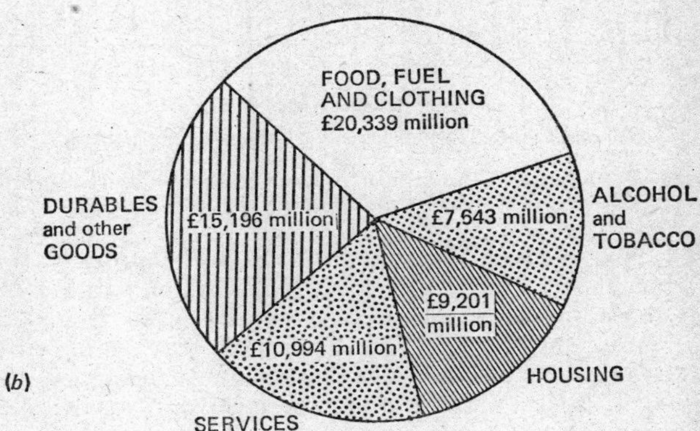

Fig. 2. Income and expenditure 1975.

as the *national income* or *national product*. This money value of the "national cake" which is to be shared out among the inhabitants of a country may be measured by valuing the total of goods and services produced, or by totalling all expenditures, or by totalling all incomes.

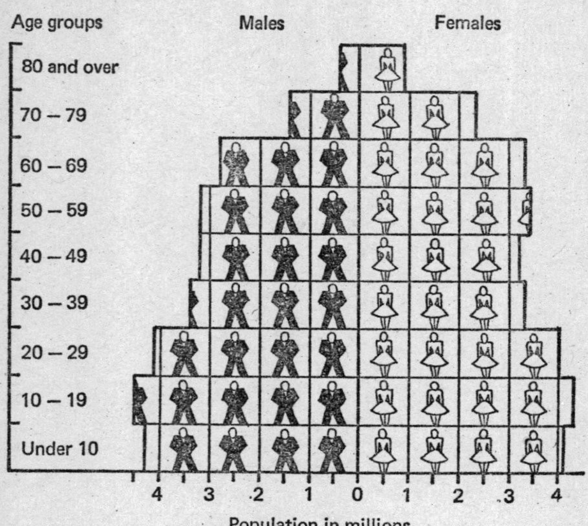

Fig. 3. Population of the UK 1975. Each complete figure represents one million people

18. The national income at 1975. The gross national product in 1975 amounted to £94,095 million. In Fig. 2 (*a*) the shares of the national product going to the various "factors of production" are shown. To give an accurately representative picture, we should allow for changes in the value of stocks and for incomes received from property overseas.

Consumer's expenditure in the same year amounted to £63,373 million and Fig. 2 (*b*) shows how this was divided among the principal categories. A comparison over a fairly long period of time would have shown how the proportion of expenditure devoted to the basic essentials of food, fuel, clothing and housing has declined as living standards have risen. Today, only one-half of consumers'

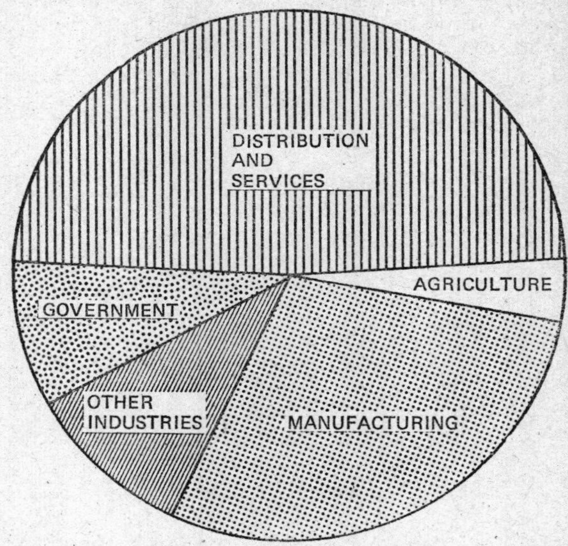

Fig. 4. Working population mid-1975. Total working population was 25.8 million, of whom 0.9 million were unemployed, a further 0.3 million were in the armed forces and 1.9 million were self-employed. Of the remaining 22.7 million employees, 13.5 million were male and 9.2 million were female.

expenditure is taken by these things. The difference between the gross national product of nearly £94,095 million and the £63,373 million of consumers' expenditure is accounted for by government expenditure on goods and services and by expenditure by firms on new capital equipment or increases in stocks.

19. Population. The population of the UK in 1975 was just over 56 million people. Fig. 3 shows the distribution of this figure between males and females and by age groups. The well-being of a community depends not only on the size of the national income but also on the number of people among whom it must be shared. Children and old people are not productive but must be supported by those who do go out to work. Many women, too, are bound by home ties and are not available for work outside the home. Fig. 4 shows the size of the working population (25.8 million) and the way in which it is divided among the principal occupations. It is notable that about one-third of the working population are women.

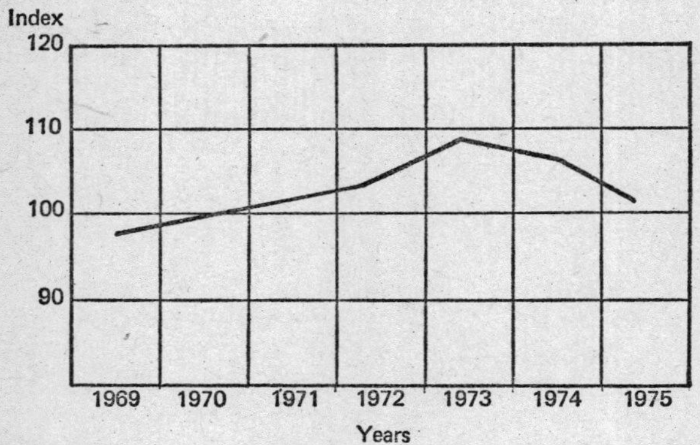

Fig. 5. Industrial production.

20. Production. Fig. 5 shows movements of the Index of Industrial Production. This index shows changes in the *volume* of production in the manufacturing industries, mining and quarrying, construction and in the gas, electricity and water industries. Although the index excludes the distributive trades, transport and all the service trades, it does give some idea of the way in which production is moving. (The Index is fundamentally a ratio of production quantities weighted for each industry. The base figure, 100, represents the 1970 figures.)

If *real income per head* is to increase, it is essential that all resources are used as well as possible, so that production grows quickly enough to keep up with increases in population. This is going to be particularly difficult in the next two decades, because the *dependent population*, the very young and the old, will be increasing in number more quickly than the *working population* which will have to support them.

21. Overseas trade. A figure and tables relating to overseas trade are shown in Chapter XVIII.

22. Keeping up-to-date. Although the figures given in this book will be useful for a number of years, they will require revision. Most of the detail shown in the diagrams discussed above (**17–20**) is based on figures taken from the *Monthly Digest of Statistics*. Other useful data can be found in the *Annual Abstract of Statistics* and in the *Blue Book on National Income & Expenditure*. The sheer amount of detail in these volumes can be intimidating, so perhaps, for a start, it would be as well merely to make a note of the most up-to-date figures corresponding to those given in this chapter and in Chapter XVIII. It may be said that it is hopeless to try to *remember* much statistical detail, but one can try to be aware of the more important round figures and of the relationships between them.

PROGRESS TEST 2

1. What was "the Industrial Revolution"? What happened during it? (**1–3**)
2. Outline some of the major industrial changes which took place between 1900 and 1938. How did they affect Britain's position in international trade? (**4, 5**)
3. Contrast Britain's present trading position with that in the mid-nineteenth century. (**1–3, 6–16**)
4. What features of the British economy today distinguish it from that of the inter-war years? Which of the new trends which you have mentioned are desirable and which undesirable? What action have governments taken to encourage the former and combat the latter? (**4–16**)
5. Discuss the extent to which government intervention in the economy between 1964 and 1970 was successful. Do you think that subsequent "non-interventionist" policies have been more successful? (**11–12**)

6. Why do some areas of the British Isles experience less prosperity than others? What has the government done to help these areas? (12)

7. Why do you think that the pound sterling has experienced so many difficulties in recent years? Do you consider that the "floating £" has helped or harmed the British economy? (14, 15)

PART TWO

BUSINESS ORGANISATION AND MANAGEMENT

CHAPTER III

FORMS OF BUSINESS ENTERPRISE: SOLE TRADERS AND PARTNERSHIPS

FORMS OF BUSINESS ENTERPRISE

Passing through any town, a traveller is likely to notice that some businesses, perhaps the larger ones, bear names such as the Brickville Engineering Co. Ltd., whereas others have merely the proprietor's name painted above the shop and others again have more than one surname displayed. The gasworks and the electricity showrooms, on the other hand, display the titles of the appropriate Area Boards and the station is distinguished by the "British Rail" sign. Obviously business can be organised in a number of different ways and each must have its distinguishing features, its advantages and disadvantages. Again, some businesses are publicly owned and others are privately owned. The chart shown below (Fig. 6) shows the various types of business enterprise, both public and private.

The remainder of the chapter will deal with the two most simple types of business organisation, the sole trader and the partnership.

THE SOLE TRADER

1. Characteristics of the sole trader. The simplest form of business is that which is owned and controlled by one man. Many people, tired of working for someone else and eager to be independent, use their savings to start a business. Needless to say, the sum of money available is likely to be small. Businesses owned and operated by a *sole trader* or *single proprietor*, as he is sometimes called, are likely to be

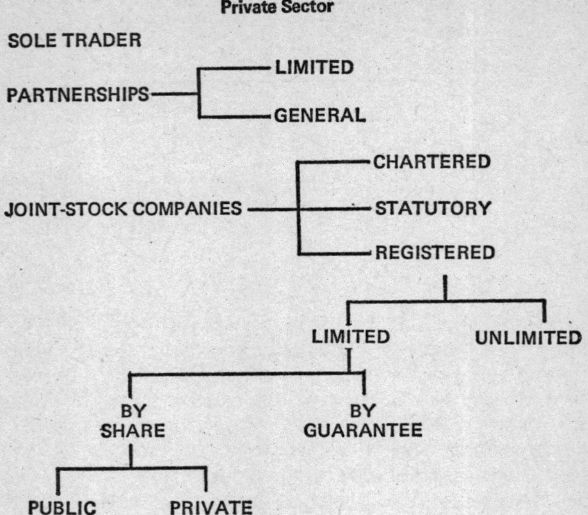

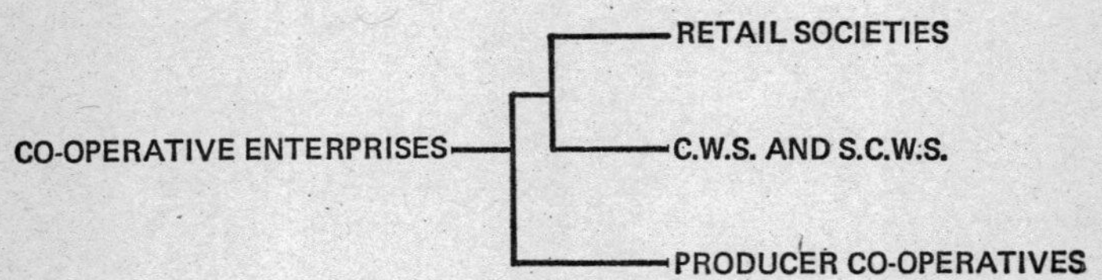

Public Sector

DIRECT GOVERNMENT SERVICES

MUNICIPAL ENTERPRISES

PUBLIC CORPORATIONS

Fig. 6. Types of business enterprise.

those to which entry is easy, requiring neither large capital expenditure nor great technical knowledge.

Many sole traders are to be found in retail trade, although here large scale retailing sometimes makes survival difficult. The sole trader is also found in crafts such as plastering and plumbing, where the initial outlay is small and a tradesman can set up on his own fairly easily after he has acquired the basic skills as an employee.

The sole trader has a special place, too, in occupations where the service given is a personal one, as in high-class tailoring, or where a great deal of discretion is needed in handling a client's affairs. Solicitors and accountants, therefore, may carry on business as a single proprietor. Where the market for a commodity is small, the sole trader will flourish because it is not profitable for larger firms, with expensive equipment and heavy overheads, to serve a restricted market.

2. Advantages of the sole trader. The advantages of the sole trader are summarised below, with explanatory comments where necessary:

(*a*) *Independence.*

(*b*) *Close supervision:* the sole trader's organisation is small; he can supervise his staff, if any, personally.

(*c*) *Simplicity of organisation:* there is no danger of bureaucracy.

(*d*) *Flexibility:* being his own master and having only the simplest organisation, he can change the whole policy of his business in a very short time. He can make quick decisions.

(*e*) *Freedom of action:* he has no Board to convince, no committees to argue with.

(*f*) *Personal contact:* he is close to both clients and employees. He can offer personal service to customers and deal with employees' problems on a "man to man" basis.

(*g*) *Direct responsibility:* his efforts are rewarded by personal profit and his mistakes by losses.

(*h*) *Freedom from regulation:* apart from the ordinary legal responsibilities incurred by anyone who trades or employs staff, the only special duty required of the sole trader is compliance with the *Registration of Business Names Act*, 1916. This is dealt with below (*see* **4**).

3. Disadvantages of the sole trader. Disadvantages may be summarised as follows:

(*a*) *Unlimited liability:* the sole trader's liability to meet the claims of his creditors is completely unlimited. If his business fails, his own possessions and wealth can be called upon to meet his business debts.

(*b*) *Small initial capital:* the sum available to start a one-man business may be too small to equip it properly or to tide it over the period during which a regular clientele is acquired.

(*c*) *Small working capital:* the sole trader may never have sufficient working capital in the business to hold large stocks or to ride-out slack periods.

(*d*) *Difficulty of expansion:* even a successful sole trader is likely to find it difficult to obtain the extra finance necessary for expansion.

(*e*) *Strain:* the sole trader, running the business on his own or with family help, is likely to have to work hard for long hours. In addition, the worry of the business is his alone.

(*f*) *Insufficient versatility:* there are many aspects to running a business efficiently. Purchasing, selling, display, and many other things must be handled by the sole trader and he is unlikely to be equally good at all of them.

The balance between the advantages and disadvantages of the unincorporated one-man business depends on the character and resources of the sole trader himself. If he is energetic, gifted and resourceful, the flexibility of this type of organisation and the sole trader's ability to make quick decisions may make his business a valuable and efficient part of the trading community. Few men are likely to have the resources needed for expansion into larger scale business, however, and at this stage the sole trader will need to think of taking partners or of opening his business to fresh capital by joining with others in the formation of a company.

4. Registration of Business Names Act, 1916. During the First World War, it was felt that foreigners trading in Britain under British names should be forced to declare their true nationality. This war-time legislation was found to have uses beyond its original narrow purpose and is still in force. The Act requires that any person carrying on a business under a name other than his own must register with the Registrar of Business Names. The true name of the trader, and his nationality if not British, must also appear on catalogues, circulars and letterheads which bear the name of the business. A Certificate of Registration must be displayed at the principal place of business.

PARTNERSHIP

If a sole trader wishes to undertake a modest expansion, one obvious way to obtain the necessary capital is to take a partner or partners. The advantages of having more capital than one person could provide are so apparent that many small businesses are formed as partnerships from the start. A good many of the sole trader's advantages are retained, but since other people are involved, the organisation of a partnership is just a little more complex.

5. Regulation. Since partnership involves more people, some additional regulation of their rights and duties must be expected. Partnerships, like sole traders, must register under the *Registration of Business Names Act*, 1916 if the firm trades under a name which does not consist of the true names of all the partners.

The main piece of legislation affecting partnerships is the *Partnership Act*, 1890. This Act consolidated and amended the law of partnership and although it does not contain the whole of partnership law, it does lay down the main principles.

6. Definition. The definition contained in *s.* 1 of the *Partnership Act*, 1890, gives a good working idea of the nature of partnership:

"Partnership is the relation which subsists between

persons carrying on a business in common with a view of profit." The Act goes on to refine this definition, which is not adequate for legal purposes.

7. Membership. An ordinary business partnership may not have more than twenty members and a banking partnership more than ten. If these numbers are exceeded, the firm must register as a company: *Companies Act*, 1948, *ss*. 429 and 434.

These prohibitions were relaxed to some extent by the *Companies Act*, 1967, which permits the formation of banking partnerships of up to twenty members with the special authorisation of the Board of Trade (now the Department of Trade) in respect of each of the members. The same Act also made an exemption in respect of certain professional partnerships, including Stock Exchange partnerships (*see* X, **5**).

8. The Partnership Agreement. No special formalities are necessary to set up a partnership; a mere verbal agreement is sufficient. Many problems and difficulties may arise between the partners in the course of time, however, and it is usual to set out their rights and duties in a formal Partnership Agreement or Deed.

The contents of the Partnership Agreement will vary with the nature of the partnership and the business concerned but are likely to include the following:

(*a*) The name of the firm and the names and addresses of the partners.

(*b*) The nature of the business.

(*c*) The capital of the firm and the proportions to be contributed by each partner.

(*d*) The extent to which the partners are to take part in the management of the business.

(*e*) The method of sharing profits and losses.

(*f*) The amounts that partners may withdraw for their personal use.

(*g*) The interest payable on loans and drawings.

(*h*) Provisions regarding the way in which the accounts of the business are to be kept.

(*i*) The duration of the partnership and the conditions under which it may be brought to an end.

(*j*) Provisions for the dissolution of the partnership.

NOTE: Where there is *ambiguity* or where the *agreement is silent*, the provisions of the law, principally as embodied in the *Partnership Act*, will apply. The ordinary rights of a partner, so far as they are not modified by the Partnership Agreement, include the right to take part in the business, to share equally in profits and losses, to prevent the admission of new partners, to examine the books when he desires and to have interest at 5% on advances which he makes beyond his agreed subscribed capital. It should be understood that these rights are overridden by any contrary clauses in the Agreement.

9. Types of partner. The status of a partner will depend on the agreement which he has made with the other partners. In the ordinary way, the partners will take a full part in the running of the business. Such partners are known as *active* partners. Other partners may agree to contribute capital and to receive their share of the profits but to take no part in the business. They are known as *sleeping*, *silent*, or *dormant* partners.

There may also be *limited* partners, but this is very unlikely today (*see* **13**).

10. Dissolution of the partnership. If the partnership is not for any fixed term and is a "partnership at will," it may be dissolved by the partner wishing to retire giving notice. If the partnership is not "at will," the consent of the other partners will be required. The Partnership Agreement may well lay down the conditions to be observed on retirement.

Sometimes a partnership is formed for a particular purpose or for a given period of time. In such cases, dissolution will take place when the stated purpose has been fulfilled or the time agreed has expired.

A partnership will also be dissolved by the death or bankruptcy of a partner or the occurrence of some event which makes the partnership illegal. Occasionally, the court may decree the dissolution of a partnership, but this would only happen in exceptional circumstances such as the lunacy or misconduct of a partner.

11. The assets on dissolution. When a partnership is dissolved, the assets of the firm must be turned into cash (liquidated) and used as follows:

(*a*) firstly in paying off the firm's creditors;
(*b*) then in repaying loans made by partners;
(*c*) then the partners' capital must be repaid, or
(*d*) if any surplus then remains, it must be divided among the partners in the profit sharing ratio. Losses must be borne in the same way if they should occur.

12. The legal responsibilities of partners. Ordinary, or general, partners are fully liable for the debts of the firm. If required, their own property and wealth can be called upon; their *liability* is *unlimited.*

Each partner is an agent for the firm and for the other partners and may make binding contracts for the purpose of carrying on the firm's business. Partners are also liable for any civil wrongs committed with the apparent authority of the firm.

13. Limited partnerships. In 1907, the *Limited Partnerships Act* was passed. This enabled the liability of partners to be limited, provided that they took no active part in the business. Even in a limited partnership there must be at least one general partner, with unlimited liability, and limited partnerships must be registered. There are very few limited partnerships since the private limited company can provide limited liability for the smaller business and can offer other advantages too.

14. Advantages of partnership. Success or failure in a partnership depends to a great extent on the relationship which exists between the partners. The resources they command must be adequate, of course, but half the battle will be won if they work well together and possess the range of abilities which their particular business requires.

The advantages of trading as a partnership are set out below, with brief comments where some explanation is needed.

(*a*) *Capital:* a number of people in business together can obviously provide more capital than any one of them on his own.

(*b*) *Possibility of expansion:* with additional capital available the business will be able to grow if trading is sufficiently successful.

(*c*) *Division of labour:* the partners are likely to have a variety of talents which can be put to work in the business. In any case, specialisation in particular fields should improve efficiency.

(*d*) *Consultation:* the sole trader was alone with his anxiety; the partners can consult with each other to "iron-out" business problems.

(*e*) *Initiative and ideas:* a number of partners are more likely to be able to produce new ideas about how to run the business, and how to react to trading conditions, than a sole trader.

(*f*) *New partners:* most businesses reach a stage, eventually, when they become stagnant and in need of rejuvenation. Bringing in a new partner can provide the stimulus that the business needs.

(*g*) *Shared strain:* partners can not only share the worry of the business, they can share the work. The excessive hours and overwork of the sole trader are no longer necessary.

(*h*) *Shared losses:* if losses should occur, they are not borne by one man. With unlimited liability, this could be important.

(*i*) *Personal contact:* most partnerships still operate on a scale that is small enough to permit personal contact with customers and employees.

15. Disadvantages of partnership.

(*a*) *Unlimited liability.*

(*b*) *Difficulty of dissolution:* assets may not be realisable easily and the death or retirement of a partner may wreck the business. The Partnership Agreement can contain a clause providing for insurance cover against such emergencies.

(*c*) *Disagreement among partners:* this is obviously possible.

(*d*) *Excessive discussion:* decisions may be reached only after long discussion. This need not imply disagreement among the partners, merely a tendency to take too great an advantage of the opportunities for consultation.

(*e*) *Difficulty of admitting new partners:* it may be difficult to secure agreement of all the partners to the admission of a new partner.

(*f*) *Shared profits:* the sharing of profits among other partners may not always be welcomed.

(*g*) *Shortage of capital:* although the partnership can command greater resources than the sole trader, it cannot approach the joint-stock company's capacity for raising capital. Successful partnerships may soon find that they are short of capital for expansion.

16. Other problems of the small business. Although the small business still has many advantages of flexibility and initiative, the growth of strong central administration in many areas of modern life has posed great problems for the smaller firm, including the smaller limited company (*see* **IV, 13**). Among the new areas of regulation to which the small firm must submit are those relating to *Value Added Tax Capital Gains Tax* and *Capital Transfer Tax*. In addition there are regulations concerning the employment, dismissal and well-being of workers (*see* VII), all of which, while necessary, make the small businessman's task more complex. In the area of taxation, the affairs of the sole trader or the partner are not separate from those of the business and this, too, has led to problems since the tendency in legislation has been to make extremely stringent regulations intended to prevent the businessman from enjoying advantages not available to the worker in employment. While much of this legislation is necessary and commendable, and while there are many exemptions freeing the very smallest firms from the duty to comply, it is unavoidably the case that small firms have tended to find their activities both more complex and more constrained.

PROGRESS TEST 3

1. Discuss the advantages and disadvantages of the sole trader. How do they relate to the kinds of activity in which this type of enterprise is found? (**1–3**)

2. Compare the legal position of the sole trader with that of a partner. What are the major statutes concerned in each case? **(4–13)**

3. Write brief notes on "The Partnership Agreement." **(8)**

4. Compare the sole trader with the partnership as a way of trading. **(1–3, 14, 15)**

CHAPTER IV

JOINT-STOCK COMPANIES

METHODS OF INCORPORATION

One of the most significant factors in the economic history of the last hundred years has been the increase in the scale of business enterprise. In both production and distribution very large undertakings have been able to cut unit costs by increasing the scale of their operations and by introducing machines of increasing size and complexity. This would not have been possible without the accumulation of large amounts of capital, and the most effective organisation for raising capital in the private sector of the economy is the joint-stock company (*see* Fig. 6).

Companies are formed for two reasons, to limit a trader's personal liability and to persuade other people to invest money in a business. The company is formed by taking the necessary legal steps to secure *incorporation.* The company then has *corporate personality* and has a legal identity quite separate from that of its individual members.

1. Incorporation. A company may be incorporated by *statute*, that is by the passing of a special Act of Parliament, by the granting of a *Royal Charter*, or by *registration* under the Companies Acts. The most important and most common method is by registration.

2. Statutory companies. Statutory companies, incorporated by Act of Parliament, used to be formed to carry out public utility services such as gas, water and electricity supply. The nationalisation of most of the utility services has made the formation of new statutory companies very rare. Statutory companies still exist where public services, such as water supply, remain under private ownership. The powers of a statutory company are defined by the special Act which created it and the liability of members is limited in the same way. The Acts of Parliament setting up statutory companies often embodied standard provisions laid down in the *Companies Clauses Act*, 1845 and other statutes.

3. Chartered companies. Some of the very oldest trading companies draw their powers from Royal Charters granted to them on their foundation. The granting of a Charter incorporates such a company, lays down its powers and confers limited liability on the members. This method is not employed for the incorporation of commercial profit-making companies today.

4. Companies registered under the Companies Acts. This is the most important method of forming joint-stock companies. *Registration*, and the issuing of a *Certificate of Incorporation* by the Registrar of Companies, brings the company into being. Members of the general public are affected by the formation of a joint-stock company both as potential shareholders and as creditors, and they must be protected. It is not surprising, therefore, that the formation of a joint-stock company involves a number of formalities and that the company is subject to detailed regulations throughout its existence.

Three types of companies may be formed by registration:

(*a*) *Unlimited companies*, which have corporate personality but the liability of whose members is unlimited. These companies are quite rare.

(*b*) *Companies limited by guarantee.* Members of these companies undertake to be liable for the debts of the company up to a stated limit. Companies limited by guarantee are not very numerous. This form of organisation is suitable for non-profit-making bodies whose normal outgoings are covered by subscription income but who might possibly incur larger debts.

(*c*) *Companies limited by share.* This is the form of organisation adopted by the ordinary commercial companies which are so familiar. The remainder of this chapter is largely concerned with companies limited by share which form the great majority of companies registered under the *Companies Acts.* There are two different types of companies limited by share, *public companies*, which invite the general public to subscribe, and *private companies*, the membership of which is restricted (*see* **12, 13**).

COMPANIES LIMITED BY SHARE: GENERAL CHARACTERISTICS

A limited company is normally formed with a view to making a profit for its members by engaging in trade or manufacture. The capital of the company is raised by each member taking "shares" in the company, the shares being paid for in cash or occasionally given in exchange for some other consideration. The members, often called shareholders, share in the profits of the company in accordance with the size of their holding. Profits are distributed in the form of a dividend which is expressed as a percentage of the "nominal value" (*see* **11** (*e*) below) of the share. Members' liability is limited to the amount paid, or agreed to be paid, for the share. Should the company fail, there will be no call on the shareholder to meet the company's debts provided that he has fully paid for his shares.

The company is a separate entity from its shareholders. Its separate identity is legally conferred by registration and is emphasised by the fact of the limited liability of the share-holders; the company's debts are not their debts. This separateness is also confirmed by the *transferability* of shares. A partner's resignation from a partnership causes a considerable disruption of the business, but a shareholder can cease to be a member of a company merely by selling his shares.

5. Control. Control of the company is ultimately in the hands of the shareholders, whose investment, after all, is at risk. This ultimate control is exercised by voting at meetings, the general rule being that voting power is in proportion to the number of shares held. The principal meeting of shareholders is the Annual General Meeting at which the accounts are presented to the members. In the ordinary way, company meetings are not well attended and the few members with large holdings are usually able to dominate and control the proceedings, although there have been a few cases in recent years when small shareholders have banded together in order to make a protest at the management of a company's affairs.

6. Directors. It would obviously be impossible for the shareholders to exercise day-to-day control over the company, nor could they effectively lay down the general policy of a complex, modern business. General policy is the concern of a *Board of Directors*, elected by, and responsible to, the shareholders. It will be realised, of course, that the election of directors is effectively in the hands of the members with the largest holdings. Frequently, the Board of a modern company will include several executive directors who are experts in their fields and have direct responsibility for the efficiency of a particular aspect of the company's work. A link is thus created between the Board of Directors and the paid managers who attend to the detailed running of the business.

REGULATION OF JOINT-STOCK COMPANIES

7. Companies Acts. The conduct of joint-stock companies is governed by the *Companies Act*, 1948. This Act is still the principal statute relating to the formation of companies, the offering of shares to the public, the keeping of accounts and many other things. The 1948 Act differed from earlier legislation in its insistence on adequate publicity, particularly in relation to the accounts of holding companies and their subsidiaries, in the more stringent regulations laid down regarding the publication of prospectuses and the allotment of shares, and in the increased powers given to the then Board of Trade in relation to companies.

Because of dissatisfaction with the safeguards of the 1948 Act, a new Bill was introduced into Parliament in 1966 and became law as the *Companies Act*, 1967. The main effects of this Act have been to compel companies to make a much more full disclosure of their affairs, to abolish the "exempt private company" (*see* **13**) and to relax certain provisions of the *Partnership Act*, 1890 (*see* III above). The provisions of the 1967 Act are discussed in more detail in appropriate sections of this chapter. The *Companies Act*, 1976, imposed additional requirements regarding reporting and disclosure.

8. Companies' powers. A company's powers are strictly defined by the documents filed with the Registrar of Companies. These documents (*see* **11**), and others filed during the life of the company, are open to public inspection at the Companies Registration Office. Each year the company must send an *annual return* to the Registrar and in most cases a balance sheet must be attached. Any mortgages or charges on the company's property must be registered, proper books of account and other records must be kept and the books must be audited and an auditors' report submitted annually.

9. Investigation of companies. If the shareholders, or a substantial minority of them, believe that the directors are mishandling the affairs of the company, they may ask the Department of Trade to appoint inspectors to make an investigation. The Department of Trade can also appoint inspectors without any application being made if there appears to be good reason for doing so. The *Companies Act*, 1967 gave the then Board of Trade increased powers to ensure the production of documents and to secure the attendance of persons for the purposes of investigation.

FORMATION OF JOINT-STOCK COMPANIES

Joint-stock companies are formed sometimes with the intention of purchasing an existing business and sometimes in order to start an entirely new business. If an existing business is purchased by the company, its assets may be exchanged for shares in the company or for cash. If the company is starting a new business, the founders will have to decide what capital is needed. Whatever the circumstances, it will be necessary to decide whether the company is to be a public or private company.

10. Formalities of registration. Once the essential details have been decided, a number of documents must be filed with the Registrar of Companies. These are:

(*a*) The Memorandum of Association.

(*b*) The Articles of Association.

(*c*) A list of the persons who have agreed to become directors (not required for private companies).

(*d*) The directors' written consents to act (not required for private companies).

(*e*) A declaration that the requirements of the *Companies Act* have been complied with.

As soon as full details are available, the Registrar must be informed of the names and other particulars of the directors and secretary and of the situation of the registered office. If everything is in order and the proper fees have been paid, the Registrar will issue a Certificate of Incorporation and will enter the company's name on the register. The company then officially exists and private companies may commence trading, since they do not have to go to the public for their capital.

Public companies are not permitted to trade until their shares have been issued to the public and sufficient have been subscribed for to give the company an adequate capital. When this has been done the Registrar will issue a Trading Certificate and the public company may commence business.

11. The Memorandum and Articles of Association. These documents are of such importance to the successful running of the company that they deserve treatment in greater detail. The *Memorandum of Association* defines the company's powers and anyone who deals with the company is presumed to have knowledge of its contents. The Memorandum is, therefore, the document which regulates the company's relations with the outside world. It gives the basic facts about the company and contains the following clauses:

(*a*) *The name clause.* Any name may be chosen which is not undesirable in the opinion of the Department of Trade. This rules out names already in use and those which are misleading or give a false idea of the company's importance. The last word of the company's name must be "Limited."

(*b*) *The registered office.* The Memorandum must state

whether the registered office is to be in England (and Wales) or in Scotland, so that it may be known whether English or Scottish law is to apply.

(*c*) *The objects clause.* This is the most important clause in the Memorandum since it determines the powers of the company. In the objects clause the company must state every type of activity which it intends to undertake. Should the company take action outside its stated objects, it will be acting *ultra vires*, or "beyond its rights." Contracts made *ultra vires* are void. The tendency in these days is to draw the objects clause very widely so that all likely activities are included. The powers of a company may be altered later in its existence if the proper procedure is followed.

(*d*) *The limitation clause.* This clause will state that the liability is limited and will indicate how it is limited, i.e. whether by shares or by guarantee.

(*e*) *The capital clause.* This clause states the amount of capital which the company has power to raise. This is known as the *nominal capital* of the company. The number and amount of shares into which it is divided are also stated. The company will not necessarily offer shares to the public for the full amount of its nominal capital, but may keep some of its nominal capital unissued for later expansion. There is no limit on the nominal capital for which a company may be registered but duty must be paid at the rate of 50p per £100.

(*f*) *The association clause.* The last clause is a formal statement by the founders of the company, indicating their desire to form the company and setting out their names and the number of shares which each has agreed to take.

The *Articles of Association* are the internal regulations of a company. They lay down the rights of shareholders of various classes, the way that meetings are to be conducted, directors to be elected and so on. Companies need not register Articles, but if they do not do so, the standard Articles set out as Table A of the *Companies Act* will apply. The Articles of private companies must contain provisions that assure their status (*see* **13**).

PUBLIC AND PRIVATE COMPANIES

There are two distinct kinds of limited company met with in business, the *public company*, usually a large organisation with many shareholders and employing considerable capital, and the *private company*, frequently a very small business indeed. The differences between them are given below.

12. Public companies. The minimum number of members for a public company is *seven*. There is no statutory maximum number. There must be at least two directors, except in the case of companies registered before the *Companies Act*, 1929. A public company has full power to advertise its shares to the public in order to raise capital and its shares are freely transferable. It is subject to the full rigour of the *Companies Acts* and to the publicity which this entails.

13. Private companies. Private companies, first permitted by the *Companies Act*, 1907, provide a form of organisation which gives limited liability to the smaller business and which has greater potentialities for raising capital than the partnership.

A private company may be defined as one which, by its Articles of Association (the regulations of the company):

(*a*) restricts the right to transfer its shares;

(*b*) limits the number of its members, excluding employees and ex-employees, to fifty; and

(*c*) prohibits any invitation to the public to subscribe for its shares or debentures (*see* IX, **13, 18**).

The effect of these provisions is to make the private company a tightly knit organisation with all the shares owned by a small group of people, mostly well known to each other and in many cases members of the same family. Before the *Companies Act* 1967, it was possible to draw up the Articles of a private company so as to exclude the possibility of outside control. Such companies, which were very popular with small- and medium-sized concerns, were known as *exempt private companies*, since they were exempt from the necessity of submitting a balance sheet to the

Registrar with their annual returns. The 1967 Act withdrew this privilege and abolished the status of exempt private company. The attractiveness of the private company as a form of business organisation has now been much reduced since the disclosure provisions of the new Act (*see* **16, 17**) are very severe, and also since recent tax legislation bears very hardly on director-shareholders of private companies. It is possible that the next few years will see a revival of the partnership for larger concerns or of the unlimited company or even, it has been suggested, of the limited partnership.

DISSOLUTION OF JOINT-STOCK COMPANIES

When a company has fulfilled the purpose for which it was set up, when it cannot pay its creditors, or when its assets are sold to another company, it must cease to exist. There are two ways of ending a company's existence, "striking off" and "winding up."

14. Striking off. This is the cheapest and easiest method of discontinuation. The company merely stops trading, pays off its creditors and dismisses its staff. If there are any assets remaining, they are sold and the proceeds used to compensate the directors. This method is very easy and cheap where there are no outside shareholders and the directors own all the shares in the company. When the assets have been disposed of, the directors and secretary resign. Since there is no one to submit an annual return and the Registrar will receive no reply to his request for a return to be submitted, he will strike the company off the register. This way of ending a company's existence is cheap but irregular. Creditors have little chance of enforcing their claims, since they are not told what is happening.

15. Winding up. Winding up, the formal method of ending a company's existence as envisaged in the *Companies Acts*, may follow a decision of the shareholders at a general meeting, or may be ordered by the courts, usually as a result of a petition from an unsatisfied creditor.

(*a*) *Voluntary liquidation.* If the shareholders decide that the company should go into liquidation, the directors must make a *Declaration of Solvency*, indicating their belief that the company will be able to meet all its debts within the next twelve months. A liquidator is appointed and advertisements for creditors are published. The assets are disposed of, creditors paid and if any monies remain, there may be a final distribution to shareholders. If the directors cannot make a declaration of solvency, or if the liquidator decides that it is doubtful that the company's assets are sufficient to pay its debts, a meeting of creditors is called. The creditors may then appoint a new liquidator of their own choice and the winding up proceeds in accordance with their direction.

(*b*) *Compulsory liquidation.* When a liquidation is ordered by the courts, the Official Receiver takes control of the company's books as soon as the order has been made. The directors and secretary must furnish him with a statement of the company's position and a list of creditors and a creditors' meeting is called. A liquidator is appointed by the meeting and the winding up follows the course outlined above.

DISCLOSURE IN COMPANY ACCOUNTS

16. The purpose of publicity in company affairs. Because of the privilege of limited liability and also because of the divorce of ownership from control, a joint-stock company is in a position to affect the affairs of both shareholders and creditors in many ways, for good or ill. There has, therefore, been a steady trend, in successive Companies Acts, towards increased disclosure of the details of a company's business. A wide disclosure of the relevant facts prevents prospective shareholders from making investments on the basis of inadequate knowledge, and enables those who supply goods or lend money to assess the credit-worthiness of the company concerned. The *Companies Act*, 1967 required much more full disclosure of:

(*a*) relationships with subsidiary and holding companies,

(*b*) the salaries of directors,

(*c*) certain aspects of trading,
(*d*) contributions to charities and political parties.

Further measures to improve and standardise disclosure in company reports and accounts were included in the *Companies Act*, 1976.

17. Disclosure provisions of the Companies Act, 1967. The principal disclosure requirements may be summarised as follows:

(*a*) *Subsidiary and holding companies*. The company's accounts must show, or must bear a note of, the *names* of subsidiary companies, the *country* in which the subsidiary is incorporated if it is a foreign company or the Scottish subsidiary of an English company (or vice versa), details of the *classes of shares* held in the subsidiary and the *proportion* of shares held in each class. A *subsidiary* company must show the name and place of incorporation of its ultimate *holding* company.

(*b*) *Directors*. Particulars of the emoluments of the chairman and directors must be shown, as must particulars of the salaries of employees earning more than £10,000 per annum. The directors' report must show details of *contracts* affecting the company entered into by directors.

(*c*) *Trading*. Directors' reports must now disclose any significant *changes in the fixed assets* of the company or its subsidiaries and any significant differences between market values and balance sheet values. Where *business of various sorts* is carried on, the turnover and attribution of profit to each class of business must be stated. The average number of employees and the total of their wages must also be shown. Particulars of *exports* must be disclosed in the case of most companies with annual turnovers of more than £50,000.

(*d*) *Share issues*. The reasons for any share or debenture issues during the year must be stated.

(*e*) *Contributions*. Any substantial contributions to political parties or to charities must be disclosed.

It will be realised that although these provisions are to the benefit of members of the public who may contemplate dealing with companies, they may also be quite onerous, particularly to the smaller company.

ADVANTAGES AND DISADVANTAGES OF JOINT-STOCK COMPANIES

The advantages of the joint-stock company are apparent from its very success, but there are disadvantages which should not be overlooked or minimised. Both advantages and disadvantages are summarised below, although some points have already been touched on in this chapter.

18. Advantages. The joint-stock company has the following factors to recommend it:

(*a*) *Ability to raise capital.* The company can mobilise the savings of the public, offering shares of various types corresponding to the risk involved and to the inclinations of investors.

(*b*) *Continuity.* The joint-stock company has a continuous existence, independent of its members or directors.

(*c*) *Transferability of membership.* Shares in a company are transferable. Membership does not commit a person to life-long involvement in the company's affairs and investments can be sold without affecting the company's capital.

(*d*) *Limited liability.* Membership of a company does not carry a liability beyond the fully paid price of the share. It may be noted that this also enables investors to spread their holdings among a number of companies without increased risk.

(*e*) *Employee's holdings.* The loyalty of employees may be increased if they are encouraged or assisted to hold shares in the employing company.

(*f*) *Goodwill can be realised.* The issue price of a share will reflect the market's assessment of the worth of the company and this will include the "goodwill" (the reputation and prosperity) of the business.

(*g*) *Specialisation of management.* The separation of ownership from control gives the opportunity for specialisation by directors, at one level, and for the employment of expert professional managers at another.

(*h*) *Economies of scale.* The power of the joint-stock company to raise capital often leads to considerable growth in the scale of the company's operations. Large-scale manufacturing and trading usually yields significant economies.

19. Disadvantages. The advantages listed above can be offset by the following disadvantages:

(*a*) *Expense of flotation.* Setting up (or "floating") a joint-stock company can be a lengthy and expensive business.

(*b*) *Regulation.* The more that an organisation involves other sections of society, the more regulation to which it must submit (*see* **7–9**).

(*c*) *Publicity.* It is difficult for a joint-stock company to conceal its affairs. The company's file is open to inspection by members of the public.

(*d*) *Divorce of ownership from control.* It is frequently thought to be a bad thing that the owners (shareholders) of a company, being scattered and having mostly small holdings, have only an intermittent and uncertain control over a company's affairs. This tends to make for a separate class of directors and managers controlling very considerable assets without being effectively accountable to the real owners.

(*e*) *Slower decision making.* Companies tend to be larger than other forms of business enterprise and this, in itself, makes for less rapid and flexible decision making. Major decisions require ratification by the Board of Directors, if not their direct consideration, and there is sometimes lack of agreement between the Board and the full-time, professional management.

(*f*) *Lack of personal touch.* It is difficult for companies to maintain close, personal contact with customers and employees.

(*g*) *Conflict.* There may be conflict between the *shareholders*, whose interest is in the short-term profitability of the business, the *Board and the management*, concerned with long-term growth and efficiency, and the *workers*, looking for better wages and working conditions. There is also room for disagreement between ordinary and preference shareholders and between shareholders and debenture holders (*see* IX). On the whole the holders of fixed interest securities will prefer safety and a conservative policy and the ordinary shareholders will look for improved dividends.

(*h*) *Bureaucracy*. The public company, tending to be a large and complex organisation, may devote too much of its resources to administration and, in particular, to petty rules and regulations designed merely to ensure a satisfying conformity in minor details.

20. The special advantages of the private company. A private company has the following additional advantages:

(*a*) It provides *limited liability* for the smaller business.

(*b*) At the same time it gives an element of *continuity* which partnerships do not.

(*c*) Since shares cannot be transferred so easily (the Articles *must* provide some control over transfers), it is not easy for outsiders to buy their way in. If the company is a family business, family control is secured.

(*d*) Although the number of members is limited, *employees* can still hold shares.

(*e*) The private company is likely to be *small enough* to preserve some degree of personal contact between the directors and the staff and customers.

With all these additional advantages, a private company retains many of the other advantages of the joint-stock company and may prosper to such an extent that it becomes a nationally known concern.

21. Changes in company taxation. The operation of joint-stock companies is necessarily influenced by the system of taxation under which they operate. The present system of company taxation in the United Kingdom was much changed by the *Finance Act*, 1965, which introduced *corporation tax* and abolished the earlier system of using income tax, with a further tax on profits, as a basis for the taxation of joint-stock companies. This, and subsequent legislation, tended to increase the tax burden falling on small private companies, particularly on "close corporations," with five or fewer members or whose members were all directors. Corporation tax, a single tax charged on the profits of companies at a given rate, tended to encourage companies to retain profits rather than to distribute them to shareholders. Although there were some advantages in this arrangement, it was felt that the bias in the system should be removed and the *Finance Act*, 1972 accomplished this by introducing the *imputation system* of corporate taxation.

It will be realised that the growth and development of companies is influenced by the accounting conventions by which profit is calculated and defined as well as by the taxation system which is in operation. This was exemplified by the need to offer special tax relief in 1974 and 1975 in order to allow for the effects of inflation on the valuation of stocks according to the current accounting methods.

PROGRESS TEST 4

1. Describe the characteristics of:

   (*a*) Chartered companies.
   (*b*) Unlimited companies.
   (*c*) Companies limited by guarantee.
   (*d*) Companies limited by share.

Which is the most important in British commercial life and why is this so? (**1, 3–6**)

2. Distinguish "incorporation" from "registration" and outline the nature and significance of the following:

   (*a*) The Memorandum of Association.
   (*b*) The Articles of Association.
   (*c*) The Certificate of Incorporation. (**1, 4, 10, 11**)

3. Outline and contrast the characteristics of private and public companies. (**12, 13, 20, 21**)

4. What are the principal advantages and disadvantages of the public joint-stock company? (**18, 19**)

5. How does a company cease to exist? In what ways is the position of a company different, in this respect, from that of a partnership? (**14, 15,** *also* III, **10, 11**)

6. What is corporation tax and how may it affect a company's policy? (**21**)

CHAPTER V

OTHER FORMS OF BUSINESS ENTERPRISE

THE PUBLIC CORPORATION

1. The nationalised industries. It is common knowledge that a number of important British industries are publicly owned. The chief industries concerned and the names of the public corporations responsible for running them are:

Industry	*Corporation concerned*
Coal	National Coal Board
Electricity	Electricity Council Central Electricity Generating Board
Gas	British Gas Corporation
Railways	British Railways Board
Freight transport	National Freight Corporation
Docks	British Transport Docks Board
Waterways	British Waterways Board
Airlines	British Airways
Aircraft Construction	British Aerospace
Ship-building	British Shipbuilders
Broadcasting	British Broadcasting Corporation Independent Broadcasting Authority
Central bank	Bank of England
Atomic energy	Atomic Energy Authority
Steel	British Steel Corporation
Posts and telecommunications	The Post Office

NOTE: Together, these industries employ one-and-three-quarter million people.

2. Reasons for nationalisation. Nationalisation is often thought of as a purely political measure and people's attitudes towards the nationalised industries and their performance are coloured by their political views. The motives for bringing an industry under public ownership may be very complex, but the principal reasons for nationalisation can be summarised as follows:

(*a*) *Political reasons.* The first post-war Labour government was deeply committed to nationalisation as a socialist measure.

(*b*) *Control of basic industries.* Some industries such as the transport industry, the coal industry and other energy-supplying industries, are so important to the economy that their performance ought to be subject to some control. It was felt that considerable "restructuring" was necessary and that private capital would prove insufficient for their modernisation and technical development.

(*c*) *Large-scale production.* Industries such as coal and gas were organised, to a great extent, in small, high-cost units. Concentration into larger units that could obtain the economies of large-scale production was essential and did not look probable under private ownership.

(*d*) *Monopoly.* Where monopolies existed, as in the local monopolies of gas and electricity, it was felt to be more desirable to have monopoly power in the hands of the State rather than of private individuals.

(*e*) *Co-ordination of services.* Competition was considered to be wasteful under certain circumstances. In the case of road and rail transport it was believed to be better to have coordinated rather than competing services, as each tended to complement the other.

(*f*) *Labour relations.* In some industries, such as coal, labour relations had become so bad in the depressed inter-war years that a "new deal" was necessary if the co-operation of the workers was to be secured.

(*g*) *Capital requirements.* Some industries would have been unable to raise the capital that they required for development in the market in the ordinary way. This was undoubtedly the case with coal, and possibly with the airways, at least in the early post-war years.

(*h*) *Price control and consumer protection.* This was felt to be easier under state ownership than by legislative control of private enterprise.

(*i*) *Security.* In the case of atomic energy, matters of

such high importance for the national security were involved that only complete state ownership and direct control would provide adequate safeguards.

(*j*) *National rather than local service.* With changing techniques, a local service of electricity generation had become obsolete and a national service was required.

Some of these reasons for nationalisation may not be considered to be valid, but it is generally accepted that most of the industries which have been nationalised are more suitably controlled under public ownership than under private. Certainly there are very few advocates of wholesale de-nationalisation.

3. Public corporations as forms of business enterprise. The public corporations are as much involved in industry and trade as other business organisations and it is important to see that they operate efficiently. On the other hand, they are also instruments of public policy and are under the control of the Government and Parliament. The fact that they are under public scrutiny has tended to make them somewhat bureaucratic but has possibly heightened their sense of public service. Often their need to be commercially competitive has conflicted with their consciousness of being publicly accountable.

4. The creation of a public corporation. A public corporation is brought into being by an Act of Parliament. Any powers that it possesses, or assets that it controls, are conferred on it by statute and it is by statute that its general organisation, functions and powers are laid down.

5. Control of public corporations. The services provided by the nationalised industries are essentially of an industrial or commercial nature and the corporations are therefore given a high degree of freedom in their methods of operation. Nevertheless, they are under Ministerial direction so far as matters of important, general policy are concerned. The exact extent of the Minister's control varies from corporation to corporation, but most of the statutes give the appropriate Minister power to give "directions of a general character" (for example the *Gas Act*, 1949, or the *Air Corporations Act*, 1949).

Day-to-day control of the industries is in every case delegated to a Board appointed by the Minister, this Board acting rather like the Board of Directors of a joint-stock company, but having wider responsibilities but less freedom of action.

Parliament has the right to discuss matters of major policy regarding the nationalised industries but not their detailed operation. Reports and accounts are presented to Parliament annually by each of the corporations, but this gives no great opportunity for discussion although Parliamentary time may be found on other occasions. There is a *Select Committee on the Nationalised Industries* which has conducted some fairly searching inquiries into particular industries.

6. Finance. The original shareholders in companies that were nationalised were compensated by issues of government stock. On the whole, compensation was generous and amounted to over £100 million in the case of coal and over £1,000 million for the transport industries. Since compensation was by means of redeemable fixed interest securities, all the nationalised industries bear heavy burdens of interest payments and contributions towards eventual redemption of the stock. New long-term capital was originally raised by issues of long-dated government guaranteed stocks. The sums required by the public sector are very large, however, and new issues of securities at inconvenient times can impede the carrying out of the government's monetary policy (*see* XIV, **22–29**). Since 1956, therefore, new capital has been provided by direct advances of money from the Exchequer.

The Acts of Parliament setting up the various public corporations require, in most cases, that the revenue of the industry concerned should be sufficient to cover outgoings "taking one year with another." This is rather vague, but it does require a nationalised industry to avoid losses extending over a period of years. In 1961, the government of the day issued a White Paper setting out more precise objectives. Future policy was to require the nationalised industries to make surpluses at least sufficient to cover deficits over a five-year period. Adequate sums were also to be set aside to contribute to capital development and interest and depreciation was to have been charged before arriving at the surplus or deficit. Each Board was set an agreed target rate of return on its invested capital in order to achieve these ends.

Alarmed at the very high rate of investment outlay in the public sector and concerned that the very large sums involved should be properly directed, the Government of the day issued another White Paper in 1967. In this a test rate of return comparable with that expected on low-risk investment in private industry was laid down and it was also established that the nationalised industries should relate their prices to costs. However, where loss-making services were required on grounds of public service, subsidies would be available. In spite of these provisions, the later experience of the nationalised industries has been far from happy. Under pressure from both government and trade unions, they have been able neither to keep their prices from rising nor, in most cases, to meet their financial objectives.

THE CO-OPERATIVE MOVEMENT

7. Origins. The co-operative movement had its beginnings in the wretched condition of the working classes at the end of the eighteenth and in the early nineteenth centuries. The first successful co-operative store was opened in Rochdale in 1844 by a group of flannel-weavers. The "Rochdale Society of Equitable Pioneers" succeeded where other attempts had failed because it followed a well-defined and sensible set of rules.

8. Rules of the Rochdale Pioneers. The objects of the Rochdale Society of Equitable Pioneers were to raise sufficient capital in shares of £1 each to found a store for the sale of provisions and clothing, to acquire or build a number of houses for the members, to set up a manufacturing establishment for the employment of members and to carry out various other worthy or charitable schemes. These broader objectives were not carried through as successfully as the running of the store, but neither were they forgotten.

The success of the store was due to the observance of the following rules:

(*a*) Goods were to be sold at prevailing local prices.

(*b*) Interest was to be paid on capital at a fixed rate.

(*c*) Profits were to be distributed in accordance with purchases.

(*d*) No credit was to be given.

(*e*) The society was to be controlled by the members, each member having one vote regardless of the size of his shareholding.

(*f*) Men and women were to have equal voting rights.

(*g*) Meetings were to be regular and frequent.

(*h*) Accounts were to be properly kept and audited.

The success of the Rochdale Pioneers led to the foundation of other similar societies in the north of England and the co-operative movement grew rapidly throughout the nineteenth century.

9. The retail societies today. Today there are some 200 co-operative societies with a total membership of thirteen million people. Most members have very small shareholdings, in many cases only the £1 minimum. The co-operative movement tends to be stronger in the North and the Midlands than in the South of England.

In addition to the ordinary retail societies there are *federal societies* set up by groups of retail societies to perform services such as laundering, dry cleaning and baking which are best operated on a large scale.

Other retail societies have joined together to form their own *retail buying groups*, such as the "Normid" groups operated by the Nottingham and Leicester societies. A development which many co-operators view with suspicion has been the expansion of the activities of Co-operative Retail Services Ltd. which was set up by the Co-operative Wholesale Society to assist small or inefficient societies which were in difficulties. The C.R.S. has taken over more than seventy societies accounting for three-quarters of a million members.

10. Formal organisation of the retail societies. Co-operative societies must register with the *Registrar of Friendly Societies* under the *Industrial and Provident Societies Acts.* They have limited liability and are permitted to raise capital by both shares or loans. Interest on capital is at a flat rate of interest and profits are distributed as a "dividend" on purchases. There is an upper limit to shareholdings of £1,000 and shares are withdrawable on demand.

Each of the retail societies is independent and is run by an elected management committee, each member of the society having one vote regardless of the size of shareholding. The elected committee, which is part-time and amateur, appoints paid officials who look after the day-to-day running of the business. A few of the larger societies are controlled by full-time management committees.

11. Problems of the retail societies. The retail societies are having to compete with the very professional, efficient large-scale private retail units. Three-quarters of all the co-operative societies' trade is in groceries and foodstuffs and yet in the last fifteen years their share of the grocery trade has fallen from 25% to about 15%.

With the total volume of sales growing only slowly and the share of the market shrinking, it has been difficult to maintain dividends. Pre-war dividends were often around 1*s*. 9*d*. (just under 9p) but by the late 60s dividends had shrunk to less than 5p in the pound and the formal declaration of a dividend has now largely been replaced by a scheme based on a trading stamp issue (*see* XVI, **20**).

12. Moves towards modernisation of retail societies. In 1958 the Co-operative Independent Commission, often known as the Gaitskell Commission, reporting on the condition of the co-operative movement, noted the slow rate of growth of co-operative sales and recommended that the number of retail societies should be reduced by amalgamation to about three hundred. The commission stressed the need for more buying groups, for national chains of specialist shops, for better pay for management and a higher degree of professionalism in management. Although there was some improvement in marketing and purchasing policies, progress along the lines suggested was slow until 1967, when a full-time chief executive was appointed at a salary which was in line with those paid for comparable jobs in private concerns.

13. The Co-operative Wholesale Society. The Co-operative Wholesale Society was founded in 1863, a change in the law in the previous year having made it possible for one co-operative society to hold shares in another. Just as individual members belong to retail societies, so the retail societies belong to the C.W.S. From wholesaling, the activities of the C.W.S. soon extended to manufacturing. The C.W.S. now has 200 factories and is the largest single unit in the wholesale trade.

14. Problems of the C.W.S. The C.W.S. finds its customers among the retail societies, but these do not provide a big enough market. The Co-operative Independent Commission suggested that the C.W.S. might improve its position by selling to outside firms. Under a plan announced in the autumn of 1965, and approved by the Co-operative Congress, the retail societies agreed to place all orders, including those for non-C.W.S. goods, through the C.W.S. This should permit bulk buying of outside lines.

15. Other co-operative activities. The C.W.S. has some of the characteristics of a conglomerate enterprise. Until recently it controlled directly a large banking business which now operates independently as the *Co-operative Bank Ltd.*, taking part in the bank clearing and offering a full range of services (*see* XIII, **3**). The Co-operative Insurance Society conducts insurance business on a large scale.

The co-operative movement has ties with the Labour Party and a number of Parliamentary candidates have been elected as "Labour and Co-operative" members. Overall control of the movement is vested in the annual Co-operative Congress.

OTHER FORMS OF BUSINESS ENTERPRISE

16. Other forms in the public sector. Public enterprise is not limited to that carried on by the public corporations.

Many important services are performed by municipal authorities. Water supply and local transport are common examples of services provided by local authorities but these are by no means the only ones.

Some services are provided by Government Departments directly responsible to a Minister of the Crown. The most important case, until recently, was the Post Office, but this is now a public corporation with powers broadly comparable with those of other corporations discussed earlier. Institutions which may trade, but which are not independent of the central government, are called *government trading bodies*. Examples are the Stationery Office, in certain of its functions, and the Royal Ordnance Factories.

17. Miscellaneous enterprises in the private sector. *Building Societies* must be registered under the *Building Societies Acts*. Originally formed to provide for the construction of houses for their members, they now lend money for house purchase on the security of the property concerned. Capital is obtained by offering shares and accepting deposits, although building society shares are not dealt in on the Stock Exchange and are withdrawable in cash.

In spite of the variety of aid rendered by the State, many people still pay periodical small premiums to *Friendly Societies*. These bodies are regulated by various Acts which confer privileges and obligations and they must be registered with the Registrar of Friendly Societies.

18. Producer co-operatives. Until recently, it was possible to dismiss producer co-operatives as small-scale, unimportant and relatively unsuccessful. While it is still true that the record of producer co-operative enterprises has been uneven, there has been a number of attempts to use worker co-operatives to keep firms in being when conventional methods have failed. It may be that producer co-operatives will have a larger part to play in industry and commerce in the future.

PROGRESS TEST 5

1. "There are no sound commercial reasons for nationalisation." Discuss. (2)

2. Write brief notes on the finance of the nationalised industries. (6)

3. Discuss the relationship between the C.W.S. and the retail societies. (9, 13, 14)

4. Describe the formal and legal characteristics of a retail co-operative society. (10) How do they differ from those of a public limited company? (IV, 12)

CHAPTER VI

MONOPOLY AND LARGE-SCALE ORGANISATION

THE LARGE FIRM IN BRITISH INDUSTRY

1. Tendency towards increased size. Most British firms are still quite small, but there has been a definite tendency for large firms to play an increasingly important part in the UK's industrial and commercial life. In manufacturing industry the three dozen largest firms control more than twenty-five per cent of the assets employed. If we consider employment, too, we find that the larger firms, although comparatively few in number, provide more than their share of jobs. This tendency for large firms to become more important in Britain's economy is caused:

(*a*) by the natural growth of efficient and progressive firms, and

(*b*) by mergers, take-overs and other re-groupings of existing firms.

2. Industrial structure. The pattern of ownership and control in any one industry will depend on many factors, some having their roots deep in the past and others being merely accidental. Any attempt to select a certain pattern as being typical of British industry is also complicated by the fact that large firms often make several products and cannot easily be said to belong to this "industry" or that. One readily identifiable form of industrial structure is that in which a few giant firms dominate an industry and any smaller firms are relegated to a subordinate role, possibly supplying specialist markets in which the giants do not care to compete. The automobile, chemical, aircraft and oil-refining industries are of this type. A more usual form of structure is that in which there are many small firms plus a number of larger firms which do not, however, dominate the industry. A great deal of British industry is organised in this way.

Since the war, there have been a number of attempts to alter the structure of industries which have failed to adapt to changing world conditions. The cotton industry was both too large and had too many small, high-cost units. Changes in the organisation of this industry have been brought about by the government, through the *Cotton Industry Act*, 1959, and, subsequently, by a series of mergers. In the aircraft industry, too, government intervention was necessary before the number of firms could be reduced. The need for re-organisation has been a factor in decisions to nationalise industries such as the railway, coal and gas industries, where existing patterns of ownership and control were out of date.

3. Some examples of large firms. The names of the largest companies are household words. The Shell company has net assets of over £3,100 million and those of Imperial Chemical Industries amount to nearly £2,500 million. Unilever, the Anglo-Dutch concern which makes such well-known lines as "Stork" margarine and the cleaning products "Omo," "Surf" and "Vim," employs capital of over £800 million. Other firms with employed capital of between £200 million and £600 million are British Leyland, the Dunlop Rubber Company, Vickers, the giant engineering firm, and Marks & Spencer. Among other organisations that have great impact on the lives of ordinary people are the insurance companies and the largest of these each dispose of funds totalling several hundred million pounds.

4. Reasons for growth of firms. The reader who has followed this book so far will be quite aware of some of the reasons for the growth of firms, but for convenience they are summarised as follows:

(*a*) The use of the *limited company* enables larger sums of capital to be raised.

(*b*) Improved *transport* has made wider markets possible, and since the size of the firm is limited by its market, this has led to larger firms.

(*c*) *Technical developments* have led to the adoption of mass production and automated production methods.

(*d*) *Improved commercial services* and communications have made the management of large concerns less difficult.

(*e*) Knowledge of the *techniques* of management has improved, so that bigger units can be controlled successfully.

(*f*) In the post-war years, there was a long period without serious business slumps and this led to *secure markets* and increased confidence in planning expansions.

(*g*) *Increased prosperity* has provided mass markets for many goods that were formerly luxuries, so that these goods have become susceptible to mass production techniques.

(*h*) The larger firm can gain *economies of scale* and so can produce at lower cost than its smaller competitors.

NOTE: This last factor in the growth of firms is sufficiently important to need a more extensive treatment. The nature of the savings that come from large-scale organisation are frequently misunderstood, as is the fact that there may be disadvantages of large-scale organisation.

ADVANTAGES AND DISADVANTAGES OF LARGE-SCALE ORGANISATION

5. Advantages. Trading or manufacturing on a large scale brings many advantages. Which of these will apply in any given situation will depend on the exact circumstances of the case. Advantages may be:

(*a*) *Technical*, concerned with the nature of the process used.

(*b*) *Managerial*, concerned with the control of the organisation.

(*c*) *Marketing*, concerned with buying and selling.

(*d*) *Financial*.

Each of these major types of advantage is dealt with below.

6. Technical advantages.

(*a*) *Specialisation.* The advantages that follow from *specialisation* and the division of labour will be familiar by now (*see* I, **1–4**). Obviously, there is more scope for the division of labour in the larger firm. As the quantity of work of a particular type increases, specialist workers can be brought in to deal with each aspect of it. Once the job has been broken down into separate tasks, specialised machines can be used and, at a later stage, the element of human control can be reduced so that the machines become self-regulating. At a still later stage, individual jobs can be brought together again as batteries of automatic machines are unified into an automated production line. The large firm also has more opportunity to combine machines of varying capacity so as to make the best use, with the least idle time, of all of them.

(*b*) *Equipment.* It is only the large firm that can use the most elaborate machines, spreading their very heavy capital cost over a large output. This applies not only to manufacturing industry but also to commerce, electronic computers, for example, being too expensive for most small firms.

NOTE: The advent of small computers of fairly low capital cost and the extension of bureaux services are now bringing these facilities within the reach of many medium-sized firms.

(*c*) *Expense of equipment.* A further set of advantages that may come to larger firms is that a single large item of equipment is often not as expensive as an equivalent number of small units. This will always be the case where *economies of increasing dimensions* apply. A 100,000-tonne oil tanker does not take so much steel, need so much horse-power to propel it nor so many crew-members to man it as would three smaller tankers of around 30,000 tonnes to 35,000 tonnes. Similarly grain-silos, blast-furnaces and so on are cheaper if built on a large scale, and with blast-furnaces there is the additional advantage of having less heat-loss than from an equivalent number of small furnaces.

(*d*) *Standardisation.* This is not a book on the technicalities of production and it would not be appropriate to spend very much time on these topics, but it will readily be appreciated that there are further advantages from having several processes carried out on the same site instead of at separate factories and that there are economies from *increased standardisation.* Finally, the larger firm has more money to spare for *research* and is likely to make more rapid technical progress than the small firm.

7. Managerial economies. The management of a large commercial or industrial enterprise involves many things; the choice of products to sell or make, the investigation and selection of markets, finding finance for the business, over-all supervision once the business is a going concern and many other tasks. The large firm will be able to engage specialist managers to look after each aspect of the work. It will employ skilled accountants, sales managers, production managers, personnel managers and so on. Top management will be able to *delegate* subsidiary tasks and will be able to concern itself with the over-all policy of the business. Really first-class management is always in short supply and the bigger firms are able to afford the salaries that will attract the best men in their fields.

8. Advantages in marketing. Firms that buy in large quantities will obtain the best discounts. A really big customer will be able to insist that suppliers quote early delivery dates and keep to them. Sometimes a single big corporation will give orders that account for the whole of a small supplier's output. In these circumstances, the customer can dictate prices, within limits, and can lay down detailed specifications for design and production.

It is probable that the large firm will have advantages in selling. It is likely to have its own highly trained sales force, can offer better after-sales service and can advertise more effectively. Large units, both in manufacturing industry and in the retail trade, may use their own wholesaling organisations.

9. Financial advantages. Since the large firm is likely to be a public limited company, probably with its shares quoted on the Stock Exchange (*see* IX, 16), it will be able to go to the public for its long-term capital. The more successful its record is, and the more secure it seems, the better the terms on which it can raise money. It is also easier for big firms to obtain bank loans and it is the larger and more prosperous firm that will be able to provide internal finance by ploughing back profits.

10. Disadvantages of large-scale organisation. As the scale on which business is carried on grows, so various disadvantages become apparent. Although it might be possible to reap further economies from standardisation, customers do not always want a standard product; they may want variety. In a large firm, too, the consequences of a mistaken decision may be disastrous, wasting hundreds of thousands of pounds and throwing many people out of work. Large companies tend to become bureaucratic in spite of the best efforts of very competent executives to keep the organisation flexible and responsive to change. Decision making becomes slow and must follow recognised procedures. When a firm has many departments it becomes difficult to co-ordinate them. As difficulties of this sort multiply, management of even higher calibre is needed to resolve them, but the supply of top executives is very limited.

11. Persistence of the small firm. There are more small firms in Britain than there are large firms. In the face of the undoubted advantages of the large organisation, it is necessary to ask why these small firms still exist. Among the reasons are:

(*a*) *Personal services.* The small firm is still more efficient where the service provided is a personal one.

(*b*) *Frequent decisions.* Where important decisions have to be taken quickly and frequently, the smaller business has an advantage. This may well be the case in agriculture, where three-quarters of all holdings are of less than seventy-five acres in extent.

(*c*) *Small markets.* The firm which produces or sells on a large scale must have a large market for its wares.

Where the total market is limited, the size of the firm is also limited.

(*d*) *Early stage of growth.* At any one time there will be firms that will grow to a large size in future years, but just at the moment their growth is still at an early stage.

(*e*) *Ease of entry.* Just as there are likely to be a number of new entrants who have not had time to expand, in trades which are relatively easy to enter, there may also be a large turnover of small businesses run by persons of doubtful capacity who enter the trade but fail within a short time. This is often seen in some sections of retail trade.

(*f*) *Shortage of executive ability.* Large-scale organisation calls for executive skill of a high order if the disadvantages of its size are to be overcome. Some firms could reap economies of scale if they had competent and forceful management.

MERGERS AND TAKE-OVERS

12. Five series of mergers. Although mergers and take-overs have received a great deal of publicity in recent years, the movement towards further concentration is no new thing in British industry. There have been five waves of mergers:

(*a*) *At the turn of the century* when foreign competition was becoming more intense and it was necessary for British firms to amalgamate in order to face their foreign rivals.

(*b*) *In the inter-war years,* which saw the amalgamation of the railway companies into the four big groups which lasted until nationalisation, the forming of I.C.I. and Lever Bros., and the rationalisation of the steel industry.

(*c*) *In the 1950s* a number of very significant take-overs made the headlines. Some of these were horizontal amalgamations designed to gain economies of scale, but many were caused by the undervaluation and under-utilisation of assets (see below).

(*d*) *In the mid- and late-sixties* this wave continued with the active encouragement of the Government and the

IRC (*see* 20). The aim of this series of mergers has been to establish larger units which are more competitive in international markets.

(*e*) *The 1970s.* In the final years of the 1960s new and powerful influences were apparent. The very big organisations expanded without regard to conventional boundaries between either industries or frontiers to form *conglomerates* and *multinational* corporations.

13. Reasons for mergers.

(*a*) *Economies of scale.* While economies of scale may be obtained through the growth of a single firm, it is often quicker and more effective to achieve larger size by amalgamating with another firm in the same line of business. This is usually done by mutual agreement between the firms concerned, but sometimes one company may attempt to gain control of another against the wishes of that company's directors or in the teeth of opposition from large shareholders. The term "take-over" is best reserved for this latter type of operation.

(*b*) *Security.* The desire to obtain the advantages of large-scale production may be one reason for mergers, but another is to gain security from competition. A larger share of the market may confer a degree of security by lowering costs or it may be considered better to merge with a rival firm than to compete.

(*c*) *Diversification.* A firm which produces or sells a single product may feel vulnerable to changes in demand in that particular market. In these circumstances a company may acquire interests in fields that are totally different from its own. Thus, the Imperial Tobacco Company controls Golden Wonder potato crisps, and a few years ago Courtaulds gained control of Pinchin Johnson, the paint manufacturers. Some of the biggest groups in British industry are diversified. Unilever, for instance, controls enterprises making a variety of products from detergents to frozen foods and animal feeding stuffs, and also owns chains of retail provision shops.

(*d*) *Realisation of assets.* When the market value of a

firm's shares is much less than the potential value of its assets, there is a standing invitation to anyone with access to sufficient cash to try to gain control of the company in order to sell or develop its assets. Reasons for the undervaluation of assets might include unimaginative and conservative management or failure to realise the potential value of assets if they were put to alternative uses. It was situations of this sort that led to the wave of take-overs that caused such a sensation in the mid-1950s. These takeovers sometimes caused hardships to employees, but they did result in a better utilisation of resources.

14. Horizontal and vertical integration. When amalgamations link firms which make similar products and are at the same stage in the process, this is called *horizontal integration.* The merger between International Computers and Tabulators and English Electric Computers brought together two major computer makers into a single group. Earlier, the government-sponsored amalgamations in 1959 put the greater part of the British aircraft industry into three major groups, the British Aircraft Corporation, Bristol Siddeley and Hawker Siddeley.

Amalgamations at different stages of the productive process are known as *vertical integration.* Vertical integration may be backwards, towards the sources of raw material or forward, towards the market. The entry of the major oil companies into the new field of petro-chemicals is an example of vertical integration as, earlier, was the acquisition by Ford of Briggs Motor Bodies.

15. The take-over code. Successive waves of take-overs have inspired criticism which the City has attempted to meet by the publication of codes of behaviour for companies and institutions involved in bids. The latest of these is the code published by the Issuing Houses Association in March 1968. This code has no legal force, but is thought to command wide allegiance among those likely to be concerned, the more so since the Bank of England has added its support to the principles embodied in it. Broadly, the code provides for dealings which are as open as possible and which are fair to all shareholders. "Insider dealings" are not forbidden, but any such "undercover" attempts to gain control must be revealed on the day after the dealings have taken place. At the time of writing, breaches of the code are again causing the question of enforcement to be discussed.

MONOPOLY AND COMPETITION

It is the common practice to talk as though monopoly was necessarily bad and competition good. The argument runs that competition is a spur towards greater efficiency and will "shake out" the inefficient firms. On the other hand, the stability of organisations having a high degree of monopoly power may allow them to allocate more funds to research or to employee welfare so that they are both technically and socially progressive. If they make good use of the economies of large-scale production, firms with a degree of monopoly power may have lower costs and be able to offer lower prices than an equivalent number of smaller, competing firms. Suspicion of monopoly is still justified, however. Groups that dispose of such huge funds have a great deal of power, and this power is not very susceptible to democratic control. Exploitation of consumers by firms enjoying a monopoly position is by no means ruled out, either.

16. Forms of monopolistic organisation. Strictly speaking, monopoly means a single seller, but any firm with a large share of the market may enjoy a degree of monopoly power. Some forms of monopolistic organisation are deliberately aimed at restricting competition, others are intended to gain economies of scale but confer monopoly power nevertheless. The principal forms of large-scale and monopolistic organisation are:

(*a*) *Amalgamations.* These have already been discussed. They are intended to be permanent organisations, the organisations concerned losing their separate identities.

(*b*) *Holding companies.* One company may gain control of another by obtaining a majority of the shares with voting rights. It is often convenient to control a group of companies by having a single company hold either all the shares of the subsidiary companies or a majority of the shares. The subsidiaries may be allowed to keep their separate identities and to retain a measure of control. The device of the holding company can give control of a group of subsidiaries with a minimum capital outlay. A shareholding which is sufficient to gain control of a subsidiary can be used to dictate policy and, if desired, to apply the resources of the subsidiary to gaining control over sub-subsidiaries. The use of minimum capital to control a succession of sub-subsidiaries is known as 'pyramiding."

(*c*) *Cartels, pools and rings.* The *cartel* is an organisation by means of which the participating firms agree to share the market, to limit profits or to define sales areas. In its strict form the central organisation has power to inspect the books of member firms and to levy fines on members who do not keep the rules of the cartel. Organisations to limit market shares or to regulate profits tend to be popular when trade is depressed, but to break up when trade improves. The cartel is an attempt to put such a grouping on a more permanent and formal basis. *Rings* and *pools* are less formal organisations intended to control the sales of a commodity or to share the profits of some joint enterprise.

(*d*) *Marketing Boards.* Although arrangements to restrict output, prices or market shares are registerable under the *Restrictive Trade Practices Act*, 1956 (*see* **18**), *statutory* organisations have been set up to regulate the marketing of some types of agricultural produce.

(*e*) *Price agreements.* Before the passing of the 1956 Act, price fixing agreements, operated through the appropriate Trade Association, were the rule in many trades. Since 1956 over 1,500 such agreements, registered under the Act, have been allowed to lapse, but informal price fixing and the following of policies set without public comment by the leading firms in an industry are less easy to regulate.

(*f*) *Syndicates and consortia.* Collaborations of firms over a limited field or to obtain particular objectives are variously known as syndicates or consortia. The term "consortium" is perhaps more appropriately used for a collaboration involving a pooling of resources in some field over a lengthy period. The Nuclear Power Group is such a pooling of resources by firms engaged in heavy electrical engineering and other activities for the design and construction of nuclear power stations. An example of a syndicate would be the temporary grouping of City interests that tried to prevent the take-over of British Aluminium by the American firm, Reynolds Metals, some years ago.

(*g*) *Conglomerates.* In the late 1960s a new type of merger, bringing together companies whose main interests were very diverse, became increasingly important. These new organisations were distinct from the merely diversified companies both on account of their very large size and of their distinctive method of operation. For the conglomerate, the important factor in its management is the securing of a high rate of return on its investment and its willingness to subordinate other objectives to this end. Admirable as this may be in ensuring an efficient utilisation of assets, it may lead to a neglect of legitimate longer-run aims. A typical conglomerate of the early 70s might be involved in entertainment, hotels, food and brewing.

(*h*) *Multinationals.* A further development of the same period is the multinational company formed by an amalgamation between companies having similar interests but previously operating within national boundaries. This is not, essentially, a new movement as the Unilever organisation and the big automobile companies testify, but the appearance of a new wave of international amalgamations, such as the Dunlop–Pirelli merger, does indicate a new freedom in the way in which business is able to transcend national frontiers.

THE CONTROL OF MONOPOLY

17. Public policy. The policy of successive governments has been to prevent the excesses of monopoly power and yet to permit and encourage the growth of large, low-cost firms. Not surprisingly, complete success in either direction has been elusive.

18. Restrictive Trade Practices Act, 1956. This Act is still a most important part of the legislation controlling monopoly. All agreements between two or more persons concerning the supply and production of goods and containing restrictions concerning prices, conditions of supply, processes of manufacture, persons to whom goods may be supplied or areas of supply, must be registered with the Registrar of Restrictive Practices. The Registrar has the power to call selected cases before the Restrictive Practices Court, which has the status of the High Court and consists of five judges and not more than ten expert lay members. The Court is required to consider restrictive agreements to be against the public interest unless the parties to the agreement can show otherwise.

Seven definite ways in which an agreement may be in the public interest have been defined and these include the protection of the public against injury, the prevention of unemployment and the preservation of export earnings. Even if one or more of these "gateways" is passed, the Court must still be convinced that the public will benefit on balance. This part of the Act was operated very strictly and was amended by a further Act of 1968, which exempted from registration agreements which might be of importance for the national economy. The 1968 Act, however, increased the penalties for failing to register and made agreements to share information, and so to avoid competition, registerable.

The second case to come before the Court was the Cotton Yarn Spinners' Association's minimum price agreement, which was believed to have had a strong chance of being found not contrary to the public interest. The failure of this case set the tone for the Court's work and many agreements have been allowed to fall into disuse rather than be defended before the Court.

The 1956 Act made collective resale price maintenance illegal (*see* XVI, **22**) and altered the size and powers of the Monopolies Commission, which had been set up in 1948 to investigate, on the request of the then Board of Trade, industries in which at least one third of the supply was in the hands of a single firm or group.

19. The Monopolies and Mergers Act, 1965. This Act restored the Monopolies Commission to its previous membership of twenty-five and extended its powers to cover services as well as goods. The Act gave greater powers to the Board of Trade to remedy abuses revealed by Monopoly Commission reports and the Board of Trade was also given powers to hold up mergers and take-overs while their desirability is investigated. Newspaper mergers require special consent if they result in total daily circulations of 500,000 or more copies. The powers of the commission were further extended by the *Fair Trading Act*, 1973.

20. The work of the IRC. The existence of the Industrial Reorganisation Corporation has already been mentioned in **II, 11**. The Corporation was influential in reorganising key sectors of British industry in the late 1960s. It was set up by an Act of Parliament in 1966 and was given power to "promote or assist in the reorganisation of any industry" and these powers included the acquisition and disposal of shares in companies and the making of loans to companies. The IRC took a leading part in promoting or assisting in the GEC/AEI merger and in the BMC/Leyland merger among others. The Corporation was much criticised for the part it took in supporting one contender rather than another in the struggle to acquire the Cambridge Instrument group in the spring and early summer of 1968. The work of the IRC has also led to some disquiet regarding its relationship with the Monopolies Commission. Mergers are only referred to the Commission if the Government so directs. The Government, therefore, had the power to promote some mergers but to hinder others. The IRC ceased to operate in 1971, issuing its final report in July of that year.

21. The National Enterprise Board. The *National Enterprise Board* (NEB) was established by the *Industry Act*, 1975 with the objectives of promoting industrial efficiency and international competitiveness. Like the IRC, it is concerned with the re-organisation of industry, but its powers also allow it to extend public ownership by purchasing share-holdings in companies. It represents, therefore, a much more forceful and radical approach to intervention in industry than was envisaged by the IRC. At the time of writing, however, its powers have only been used in a limited way and the funds placed at its disposal have been comparatively small.

PROGRESS TEST 6

1. What social and economic factors have encouraged the development of large industrial and commercial organisations? **(1–4)**

2. Discuss the advantages and disadvantages of large-scale organisation. **(5–10)**

3. Distinguish carefully between horizontal and vertical integration, giving examples of each. **(14)**

4. Write short notes on the following topics:

(*a*) The survival of the small firm. **(11)**
(*b*) Take-overs. **(15)**
(*c*) Holding companies. **(16)**
(*d*) *The Restrictive Trade Practices Act*, 1956. **(18)**

5. "Those who frame public policy towards monopolies never seem sure whether they should restrict the power of the large firm in order to protect the consumer or should encourage it in order to gain economies of scale." Discuss. **(17–20)**

CHAPTER VII

LABOUR AND TRADE UNIONS

In many fields of economic policy, it is possible for the government to intervene directly. Industries can be subsidised, tax rates altered and so on, but where industrial relations are concerned, direct action is difficult. Good industrial relations depend on social and personal relationships and these are not amenable to control and regulation. On the other hand, much economic policy depends for its success on high productivity and freedom from industrial unrest and this has forced successive governments to consider the possibility of intervention in a field where direct government action is likely to be difficult. In outlining the structure of labour relations in Britain, it is useful to begin with the voluntary aspects, therefore, and then to go on to see how this voluntary system has had to be modified.

LABOUR AT THE WORKPLACE

1. Productivity and the working group. The level of workers' morale and the amount of effort which they put into their work generally depends on standards set within the comparatively small groups of people who work closely together day after day. These groups, sometimes referred to as "primary work groups," are small enough for all the people concerned to know each other well and to be aware of each other's capabilities and characteristics. The people involved in such a group are aware of who is reliable and to be respected and who is not. Many investigations have shown that it is in these primary groups that practical standards or "norms" of work are established and it is with these groups that a study of labour relations ought to start.

2. Leadership in work groups. The small, primary, work groups tend to throw up their own leaders without any formal process being necessary. There is some evidence to show that the persons chosen as leaders tend to vary with the circumstances in which the group finds itself, so that when conditions are tense and difficult the militant, who is possibly regarded as a "hothead" in normal times, becomes the natural person to express the group's discontent. In larger workgroups, which consist of several primary groups, it is not so easy for leaders to emerge in a natural way and some more formal process is needed. The employer, or the management, *appoints* charge hands and foremen to ensure that the work is carried out according to instructions and is properly controlled. The work-people also need someone to speak and act for them in matters affecting their pay and working conditions and, where there is adequate trade union organisation, they *elect* representatives, who are often called shop stewards, although this is not always their official title. In many factories another group of representatives is elected to represent the workers on consultative committees (*see* 5).

3. Negotiation at the workplace. A pattern of negotiation which is common in much of British industry is for a negotiating body consisting of representatives of both employers and trade unions to agree on *national* scales of wages and conditions. These national scales apply to all the firms in an industry, or in some cases, to all workers in particular trades. The detailed application of national agreements necessarily involves special knowledge of the jobs done by particular workers at individual factories and this knowledge only exists at *local* level. Much of the application of a new national agreement is likely to be routine but where disagreements arise, these have to be settled by negotiation between the local management and the workers' representatives. A great deal of workplace negotiation will also be needed when workers are paid according to their output under "piecework" or "bonus" schemes. Obviously changes in working methods or the introduction of new machinery is likely to affect earnings and discussion about rates and required levels of output will be needed. A great deal of such discussion is entirely successful and undramatic; it is the comparatively rare breakdown of negotiations which is given publicity.

Two further tendencies have given rise to increased negotiation at workshop and factory level in recent years. Schemes of payment by results have grown unpopular since they tend to obstruct the introduction of new methods and equipment. Consequently they have tended to be replaced by schemes for hourly or weekly payment, the terms of which have to depend on the detailed practices in operation. The second movement has been the introduction of productivity bargaining, under which a mass of traditional and obstructive rules are swept away in exchange for agreed higher payments. Again, the elimination of traditional work methods can only be accomplished with the agreement of the men on the spot.

4. Shop stewards. The workers' elected representative at factory or office level is usually called the shop steward. Sometimes several trade unions will be involved in a single firm or factory and then it is likely that the members of each union will elect one or more shop stewards to act as their spokesman and local negotiator. This is quite sensible when the unions represent different trades and skills. In some firms the shop stewards are chosen to represent all the people working in a particular department and so may speak for members of several unions. This system is adopted in some of the large automobile assembly plants. Where there are a number of shop stewards in an undertaking, it is desirable for them to meet together in a *shop stewards' committee* under the chairmanship of a "*convener*."

5. Joint consultation. In addition to matters of pay and conditions of work, which are the subject of negotiation between employers and trade unions, there are many other matters on which discussion and consultation are necessary. In many companies joint consultative committees have been set up to facilitate such discussions. Matters with which these committees are concerned include

(*a*) Improvements in methods of production.
(*b*) Changes in organisational structure.
(*c*) Training and education of employees.
(*d*) Health, safety and welfare.

It is usual for the constitutions of joint consultative committees to forbid discussion of wages and conditions of employment, thus avoiding any charge of attempting to circumvent the trade union channels of negotiation.

THE TRADE UNIONS

6. Origins. Although the trade unions may be said to have their origins in the medieval guilds, particularly in the "journeymen's guilds" which were formed to protect the interests of craftsmen who had little opportunity of becoming masters, their real significance came with the Industrial Revolution. Their early days were marked not only by opposition from the governing classes but also by the fact that their activities were actually against the law. After 1825 the laws which had made combinations of workmen illegal were repealed and the trade unions made slow but continual progress towards legal and social acceptance.

Attempts to form very large unions during the 1830s failed, but in the next decade more solidly based unions grew up among the skilled trades and some of these were the predecessors of present day unions. Thus, the Miners' Association was formed in 1841 and the Amalgamated Society of Engineers ten years later. These early unions were partly concerned with obtaining adequate wages and good working conditions for their members and partly with the provision of insurance and social benefits. This dual nature continues in many trade unions today.

It was natural in the nineteenth century climate of opposition to trade unionism that many of those involved in the emerging labour movement should look for political solutions to their problems. Further legal difficulties in the last years of the nineteenth century confirmed their belief that a political movement was needed and a Labour Representation Committee was formed. It was this committee which, a few years later, became the Labour Party and thus established a link which is a prominent feature of British political and economic life. It should be said, however, that there was no political uniformity among the early trade unionists and that a close connection between the trade union movement and a single political party is by no means the rule in other countries.

7. Craft unions and general unions. The traditional categorisation of British trade unions was into *craft* and *general* unions. The craft union was formed to look after the interests of workers pursuing some particular trade. It was frequently a small organisation and controlled very closely the conditions of entry and apprenticeship in the trade concerned. Two factors have led to the relative decline of the craft unions. Firstly, technological change has made many of the old skills obsolete and, secondly, the larger craft unions have opened their ranks to semi-skilled and even unskilled workers.

The general unions may be defined as large trade unions, the membership of which is not confined to a single trade or to a single industry. The typical general union would be the Transport and General Workers' Union with a membership of nearly two million scattered over many industries including road transport, oil refining and the ports. Although some unions are clearly of this general type, the distinction is no longer entirely clear, since other unions which formerly had a base in some well defined skill now organise workers of all grades over a range of industries.

8. Industrial unions. An industrial union is one which purports to organise all the workers in a single industry, thus facilitating negotiation and possibly increasing the union's power and influence. Industrial unionism has had much support at various times, not only from workers but also from industrialists, since it would appear to avoid the troublesome and difficult negotiation with several unions and also the folly of inter-union disputes. However it is increasingly difficult to define an "industry" and the existing pattern of unionism makes it difficult to impose a new scheme, however attractive it may seem. Unions such as the National Union of Railwaymen (NUR) have some claim to be industrial unions, but even here important sections of the industry owe their allegiance to other unions, in this case to the Associated Society of Locomotive Engineers and

Firemen (ASLEF) and to the Transport Salaried Staffs Association.

9. White collar unions. A feature of recent years has been the rapidity with which clerical and supervisory staffs have entered the trade union movement. In local government and the nationalised fuel and power industries, these workers are organised in the National and Local Government Officers Association, a major union with nearly 630,000 members. In the private sector, too, white-collar unionism has become a powerful force, the principal union being the Association of Scientific, Technical and Managerial Staffs.

10. Trade union membership. The foregoing outline of trade union structure may tend to give a rather false impression of the extent to which labour is organised. The fact is that out of a working population of 26 million people, some 11 million are members of trade unions. Thus only 40% of British workers are unionised. A further fact of life in the British trade union movement is that this membership is increasingly concentrated in a few very large unions, the smaller unions having been absorbed by a succession of amalgamations.

11. Trade union organisation. It is usual for trade unions to be organised locally into *branches*, these branches being responsible for routine administration. Increasingly the local negotiating responsibilities of the branch have been taken over by shop stewards who are in closer touch with the situation at shop-floor level. Officers of the branch are elected and frequently form a link with higher levels of union organisation since they are likely to be entitled to sit on district or area committees. The branch secretary may therefore be quite an important figure even though the influence of the branch itself is not great. Major questions of policy are usually decided at an annual *conference*. Representatives at the conference are likely to be branch secretaries, members of district committees and senior shop stewards. Unions employ a small number of full-time paid officials and these will also be present and will be very influential. While the conferences are able to decide policy in broad outline, the detail and, indeed, much of the substance of union strategy is often decided by the union *executive*, the top level body of senior elected members and paid officials. This is in most cases a very small and powerful group and since it meets frequently and is in touch with the major issues concerning the union, it may tend to dominate both the conference and the general running of the union's affairs. There is great variety in the pattern of trade union organisation but the elements outlined are present in most cases.

12. The T.U.C. One hundred and ten trade unions, representing 90% of total union membership, are affiliated to the Trades Union Congress, the central co-ordinating body of the British trade union movement. Now that the National Union of Teachers has become affiliated to the T.U.C., the remaining unaffiliated unions are, almost without exception, very small indeed. The affiliated unions send delegates, about a thousand, to an annual meeting, the main function of which is to elect a thirty-eight member General Council. The General Council is the dominant body of the T.U.C. and it, rather than the Congress as a whole, determines policy. The General Council of the T.U.C. is an important and influential body and is frequently consulted by the government on matters of industrial and economic policy. The General Council acts as a powerful "lobby" for the interests of organised labour and its opposition to legislation or to a particular government policy cannot be lightly dismissed. The General Council of the T.U.C. may also intervene in the settlement of inter-union disputes and a union which disregards its decisions may find itself liable to suspension from membership of Congress.

LEGISLATION ON LABOUR RELATIONS

13. The trade unions in the economy. The difficulties of adapting the British economy to the harsh conditions of the post-war world were mentioned in II, **10.** In order to keep British prices competitive in world markets, it is necessary to make sure that the costs of British goods do not rise too quickly. In order to curb inflation, it is important to make sure that incomes do not rise faster than productivity. Governments have not been successful in securing these objectives and one reason for this is that the trade unions have used their considerable power without regard to the over-all economic consequences. Too often essentially trivial disputes have been settled only after damaging strikes or other industrial action. Consequently it was felt that legislation should be introduced in order to make it rather more difficult to engage in strike action without very careful thought and a full exploration of alternatives. At the same time, the opportunity existed to safeguard the position of workers in several important respects. These principles were embodied in the *Industrial Relations Act*, 1971 but this proved wholly unacceptable to the trade unions and it was repealed in 1974. The *Industrial Relations Act* had provided for a *National Industrial Relations Court* and for a *register* of trade unions and employers associations. It also contained elaborate regulations concerning disputes and the way in which they could be conducted, the existence of "closed shops" and many other matters. Some parts of the *Industrial Relations Act*, although repealed, were re-enacted in the *Trade Union and Labour Relations Act*, 1974 (*see* **14**). These were the sections relating to unfair dismissal, to industrial tribunal procedures and to the "Code of Practice" for industrial relations.

14. The Trade Union and Labour Relations Act, 1974. This Act was the instrument by means of which the *Industrial Relations Act* was abolished. The effect of the *Trade Union and Labour Relations Act*, 1974 was to restore the legal position regarding labour relations in many respects to the state which had existed before the passing of the *Industrial Relations Act*. The traditional concept of free collective bargaining, with the two sides of industry settling the conditions of pay and employment between themselves without outside interference, at least so far as the legal system was concerned, was therefore reinstated. The new Act also freed the trade unions from a great deal of the liability which might arise from industrial disputes. Whether this privileged position in law, which was needed when trade unions were lacking in almost all power except that conferred by industrial action, is justifiable today, must be a matter for discussion.

As indicated in **13**, the *Trade Union and Labour Relations Act* (this cumbersome title is often abbreviated to TULRA) re-enacted the provisions of the previous Act which protected employees from unfair dismissal. Every employee, with a few exceptions, now has a right not to be dismissed unfairly and, in general, the onus of proof is on the employer to show that the dismissal was, in fact, fair. The Act also contained formal provisions defining a trade union for legal purposes, requiring the Registrar of Friendly Societies to keep and maintain a register of them, and similar matters.

15. Closed shops and unfair dismissal. The *Industrial Relations Act* had contained provisions intended to protect workers from the unfair practices of trade unions as well as from those of employers. Among these unfair practices was the coercion of workers to join a particular union. Workers, it was considered, should be free from pressure to join a union and should have the right, if they wished, to join no union at all. This was a blow at the practice of declaring a "closed shop," a workplace in which all the employees were required to be members of designated unions. This custom was, and still is, necessary in the eyes of many trade unionists both in order to prevent non-members from enjoying benefits stemming from union activity and, as well, to ensure solidarity among the workers concerned. The now repealed *Industrial Relations Act* allowed merely "agency shops," in which it could be agreed with the employers that workers could be required to join a union, but which provided exemptions in cases of genuine conscientious objection. The new Act (TULRA) allows a *union membership agreement* which effectively restores the closed shop. The effect of the new Act is that dismissal on the grounds of refusal to join an appropriate trade union is not unfair dismissal. There is still doubt, however, about what, precisely, constitutes an appropriate trade union. The new Act, too, contains provision for exemption from the requirement to join a particular union on the grounds of religious objection or on "other reasonable" grounds.

16. The protection of employment. Although the *Trade Union and Labour Relations Act* preserved and strengthened the workers' rights against unfair dismissal, there were still other areas of concern in which the government felt that new legislation was needed. There was, for instance, the problem of the employee's position if the firm he or she worked for should go into liquidation. Also, having restored free collective bargaining by the provisions of TULRA (*see* **14**), it was necessary to make sure that the bargaining processes themselves were effective. The provisions of the Act dealing with these matters, the *Employment Protection Act*, 1975, are complex and detailed and, as with the legislation discussed in the previous section, it is not possible to do more than indicate the approach taken by the law. The main safeguards offered by the Act are:

(*a*) Protection from loss of earnings due to short-time working.

(*b*) Payment when suspension is due to the existence of a health hazard.

(*c*) Maternity payments to be made under certain conditions and protection provided against dismissal which is solely due to pregnancy.

(*d*) The right to a written statement of reasons for dismissal of employees with at least twenty-six weeks' service.

(*e*) Consultation when redundancies are considered.

(*f*) Reasonable time off for trade union duties.

(*g*) The right to claim from the redundancy funds any amount owing to employees on the insolvency of an employer.

The collective bargaining machinery is strengthened by requiring the *Advisory, Conciliation and Arbitration Service* to promote the improvement of labour relations and to give and publish advice on industrial relations and collective bargaining. In addition to its conciliation and arbitration functions with respect to disputes, the Service may also make recommendations concerning the recognition of trade unions by employers. These recommendations are not to be taken lightly, since employers have duties of consultation and disclosure of information, imposed on them by the Act, towards recognised independent trade unions. The Act also sets up other institutions including a *Central Arbitration Committee.* The provisions of the Act place heavy duties upon employers and so are being introduced gradually to enable full preparation to be made.

17. Changes in legislation. Legislation regarding industrial relations is a matter for political dispute, as may have been gathered from the previous sections. The unions feel that negotiations between workers and employers should not be regulated although there should be legal protection for workers. Many other people, including some trade union members, feel that union power should be regulated. Consequently, it is likely that there will be many further changes in this area of legislation as the balance of political power in the country changes. Perhaps the process could be seen as a gradual movement towards a compromise that is appropriate to the times and acceptable to the nation as a whole.

18. Other legislation concerning labour relations. There is, naturally, a great deal of legislation concerning the safety and well-being of employees and that is not our concern for the moment. However, in the field of labour relations some attention should be given to recent enactments to prevent discrimination on the grounds of race or sex. The two Acts concerned are the *Race Relations Act*, 1976 and the *Sex Discrimination Act*, 1975. These Acts cover a much wider range of activities than work and employment, but they should do much to prevent obvious and blatant discrimination.

PROGRESS TEST 7

1. What is meant by workplace or shop-floor negotiation and why is it important? (1–3)
2. "Shop stewards are unnecessary if there is adequate union branch organisation." Discuss. (4, 11)
3. Describe the evolution and structure of trade unions in Britain. (6–12)
4. To what extent is it true to say that the T.U.C. controls trade union policy? (12)

5. Discuss the way in which the changed position of the trade unions has been reflected in recent legislation. (13–17)

6. What is a "closed shop" and how has it been affected by changes in the law in recent years? (15)

7. Outline the main provisions of the *Employment Protection Act,* 1975 and discuss the extent to which these are likely to increase the security and well-being of workers. (16)

CHAPTER VIII

DOCUMENTS AND DATA-FLOW IN A BUSINESS

INFORMATION AND THE BUSINESS

1. The business as a system. In order to understand the part which information plays in the efficient functioning of the business, it is convenient to use the concept of the firm as an *open system*. We refer to the business as a system because its functioning can only be effectively understood when each of its parts is seen in relation to the business as a whole; it is not enough to see how each section of the business works because the operation of each part, each department or workshop, affects every other part. We must consider the system as an "open" one because it is in constant interaction with its *environment*, the outside world. This interaction with the community at large consists of three parts:

(*a*) Flows of energy and of material things.
(This category would include not only flows of electricity, fuel, raw materials and so on but also inputs of labour and the use of capital equipment.)
(*b*) Monetary and financial flows.
(*c*) Flows of information.

While the existence of the business depends on the maintenance of physical (or "energic") flows, these can only continue if monetary and financial flows are also maintained. If revenues fail, goods cannot be paid for nor can the wages and salaries bill be met. Neither of these first two categories of flow can be either measured or controlled, however, unless the information flow is adequate and prompt.

2. The firm and the outside world. A business can only succeed if it responds to changes in the community. It is useless to make products for which there is no longer any demand. It is also necessary to take account of the state of trade in general and of the policies and trading practices of rival firms. This means that there must be an *inflow* of information about all these areas of interest. In the terminology of the preceding section, we could say that information was required about the economic, social and trading environments of the firm. Similarly there must be adequate *outflows* of information from the firm in order to tell people about the goods and services which the firm provides. It is also necessary to tell possible investors and shareholders about the worth and prospects of the business. In addition *statutory* information must be published in the accounts if the firm is a limited company. Increasingly, too, large firms often find it prudent to publish general information about their activities in order to improve and preserve their "corporate image," the view of the company which it is wished to present to the community at large. While there is much that could be said about every one of these types of information flow, much of the remainder of this chapter is concerned with the detail of the ways in which information is received, stored and used within the business. We are also concerned with the specific techniques by means of which information is communicated to customers, creditors and others with whom the firm has dealings. The relationship between the firm and its environment is shown diagrammatically in Fig. 7.

3. Information flows within the business. Once a business becomes at all large, problems of internal communication arise. These concern:

(*a*) The way in which policy decisions are transmitted to those who must turn policy into specific instructions and procedures (from *policy* level to *administrative* level).

(*b*) The methods by which instructions are given to workers who must carry out the operations by which the business discharges its essential functions (from the *administrative* level to the *operational* level).

(*c*) The provisions for passing information back to the administrative level and to the policy level so that the effectiveness of decisions may be assessed and corrections made (feedback).

(*d*) The procedures by means of which operational information is passed *between* the working departments.

(*e*) The arrangements for collecting data into permanent or temporary records and for ensuring its prompt recall when it is required.

Each of these categories of information transmission, processing and storage deserves extensive discussion, but our present concern is with practical problems rather than

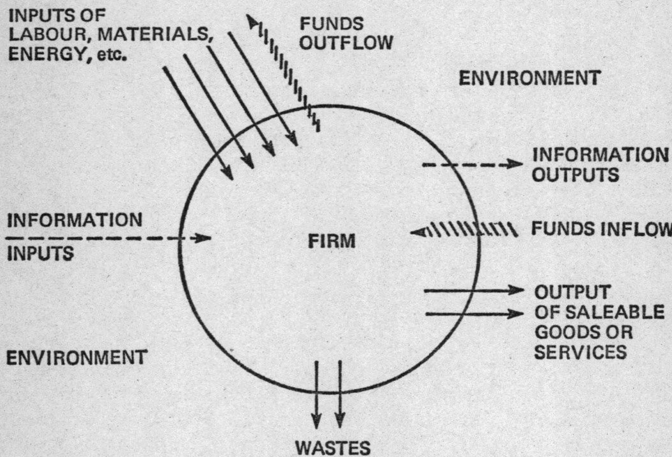

Fig. 7. The firm as an open system.

with managerial aspects of internal information flows. However, the essential functions of business information both within the business and between the business and the outside world must be kept in mind when considering the conventions and practices currently in use.

THE ACCOUNTING SYSTEM AND BUSINESS INFORMATION

4. Measuring performance. The owners of a business need to know whether the concern is efficient and well-run. It is by using money as a measure or "unit of account" (*see* XI, 9) for the various expenses of a business, whether payments have been made to outsiders or not, and by calculating the money value of its assets and of the various receipts, that the profitability of a business can be assessed.

The information necessary to calculate the profitability of a business and other measures of its performance are collected in the course of routine accounting operations. Unfortunately it is true that in many businesses great quantities of data are collected and never properly used, while information that is urgently needed never seems to be to hand.

5. Accounting information. Accounting information is required:

(*a*) so that the owners of the business may know its financial position,

(*b*) so that management may assess the profitability of the business in all its aspects and may estimate its financial needs, and

(*c*) so that the statutory requirements concerning the publication of accounts may be fulfilled and the tax position of the business may be calculated and all due allowances claimed.

6. Cost accounting. Financial accounting, the conventional accounting of the book-keeper, is not adequate for all the needs of a modern business. Systematic analysis of accounting data, however, can be used to reveal the actual cost of goods produced or of contracts carried out. Accurate costing is absolutely necessary for competitive pricing and the reduction of waste and inefficiency.

Although the data used by the cost accountant is essentially the same as that used by the financial accountant, the cost accountant's analysis is carried out independently. Strictly speaking, cost and financial accounts should be exactly reconcilable. In some businesses, systems of integrated accounts are used, so that the one accounting system produces both cost and financial accounting data.

7. Budgetary control. If the sales of a firm can be forecast with some degree of accuracy and past costing figures are available, a projection of future costs, revenues and profits can be made. In these circumstances, "budgets" can be established and if revenue or costs vary from the budget, investigations can be made and policies modified if necessary. A "flexible budget," in which budgeted costs can be adjusted according to fluctuations in output, can be a most effective instrument in the control of a business.

8. Information for business decisions. Information is required not only as a record of a business's past performance but also as a basis for current decisions. It is important that business decisions should be made as rapidly as changing conditions require and that, as far as is possible, the decisions made should be the correct ones. Good decision making requires accurate and up-to-date information and the provision of this information depends on the careful design of systems of data collection and data-flow.

SOURCES AND USES OF INFORMATION

9. Business documents. Control of the flow of information within a business depends to a large extent on the design and proper use of business documents. The actual documents and systems in use will vary from business to business, but some of the more important ones, which are in use in virtually every business, are discussed below. Some of the ways in which business documents can be used to control the flow of information have been described above (5–8).

10. Customers' order forms. Business documents are not standard. Life would be simpler if they were and there have been some attempts to encourage standardisation. Customers' orders will be of all shapes and sizes, therefore. Sometimes it may be desirable to transcribe this multiplicity of orders on to standard, internal stores requisitions or job sheets before they are acted upon further, but unnecessary copying and transcription is to be avoided.

11. Advice notes. When goods are sent to a customer, it is usual to enclose an advice note, showing particulars of the items supplied.

12. Invoices. The invoice tells the customer exactly what has been sold to him, the amount that is due and any discounts that may be deducted. It may also show transport or postage charges.

13. Credit notes. From time to time goods will be returned by customers because they are faulty, or invoices will overstate the amount due. Credit notes will be sent to customers making the necessary adjustment.

14. Statements. In the course of a month, a customer may receive several consignments. The invoices relating to these consignments will be listed on a statement, showing the sum due over the month, together with any balance carried forward.

15. Firm's own order forms (purchase orders). Every time a purchase is made, an order will have to be sent to the suppliers. Orders should be serially numbered and will state exactly the items required, quoting part numbers or other indentifying information and will bear the signature of a responsible official.

16. Arranging payment. Payment will only be authorised when goods have been supplied against the firm's order. Suppliers' invoices will be checked to see that they correspond with the orders, that all calculations are correct and that discounts have been given. If all is correct, payment will be authorised and cheques prepared. The normal practice is to make a single monthly payment to each supplier.

17. Payroll. Wages and salaries are a major expense of most firms. There are various methods of preparing the payroll, but some record of workers' hours is necessary and this will be provided by time-recorder sheets or cards giving a record of the times that work commenced and ceased each day. This mechanical record may be supplemented by detailed time sheets showing jobs worked on and extra rates claimed.

18. Stores records and stock control. Stocks, or inventories as they are sometimes called, are so closely connected with a firm's productive and financial efficiency that some of the most advanced methods have been applied to their control.

The value of stocks of materials, components, part-finished and finished goods is an item of information that is essential for the calculation of a firm's profit. For an effective purchasing and re-order policy, an up-to-the-minute record of stock levels is also necessary. Production could be held up completely for lack of some vital component and yet the high stock levels that would give absolute security from this sort of breakdown would necessitate unduly large amounts of capital being tied up in idle stocks.

Whatever methods of stock recording are used, they must provide

(*a*) immediate warning when stocks reach re-order level,

(*b*) adequate information for subsequent analysis of rates of materials, usage, delay in delivery, etc., and

(*c*) the value of stocks held.

19. Technical and production data. In addition to the information emanating from the accounting or inventory control systems, another important category of information is that relating to the actual process of production. In an engineering works, for example, it will be necessary to schedule the work on hand so that every machine is fully employed and queues of work are avoided as far as is possible.

Production data will also form an essential part of the costing system, since output figures will be needed to calculate unit costs or marginal costs and other data may be required for the allocation of overheads to particular jobs or departments.

20. Personnel. Information about personnel includes not only routine data, obtainable from an analysis of the payroll, but also detailed information about employees' skills, potentialities and experience. The second type is very important since it enables a firm to relate its labour force to its present and future needs and to operate a rational policy of recruitment and employee development.

21. Systems of information flow. The accounting system is the most easily recognised system of data collection and analysis, but it will now be appreciated that other systems exist simultaneously with it. The various flows of information are not entirely independent, production figures being incorporated into accounting information, figures from the accounts complementing sales office figures and so on. If all the systems of information collection are operated separately there is likely to be duplication of records and waste of time. Moreover, no one will know exactly what information is available. In a small firm, personal contact may overcome this, but in a larger business some form of *integrated data processing* is required.

METHODS OF HANDLING DATA

22. Book-keeping systems. *A manual book-keeping system* consists, essentially, of a set of ledger accounts in which transactions are recorded according to a laid-down procedure. Systems using bound ledgers have largely given way to *loose-leaf systems* which permit information to be typed on to a loose-leaf sheet or ledger card. By using double-feed typewriters, or other fairly simple devices, a summary of the entries can be kept and periodical totals produced. The marrying of the typewriter to the adding machine produced the keyboard accounting machine which permitted the necessary arithmetic to be carried out mechanically as the entry was being made. A modern direct-entry accounting machine may embody electronic as well as mechanical components.

23. Double entry. Conventional accounting methods, whether mechanical aids are used or not, embody the double entry principle. This system of book-keeping has the advantage of being self-checking to a high degree and of providing a set of rules which permit a simple and easily understood "model" of a business to be produced.

The rules of double entry book-keeping recognise that every business transaction involves a transfer of value. A sale of goods on credit, for example, represents a transfer of value from the seller to the buyer. This transfer is recorded in both its aspects in the selling firm's books, the sales ledger account being credited and the debtor's (buyer's) account being debited.

Since this book is not a treatise on book-keeping, no further attempt will be made to explain the mechanics of the system except to point out that its procedures regulate a flow of information so that it gives a picture (model) of the financial position of the business. This is illustrated in Fig. 8.

24. The main accounting statements. The diagram in Fig. 8 shows that the flow of data through the accounting system culminates in the production of the *profit and loss account* and the *balance sheet.* The profit and loss account shows the totals of expenses and receipts over the period under consideration. Expenses will include "virtual expenses" such as depreciation, as well as actual expenses representing payments of money. The profit and loss account shows the *net profit* available for disposal in whatever way the owners of the business may decide. The balance sheet does not record the totals which have accumulated over a period, but is a "point-of-time" statement, a snapshot showing the position of the business at a certain instant. It is concerned with the *assets* owned by a business and the *claims* which may be made against them (*liabilities*), including the claims of the owners. A simple form of balance sheet is shown in Fig. 9. It should be noted that the shareholders' capital represents a claim against the business and is not the same as the *real capital*, the machines, buildings and other resources employed in the business. The two ideas could be distinguished as the accountant's concept of capital and the economist's concept of capital. The *net worth* of the business to the owners is the *total of assets*, less claims due to outsiders.

25. Accounting for inflation. The conventional accounting system tends to be ineffective in revealing the state of a

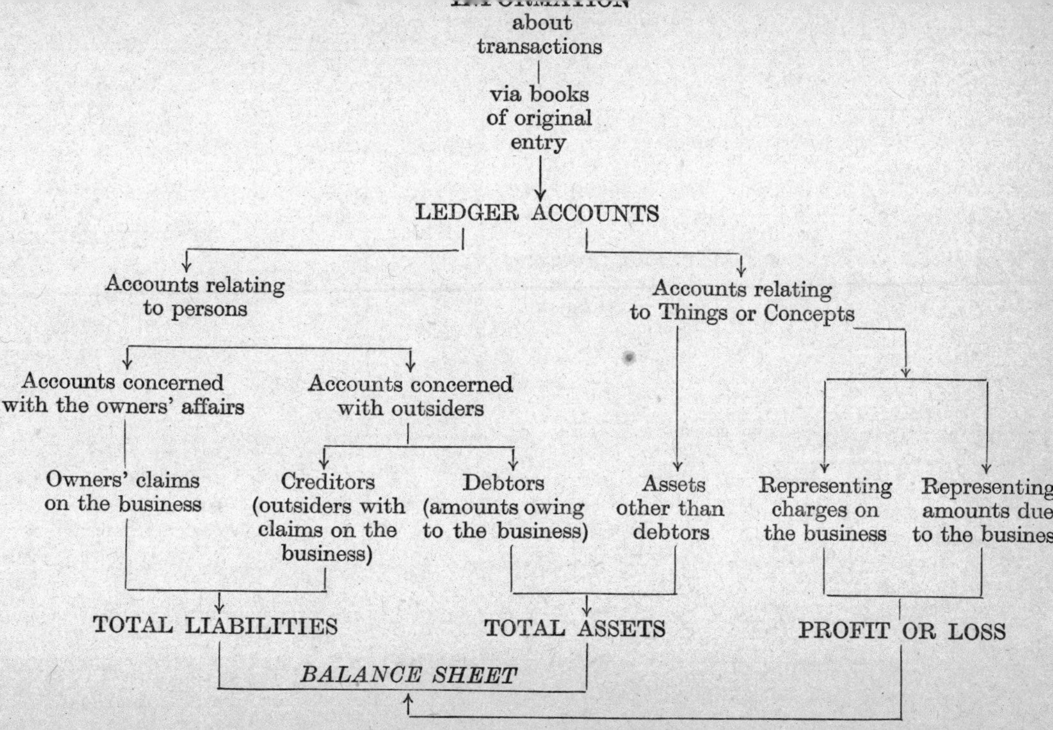

Fig. 8. The accounting system.

The Manufacturing Co. Ltd.

Balance Sheet as at 31 December 1975

	£ Authorised	£ Fully paid		£ Cost	£ Depreciation	£
SHARE CAPITAL			FIXED ASSETS			
20,000 6% Preference			Freehold land and			
Shares of £1 each	20,000	20,000	Property	90,000	—	90,000
200,000 Ordinary			Plant and Equipment	135,400	24,700	110,700
Shares of £1 each	200,000	200,000				
						200,700
	220,000	220,000				
REVENUE RESERVES			CURRENT ASSETS			
Undistributed Profits		20,000	Stocks of Materials			
			and Work in Pro-			
		240,000	gress		42,000	
			Stocks of Finished			
CURRENT LIABILITIES			Goods		16,000	
Creditors	52,000		Debtors		31,500	
Proposed Dividends			Bank Balances and			
(net)	16,200	68,200	Cash in Hand		18,000	107,500
		£308,200				£308,200

Fig. 9. A simplified balance sheet.

business in times of rapidly rising prices. The values of the several kinds of asset are distorted and profits may tend to be over-stated since depreciation charges are likely to be

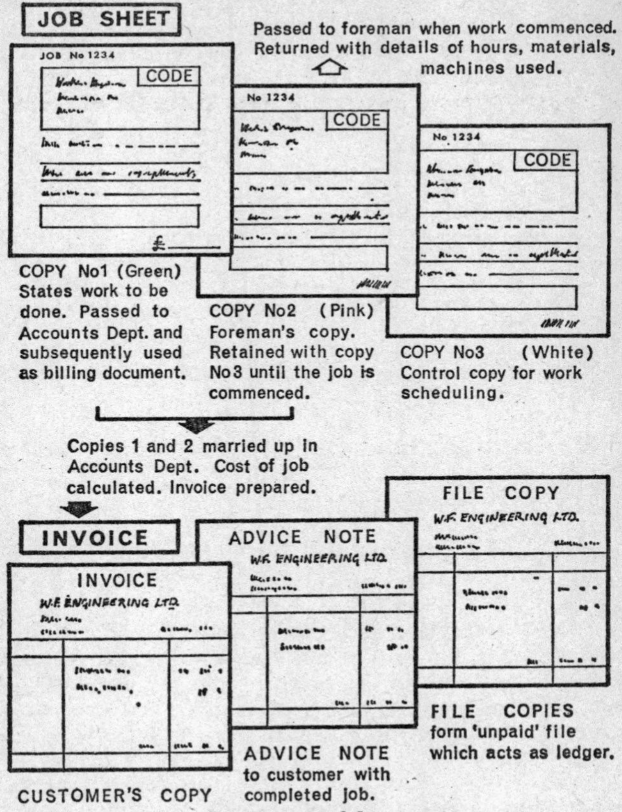

Fig. 10. The use of documents.

based on the book values of fixed assets. In the autumn of 1975 the government accepted the main recommendations of the *Sandilands Committee* (which had worked under the chairmanship of Sir Francis Sandilands) and endorsed the concept of *Current Cost Accounting*, or CCA. The main features of this system are that assets and liabilities are shown in the accounts at the *current* value of the item to the business. There are many technical problems in valuing assets under this system and while the *replacement* cost may often be the correct valuation, in other circumstances the *net realisable value* or the *present value of future earnings* from the asset would be appropriate. At the time of writing the government has proposed that CCA should be applied

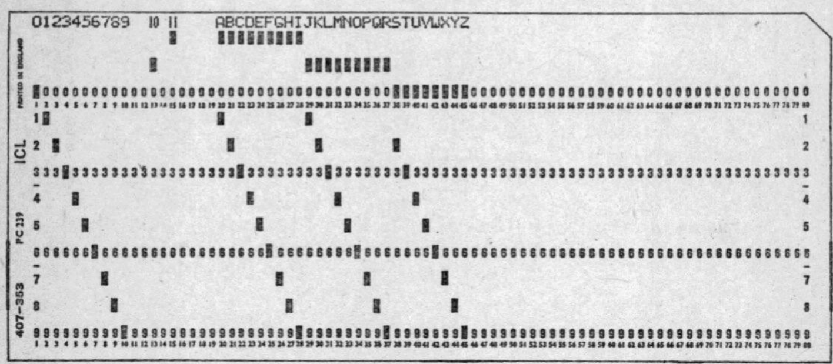

Fig. 11 An 80-column punched card.

to published accounts for all periods beginning after 24th December 1977, "if this proves feasible."

26. Improvements in data-processing. The efficiency with which data is handled does not depend entirely on the use of accounting machines or other expensive equipment. Even a small firm can improve and streamline its data-processing by giving careful attention to the design of its documents and procedures. The use of multi-copy stationery, for example, so that information required at several points in the firm's organisation is produced in one typing or writing operation, can save time and reduce errors. Copy documents can take the place of the ledger, each outstanding account, for instance, being represented by a copy of the invoice in the "unpaid" file. When payment is made the account concerned is removed from the file, the total of the copy invoices remaining in this file being the total due from the firm's debtors. Fig. 10 shows a single system of this kind. Coding systems can simplify the analysis of cost or other data.

27. Punched cards. A comparatively early development in the processing of data was the punched card installation. Coded references, quantities or values are represented on the card by holes punched in appropriate positions. An example of a punched card is shown in Fig. 11. The basic equipment used with punched cards comprises:

(*a*) *The punch*, which may be automatic and quite elaborate.

(*b*) *The sorter*, which sorts cards mechanically, at high speeds.

(*c*) *The tabulator*, which can perform arithmetical operations and prints out information read from the cards.

Punched cards still form a much used input and storage medium in computer systems.

28. Electronic computers. Electronic computers caused a great stir when they were first put to commercial use in the early 1950s. The superiority of the computer lies not only in its ability to carry out calculations at great speed, but also in the fact that it has a memory and that instructions as well as facts may be stored in its memory. The memory may consist of magnetic tape, magnetic cards, magnetic drums, discs, ferrite cores or ordinary punched cards. The speed with which the computer can retrieve material from its memory store depends on the type of storage device used, and most computers incorporate a combination of the devices listed. A block diagram of an electronic computer is shown in Fig. 12.

29. Programming. The computer is a very fast calculator but it is no "electronic genius." Instructions must be fed into the machine in a form which it can understand and this means breaking down every command into its simplest parts. These precise and detailed instructions must then be coded and transformed into impulses on magnetic tape or holes in punched paper tape or some other acceptable form, depending on the input medium used. A sequence of instructions is called a *program.* Once a program has been devised for a certain operation, the preparation of the payroll, for instance, it can be used over and over again.

In order to avoid the translation of every step of the program into "machine language" a translator program can be stored in the computer and instructions given in "symbolic" form using standard abbreviations. A further

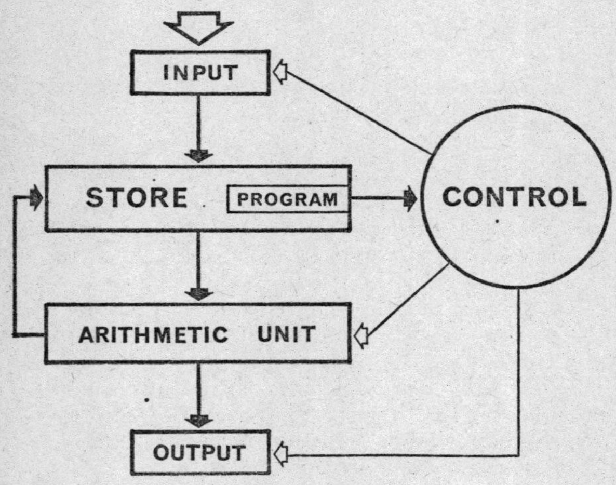

Fig. 12. The electronic computer.

refinement is the standardisation of sub-routines that are in frequent use. When a program involves one of these standard sub-routines, the program can use a single *macro-instruction* which will cause the computer to follow the predetermined sequence of operations.

In the last few years, these *autocodes* have been developed to the point where it is possible to talk of "computer languages." These languages can simplify programming considerably, but unfortunately standardisation of computer languages has not been achieved. Among the best known computer languages are COBOL and FORTRAN.

30. Input and storage media. The acquisition, transfer, processing and storage of information is a complex affair. In recent years, however, the range of available input and storage media has increased to such an extent that the information aspects of the business system have become ever more dovetailed with the physical processes of trading or of providing services. Some of these new methods of recording data are:

(*a*) *On line terminals*, which allow an operator to interrogate and communicate directly with a computer.

(*b*) *Magnetic ink characters*, which, with the necessary reading equipment, permits the reading of special type directly from documents into the computer.

(*c*) *Mark readers.* These allow pencil marks placed in specific places on forms to be read directly as do *mark sensing* devices with punch cards.

(*d*) *Perforated tags.* Readers may have seen these tags on garments or other items in large stores. Fed into an appropriate mechanism these tags convert sales and cost data into punched card form.

These methods are, of course, in addition to the well-known punched cards, paper tape and magnetic tape input and storage devices.

The increasing flexibility and versatility of recording and input devices has been matched by that of storage devices. The appropriate device to be used will depend on how *quickly* the stored information is required, how *long* the information must be retained, the *volume* of the material to be stored and the *cost* of the medium chosen. Modern *file media*, the usual term for the method used to store information for later use, include magnetic tape, magnetic drums and magnetic discs as well as the familiar punched cards, which are now used for input and output rather than storage.

31. The effect of the computer. Accounting routines are usually among the first applications when a computer is introduced into a business. Payroll, consumer billing and stores accounting are obvious examples of operations that involve much routine and repetitive clerical work. Both before the computer is ordered and afterwards when the flow of work is being planned, all the accounting systems involved will be subjected to a thorough scrutiny and analysis. This critical appraisal of existing routines and the streamlining which follows may be one of the major benefits from installing a computer.

The use of a computer tends to centralise the storage of information. Centralised files and the ability of the computer to recall data rapidly and to analyse it in different ways for different purposes are steps towards the integrated data-processing system mentioned in **21**.

32. **Operational research.** Operational research represents the application of scientific and mathematical thought to business problems. Essentially, operational research demands a thorough study of the problem concerned, the construction of a "model," which is a mathematical representation of the situation, and the manipulation of the model to produce an optimum solution. The availability of information and the calculating power of the computer both have relevance here.

PROGRESS TEST 8

1. What is meant by referring to the business as a "system" and how does this affect your view of the use and control of business information? **(1–3)**

2. Discuss the ways in which accounting information may be used in a manufacturing business. **(4–8)**

3. Write notes on the following documents, explaining clearly the function of each:

    (*a*) Credit note.
    (*b*) Invoice.
    (*c*) Advice note.
    (*d*) Statement.
    (*e*) Purchase order. **(11–15)**

4. Distinguish between a profit and loss account and a balance sheet, describing the contents and purpose of each of these accounting statements. **(24)**

5. The following items refer to the XYZ Co. Ltd. on the 31st December 1965. Arrange them in balance sheet form:
Share capital, 20,000 £1 ordinary shares fully paid, £20,000;
Sundry creditors, £7,500;
Value of premises, £12,000;
Machinery, £6,000;
Stocks of materials, £2,000;
Debtors, £5,000;
Cash, £2,500. (24)

6. Why does rapid inflation make traditional accounting methods inappropriate? What can be done about this problem? (25)

7. What is meant by "computer programming?" What advantages may be gained by introducing a computer into an organisation? (26–31)

8 Write brief notes on "Providing information for management." (1–32)

PART THREE

STOCKS AND SHARES

CHAPTER IX

RAISING CAPITAL FOR JOINT-STOCK COMPANIES

THE SHARE CAPITAL OF A COMPANY

The success of the joint-stock company as a form of business organisation rests on its ability to tap the savings of wide sections of the general public. Investment in joint-stock companies may be made directly by individuals or indirectly through institutions (*see* **23–26**). Whatever form the investment takes, the shares that the company offers must form an attractive "package," giving both a good return and reasonable security. A company can offer a great variety of rights and privileges to attract different types of shareholder and to suit different market conditions, but they fall into a few main categories which are dealt with below.

1. Preference shares. The holders of preference shares are entitled to a dividend before any dividend is paid to holders of other classes of share, but this dividend is given only at a fixed rate. Preference shareholders are reasonably sure of their fixed dividend even when profits are not sufficient to give a return to other shareholders. In years when the company makes no profit, or makes a loss, however, there can obviously be no distribution to the preference shareholders. Most companies, recognising that preference shareholders do not share in the "plums" of the very good years, and that it is unjust that in an occasional bad year they should even forfeit their relatively low fixed dividends, issue *cumulative preference shares.* Dividend unpaid on these shares in one year remains due in succeeding years. Preference shares are legally deemed to be cumulative unless the company's Articles specifically make them *non-cumulative*, in which case they will carry the right only to a fixed dividend from the profits of the year in question and will have no right to arrears of dividends from previous years.

Companies may also issue *redeemable preference shares* which may be "bought back," or redeemed, by the company at some future time. This gives the company the opportunity to issue a new class of shares, carrying different rights and possibly a different rate of dividend.

2 Participating preference shares. A company's articles may provide for the issue of participating preference shares, which carry a prior right to a fixed dividend, like other preference shares, but in addition are permitted to share in any profit remaining to be distributed after other classes have received dividends up to some agreed limit.

3. Ordinary shares. Ordinary shareholders take the main risk of a business and are entitled to the major part of the profit after the preference shareholders, if there are any, have been paid. Their dividend depends on the success of the business; in a good year they may receive a very handsome dividend indeed, in a bad year nothing. Since they take the risk, they usually possess the voting power to control the company.

4. Non-voting ordinary shares. In recent years, there has been a tendency for companies to issue ordinary shares which have the usual rights to dividends but which have no voting powers as regards the general policy of the company. These shares are sometimes known as "A" ordinaries. They permit the original majority shareholders to increase the capital of the company without relinquishing control. Although the issue of non-voting shares has been criticised on the grounds that ordinary shareholders take the risk and should share in the control, it has also been pointed out that those who purchase non-voting shares know what they are buying and the loss of voting rights is presumably reflected in the market price of the shares.

5. Deferred and preferred ordinary shares. Other classes of ordinary shares with special conditions attaching to them are *preferred* and *deferred* ordinaries. Preferred ordinary shares carry a preferential right to a dividend at some fixed rate and deferred ordinaries are entitled to a share in the profit remaining when dividends have been paid on all other classes of shares.

6. Founders' shares. Occasionally a special class of shares is issued to the original founders of a business, often as part of the consideration for the business when it is purchased by another company, or perhaps in recognition of some special service. Founders' shares, or management shares, are usually very few in number and carry a right to the residual profit when other shareholders have been paid. In a successful business, this will result in the fortunate few who hold founders' shares receiving a large dividend year after year. The issue of founders' shares is far less common than it used to be and is generally felt to be unfair to the ordinary investor.

7. Equity capital. Shares which carry a right to the residue of profits after a dividend has been paid to classes of shares with prior rights are often known as the *equity* of a company. The term *equities* is in general use to mean any shares (but particularly ordinaries) on which dividends may be paid without limit so long as profits are sufficient.

8. Stock. Although the terms *stocks* and *shares* are sometimes used in ordinary speech as if they were interchangeable, there is a clear distinction between them. A share is a distinct individual unit of capital in a company and shares can only be bought and sold in whole units. When all of a particular class of shares in a company's capital have been fully paid, that class of shares may be turned into *stock*. When a class of share capital is turned into stock it becomes a mass of capital rather than a number of separate units. Unlike shares, stock, even if divided into units for convenience, bears no distinguishing numbers and stock units may be bought and sold in fractional parts, unless the company's Articles expressly forbid it. The conversion of an issue of shares into stock simplifies the work to be done when holdings are transferred and makes the company's capital more marketable, since it can be transferred in any convenient amount.

9. Nominal values and shares of "no par value". In Britain, shares bear a value which is fixed when the capital of the company is registered (*see* IV, **11** (*e*)) and which forms the basis to which dividend percentages are referred. This nominal value bears little relationship to the price paid for shares on issue or to the market price of the shares at any later time. In the United States and some other countries shares of "no par value" are issued. These shares, as might be inferred, have no nominal value and entitle the holder to a certain proportionate interest in the ownership and profits of the company. Dividends can then be expressed as a money sum per share held. The Gedge Committee reported in 1954 that there were distinct advantages in issuing ordinary shares of no par value but that it would be unwise for preference shares.

10. Capital gearing. A company's capital may consist entirely of ordinary shares or of a variety of shares carrying different rights. Investors will not take fixed interest shares unless the company concerned is a safe one and so new companies without any background of successful trading and companies whose business is essentially risky must issue ordinary shares. Established companies with a good profit record can issue a proportion of their capital as preference shares.

The ratio in which a company's profit is divided between fixed interest shares and ordinary shares is known as the *capital gearing* of the company and depends on the number of ordinary and preference shares issued. A high proportion of preference shares results in a heavy burden of preference dividend to be borne before the ordinary shareholders get anything, but a relatively small number of ordinary shareholders to share any excess after the preference shareholders have been satisfied. Companies with capital structures of this type are said to be *highly geared* since a small increase in profit results in a large increase in the ordinary dividend.

Although capital gearing has been discussed above in terms of ordinary and preference shares, recent market conditions have favoured the raising of capital by means of *debentures* (*see* 13). An exactly similar situation arises, in terms of gearing, when the proportion of debt in a company's capital structure is high as when there is a high proportion of preference to ordinary shares.

11. Example of high capital gearing.

Issued capital of company

	£
250,000 6% £1 Preference shares	250,000
100,000 25p Ordinary shares	25,000
	£275,000

Year 1

Profit £16,000

	£
Preference dividend at 6%	15,000
Ordinary dividend (4%)	1,000
	£16,000

Year 2

Profit: £20,000

	£
Preference dividend at 6%	15,000
Ordinary dividend (20%)	5,000
	£20,000

12. Example of low gearing. Low geared companies, on the other hand, require a very large increase in profits before there is any significant increase in ordinary shareholders' dividend. In the example below, an increase in profit of over 35% has provided only an extra 2% for the ordinary shareholders.

Issued capital of company

	£
25,000 6% £1 Preference shares	25,000
1,000,000 25p Ordinary shares	250,000
	£275,000

Year 1

Profit: £14,000

	£
Preference dividend at 6%	1,500
Ordinary dividend (5%)	12,500
	£14,000

Year 2

Profit: £19,000

	£
Preference dividend at 6%	1,500
Ordinary dividend (7%)	17,500
	£19,000

LOAN CAPITAL

A company which is faced with the need for additional cash may choose to obtain it not by an issue of shares but by raising a loan. A person who *lends* money to a company is a *creditor*, not a shareholder. He is not a member of the company and, if the company should fail, he will have a right to be paid before any distribution is made to the shareholders.

13. Debentures. A debenture is the written acknowledgment of a loan made to a company. It normally contains provisions for the payment of interest and the eventual repayment of the sum loaned. Debentures are therefore a form of security and may be bought and sold in much the same way as shares. In order to give lenders some security against non-repayment of their loan, a charge is often made against the assets of the company, so that if the claims of the debenture holders are not met, assets can be sold and the debt repaid. The terms under which this can be done may be set out in a *debenture trust deed* which provides for the appointment of trustees who may act for the debenture holders if the company should default. Such debentures which create a charge on the property of the company are known as *mortgage debentures*. Debentures which are unsecured and make no charge on the company's assets are often known as "naked" debentures. Mortgage debentures may be secured on some particular asset, in which case there is said to be a "fixed charge," or they may be secured upon the whole assets of the company without any particular piece of property being specified. In this latter case there is a "floating charge."

Debentures may be registered in the holders' names and transfers made in much the same was as with shares, or *debenture stock* may be issued. It is not necessary for an issue of debentures to be fully paid and then turned into stock; the issue can be made in the form of stock from the start. If a company makes more than one issue of debentures, some may carry higher priorities for repayment in the event of default than others. In this case they are usually known as first debentures, second debentures and so on. Debentures are usually redeemable at some stated date, but occasionally they may be irredeemable.

The return which debenture holders receive is not a dividend, it is *interest* on the loan made. As such, it must be paid whether the company makes a profit or not. It is a charge against the profit and loss account of the company and is deducted *before* the net profit is calculated.

THE ISSUING OF SHARES TO THE PUBLIC

14. Methods of issue. There are several ways of issuing shares to the public. Which way the company chooses will depend on the size of the issue and the market conditions. Methods in use are as follows:

(*a*) Private placing.
(*b*) Stock Exchange introduction.
(*c*) Stock Exchange placing.
(*d*) Public Issue by Prospectus.
(*e*) Offer for sale.
(*f*) Offer for sale by tender.

The first three methods are suitable for smaller issues and the last three for full-scale major issues. Each of these methods is dealt with briefly below and the following part of the chapter deals with ways of issuing shares to people who are already shareholders.

15. Private placing. It is often convenient for a company wishing to make a fairly small issue of shares to make arrangements for their purchase privately by a single investor or by a few investors. The company's stockbroker will probably be well placed to act as an intermediary in such transactions. He may have possible purchasers among his own clients or he may be in touch with large investors who would be willing to take a block of shares. When a company needs additional capital it may be provided by a finance company taking up a block of shares in this way rather than by the provision of an ordinary loan.

16. Stock Exchange introduction. Stock Exchange introductions are a method of introducing the shares of a company onto the Stock Exchange. Unquoted shares are not very easy to sell and are difficult for executors to realise when a shareholder dies.

A company that wishes to have its shares introduced on the London Stock Exchange must arrange for its broker to apply to the Council of the Stock Exchange for a quotation and both the company itself and the issue of shares concerned are carefully "vetted." The public must be informed that the shares are available and an advertisement, also approved by the Stock Exchange authorities, is inserted in two leading London dailies and is circulated to the Exchange Telegraph and to Moodie's Statistical Services. In order to ensure that there are shares actually available for sale, the company must secure the support of two jobbers (*see* X, **5**) and must arrange to supply sufficient shares to create a free market. A private company that wishes to "go public" will seek a Stock Exchange introduction if it wants its shares to be quoted.

17. Stock Exchange placing. When a company wishes to raise a fairly large sum, but not more than about £500,000, the most convenient way is by a Stock Exchange placing. This combines features of both the methods previously described. The company's broker arranges for a number of institutional investors to take up a substantial proportion of the issue (*see* X, **9**). Application for a quotation is made to the Council of the Stock Exchange, and the issue is advertised in two London dailies and through the commercial information services. Jobbers in the appropriate market (*see* X, 5) are supplied with shares and ordinary investors can then buy the shares through their brokers in the normal way.

Placings are generally thought to be a little unfair to small investors who do not have a very good chance of getting their share of the issue. Nevertheless, they are a very popular way of making medium-sized issues. The Council of the Stock Exchange discourages placings for larger issues and insists that enough shares are available for general sale to ensure an active market.

18. Public issue by prospectus. This is the "full dress" method of floating a new share issue. The problem is to sell to the public in this one operation as many of the company's shares as they would normally take over a long period. This involves:

(*a*) Deciding what type of share is appropriate.

(*b*) Advertising the issue to the public.

(*c*) Making the necessary administrative arrangements for handling the flood of applications which is expected.

(*d*) Selling the shares at exactly the right price.

(*e*) Making arrangements for the "underwriting" of the issue, that is for any shares unsold to the general public to be bought by other persons or institutions.

A joint-stock company formed for manufacturing or trading is not equipped to carry out these tasks and so seeks the help of an *issuing house*. The issuing house may be a merchant bank or it may be one of the newer issuing houses specialising in share issues. A good issuing house will not handle an issue unless the company concerned is sound and the share issue has a good chance of success. The issuing house will advise the company on all the details of the issue and will arrange to have the issue underwritten. Frequently, the issuing house itself will be the main underwriter but will pass on some of the responsibility for the issue to sub-underwriters. If the issue is fully subscribed, the underwriters will earn their commission without any further service being required. If some shares remain unsold, the underwriters will take up their proportion of the shares at the issue price less their commission, thus obtaining a good security at a *cut-price*.

When the exact terms have been decided, the issue must be advertised to the public. Information about the company and the issue will be given in a *prospectus* which, according to Stock Exchange regulations, must be published in at least two London dailies. The published advertisement will include a form of application for the shares. If prospective investors are not to be misled, it is essential that the prospectus neither conceals nor misrepresents any material fact. The directors, in whose name the prospectus is issued, may be personally liable if the prospectus contains untrue or misleading statements. The *Companies Act*, 1948 sets out in some detail the particulars which must be contained in a prospectus. The prospectus will include a statement of the "minimum subscription," the minimum amount which is necessary, in the opinion of the directors, to enable the business to be started and to provide a reasonable working capital. Unless this minimum is subscribed, the Registrar will not issue a Trading Certificate (*see* **IV, 10**).

It frequently happens that an issue is *oversubscribed*, that is that more applications are received than there are shares available. When this happens, the directors may allot the shares in any way that they think fit. A very common way of doing this is to satisfy small applications in full and to allot only some given percentage of larger applications. The success of a new issue may be assisted by the activities of speculators known as *stags*, who buy shares in order to sell them at a profit as the market price rises.

On the whole *stagging* is not welcomed, as some of the less scrupulous speculators resort to practices which merely add to the difficulties of making the issue.

19. Offer for sale. When an "offer for sale" is made, the shares are offered to the public not by the company, but by some intermediary to whom the issue has already been sold. The intermediary is usually the issuing house, and the offer will be made to the public at a price which is high enough to cover the expenses of the issue and to yield a profit. From the public's point of view, there is little difference between an offer for sale and a public issue by prospectus. The advertisement will contain substantially the same information, although the observant will notice that it is given in the form of a "chairman's letter" and not presented as a straight prospectus. Issues of ordinary shares are far more often made by offers for sale than by public issues by prospectus, which are more frequently used for preference shares or debentures.

20. Offer for sale by tender. When an issue of shares is made by tender, details of the offer are advertised in the usual way, but the intending investor is required to state the number of shares he wishes to buy and the price that he is willing to pay. A minimum price is laid down, below which no applications will be considered. When all the applications are received, an allotment is made at the lowest price that will dispose of all the shares. It is usual for offers for sale by tender to require that cheques be submitted with applications and intending investors are warned that cheques may be presented for payment. This effectively frustrates those stags who make a practice of sending in cheques without having the funds to back them.

Until some three years ago, offers for sale by tender were comparatively rare, but recently they have become more popular.

ISSUES TO SHAREHOLDERS

21. Rights issues. A very common way of making new issues of ordinary shares is by offering them to existing shareholders at a preferential price. Naturally, this can only be done by established companies whose shares are already quoted. Shareholders are offered the right to purchase new shares of the same type that they already hold, in some stated proportion of their existing holdings. Thus, shareholders might be offered one new share for every two existing shares. They may either take up their rights to the new issue or they may sell their "rights" to an investor who does want the new shares.

Since a new issue of shares identical to the old will tend to depress the market price, shareholders who do not take up their rights are likely to find that the value of their previous holdings has fallen. In order to avoid a loss, they must either sell their rights or take advantage of the low price at which the new issue is offered. Rights issues by companies whose shares are standing well above par are, therefore, extremely unlikely to fail. No shareholder need suffer any loss, but purchase of the shares or sale of the rights will guarantee the success of the issue.

22. Bonus issues and internal finance. "Ploughing back" profits instead of distributing them to shareholders has always been an important way of providing capital for development. When substantial sums have been ploughed back over a number of years, however, the net assets employed in the business are much greater than the share capital of the company. Profits tend to be high compared with the nominal value of the shares issued. Consequently dividends are likely to be at a high rate and the market value of the shares much above their nominal value. Investors tend to be suspicious of excessively high share values and employees resent excessively high rates of dividend.

Bonus issues:

(*a*) bring the issued capital into line with the real assets owned by the shareholders,

(*b*) depress the market price of the shares to a more realistic level, and

(*c*) reduce the rate of dividend.

Since neither the company's assets nor its power to earn profits have been increased, bonus shares are not a free gift to shareholders.

SOURCES OF CAPITAL FOR JOINT-STOCK COMPANIES

23. Savings and capital. The accumulation of real capital, the machines, buildings and equipment that make efficient production possible, depends on saving. If a community spends all its income on consumption goods, it cannot add to its stock of capital or even renew capital equipment that has worn out. The source of capital is savings, whether of individuals or of institutions.

Savings may be regarded as the amount that remains from total income after spending on current consumption. The savings of businesses will be represented by their undistributed profits, depreciation funds and taxation reserves. Government saving is represented by budget surpluses. Savings will normally result in the acquisition of assets, which may be cash, real property, marketable securities, insurance policies or other miscellaneous assets. The savings of official bodies are most likely to be channelled into government securities, but a considerable proportion of the savings of persons and of business is invested in British companies.

24. Direct and indirect investment. The savings of persons may be invested directly in marketable securities. People of modest means, however, are more likely to use their savings:

(*a*) In paying for their own homes, *i.e.* by investing in real property.

(*b*) In increasing their holdings of "liquid assets," by accumulating cash, building up deposit accounts, buying National Savings Certificates, Premium Bonds, Defence Bonds, etc.

(*c*) In acquiring "whole life" or endowment assurance policies.

(*d*) In contributing to superannuation schemes.

When these more urgent needs have been met, the ordinary person may look for some attractive security in which to invest any remaining funds. In these days, he will probably do this through a *unit trust.* It will be realised that since insurance companies and pension funds invest a large proportion of their funds in the stocks of British companies, much of the capital for joint-stock companies comes from the indirect investment of personal savings.

25. Investment trusts and unit trusts. An individual's capital is limited. If he invests in a particular stock, he may choose unwisely and lose his savings. It is more satisfactory if a number of small investors can pool their capital and spread their investment over a wider range of securities, preferably under the skilled guidance of an expert manager. Both *investment trusts* and *unit trusts* provide a service of this type.

(*a*) *The investment trust* is, in fact, a joint-stock company, raising its capital by issuing shares to the public and investing the proceeds in securities of various kinds.

Some investment trusts specialise in particular markets, but most spread their "portfolios" (the complete list of securities invested in by the company) over a wide variety of shares in different industries and in different countries. Investment trusts normally distribute only about 80% of their net profits, the remainder being ploughed back into further investments. A useful, though small, supplementary income for many investments trusts comes from commission earned by underwriting new issues.

(*b*) *Unit trusts* do not issue shares in the ordinary way. They are basically a pooling of resources to buy shares through a professional management company. The shares themselves are held by trustees who take no part in the management but are merely responsible for the safe-keeping of the securities.

Funds for investment are obtained by selling "units" to the public, each unit representing a certain fraction of the portfolio. Unit trusts spread to Britain from the United States in the early 1930s and at first investors insisted on knowing exactly what investments their units represented. Funds were, therefore, invested in a quite narrow range of previously selected securities and such trusts were known as "fixed trusts." Modern trusts are normally flexible trusts which give the managers much wider discretion in the selection of investments.

26. Finance companies. Capital for promising new ventures is sometimes provided by finance companies. Although these companies, like investment trusts, raise money from the public which they then invest in other concerns, they are not merely interested in investment income, but are deeply involved with the management and control of the companies in which they have holdings. Some of the larger finance companies provide central administrative services for a group of companies in which they have a controlling interest.

27. Institutions providing special finance. Over thirty years ago, the Macmillan Committee drew attention to the difficulty that small but growing businesses found in raising adequate finance. The problem still continues and the provision of finance for the smaller business has, since 1945, been the concern of the *Industrial and Commercial Finance Corporation.* This Corporation is able to make loans of up to £200,000. The *Finance Corporation for Industry* provides larger sums for companies operating in the United Kingdom by making loans of up to £25 million for projects which could not be financed in the ordinary way. Both of these institutions are subsidiary companies of *Finance for Industry Ltd.*, a holding company set up in 1973 with the English and Scottish clearing banks having the major shareholdings and the Bank of England holding a minor (15%) share.

A number of other organisations have been set up to assist particular industries. The *Agricultural Mortgage Corporation* was formed in the inter-war years with capital supplied by the Bank of England and the commercial banks and with government backing. More recently, in 1957, the *Ship Mortgage Finance Co. Ltd.* was formed to assist shipowners who had ships built in British yards.

PROGRESS TEST 9

1. What are the main characteristics of preference shares? How may these characteristics be varied to suit differing market conditions and different types of investor? (**1, 2**)

2. Discuss the difference between debentures and preference shares. (**1, 13**)

3. What is meant by the "equity" of a company? What is the significance of this concept and what classes of share are likely to be involved? (**3–7**)

4. Write brief notes on "capital gearing." (**10–12**)

5. List six ways of issuing capital to the public and describe the main characteristics of each of them. (14–20)

6. What is a "rights issue"? How does it differ from a "bonus issue"? (21, 22)

7. Discuss the role of special financing institutions. (27)

CHAPTER X

THE STOCK EXCHANGE

THE FUNCTIONS OF THE STOCK EXCHANGE

1. The Stock Exchange is a market. The workings of the Stock Exchange are not difficult to understand if it is remembered that it is a market, a market for securities. If no such market existed, people with stock or shares to buy or sell would be put to considerable inconvenience and expense in finding anyone with whom to trade. A market enables buyers and sellers to come together.

It is not sufficient that buyers and sellers should find each other eventually; it must be possible for business to be transacted without any appreciable delay. It is also necessary that trade should take place at prices which reflect the true worth of the securities at that time. If the stock market is to fulfil these conditions it must be active, with many bargains being made and with many buyers and sellers taking part. Buyers and sellers must be in close touch with market conditions and must be fully informed about prices ruling and the factors affecting them. There must be as few restrictions on trading as possible. An effective market in securities, in short, must be as close as possible to the "perfect market" of economic theory.

2. The securities sold. The Stock Exchange is described above as a market in securities. The securities concerned are claims on:

(*a*) Joint-stock companies (the familiar stocks, shares and debentures discussed in IX).
(*b*) The central government.
(*c*) Local authorities.
(*d*) Foreign governments.
(*e*) Foreign companies.

Securities bought and sold on the Stock Exchange are not "new" securities, issued to a holder for the first time (although the Stock Exchange does play a part in making some new issues), but "secondhand" securities.

3. Summary of Stock Exchange functions. The part played in the economy by an active, competitive market in securities may be summarised as follows:

(*a*) *Liquidity.* Securities of any sort would not be attractive to hold unless they could quickly be turned into cash. The Stock Exchange provides a ready means for converting investments into liquid form.

(*b*) *Transferability of investments.* Sale of existing holdings on the Stock Exchange makes it possible for investors to take advantage of more attractive investment opportunities as they appear.

(*c*) *Price.* The existence of an active market for securities means that a price can be set on them whether they are actually being offered for sale or not.

(*d*) *New issues.* As described earlier (*see* IX) the Stock Exchange has a part to play in the raising of new capital. It should be remembered that the terms on which a company can raise new capital depends to a large extent on the market's assessment of its existing shares.

(*e*) *Direction of savings.* The market's assessment of a security determines its price at any time. In the case of fixed interest securities, the price also determines the return, or yield. Investors will look for the best possible bargains, either in terms of income or of growth. The influence of the market on prices and on new issues is therefore very important in determining how savings are directed into this or that form of investment.

THE ORGANISATION OF THE STOCK EXCHANGE

4. Origins. Dealings in stocks first became important towards the end of the seventeenth century. Professional dealers in stocks were regarded with disapproval in the early years and a number of attempts, none of them very successful, were made to regulate or abolish "the infamous Practice of Stock Jobbing." The stock-jobbers at first used the Royal Exchange for their dealings but later moved out into

'Change Alley and to the coffee houses round about, particularly Jonathan's. Attempts to make Jonathan's an exclusive club for the use of the more wealthy and reputable dealers failed and in 1773 a group of brokers acquired for their use a building in Sweetings Alley, the first premises to be called "the Stock Exchange."

By the end of the eighteenth century plans were afoot for a move to new premises in Capel Court. The new Stock Exchange was opened in 1802. Membership of the new Exchange was exclusive, use of the building and its facilities being open to subscribers only. A Deed of Settlement, signed in March 1802, provided for the management of the premises by nine Trustees and Managers and for other matters to be entrusted to a Committee for General Purposes. This constitution lasted until 1945 when the Trustees and Managers and the General Purposes Committee were merged into a new Council of the Stock Exchange.

5. Membership. There were some 2,260 active partner-members of the London Stock Exchange in 1975 of whom about 2,130 were *brokers* and 130 were *jobbers*. In addition, there were some 1,700 *associated* members, who were not partners but employees of member firms. Of these employee-members, 1,360 were brokers and the remainder jobbers. There was also a small number of dual capacity members. This distinction between the two types of member is unique to the London Stock Exchange.

Brokers are agents, dealing with both members of the public and other members of the Stock Exchange, both brokers and jobbers. Since they follow their client's instructions, making the best bargain they can on his behalf, they are rewarded by a *commission*. Brokers do not specialise and are prepared to obtain shares of any type required by a client.

Jobbers specialise in shares of a particular type, they deal on their *own behalf* and not as agents, and are rewarded by the profit, known as the jobber's "turn," which they make on the deal. Jobbers do *not* deal with members of the public.

Both brokers and jobbers now trade not as individuals but as firms, either partnerships or, since 1969, limited companies. It is felt to be essential that members should be fully responsible for any liability incurred by their transactions. In recent years, the tendency has been towards fewer and larger firms. There are now about fifty jobbing firms and under three hundred stockbroking firms. Each firm may employ a limited number of *authorised clerks*, who are elected members of the Stock Exchange, having access to the floor of the "House" and able to make deals on their employers' behalf. Firms may also employ *unauthorised clerks*, known as "blue buttons" from the blue badges that they are required to wear, who have access to the floor but are not permitted to deal. Firms may also employ *Settling Room clerks*, who do not have access to the floor of the Stock Exchange and, of course, numbers of clerical workers to deal with the ordinary routine.

Any British subject who is not engaged in other business is eligible for membership. Prospective members must be proposed, seconded and elected by the Council. Membership is for one year and all members come up for re-election annually. Before a member can be elected, he must purchase a nomination, which may cost around £1,000. After election, he must pay a heavy entrance fee and an annual subscription. Conditions of entry for authorised clerks are less onerous.

6. Control. The Stock Exchange is governed by a Council of forty-six members who are appointed by a ballot among members of the Exchange, with the Government Broker as an additional, *ex officio*, member without the right to vote. The Council elects a Chairman and two Deputy Chairmen each year. Detailed business is delegated to a number of committees, including those on Admission of Members and Clerks, Quotations (*see* 7), Official Lists and Publications, Central Administration, and Public Relations.

The tremendous amount of routine work involved in keeping track of the vast number of transactions taking place is handled by the Delivery and the Settlement Departments. The *Delivery Department* provides facilities for brokers' and jobbers' staffs to meet to arrange for payment and delivery of stocks. The *Settlement Department*, which is now highly mechanised, sorts out dealings in the more active stocks, cutting out intermediate transactions and bringing together original sellers and the final buyers.

7. The Official quotation. It is of great advantage to a joint-stock company if there is an active market in its shares. The shares become well known among investors, who can buy them with confidence, knowing their exact market value and being able to dispose of them if necessary. If a company's shares are marketable in this way, it is much easier to raise fresh capital when it is required. The highest degree of marketability is enjoyed by those shares which have a Stock Exchange quotation, their prices being shown on the Official List, which is published daily.

Before a quotation is given to a company's shares for the first time, the most thorough inquiries are made into the company's past history and its financial position. The issue of shares for which a quotation is sought must be of a reasonable size with sufficient shares in existence to make active dealing possible. It must also have been publicly advertised and two thirds of the total amount applied for and issued to members of the public.

8. The scale of the market. There are over 9,000 different types of security available for sale on the London Stock Exchange and their total market value is probably in excess of £200,000 million. Rather more than a quarter of this sum is accounted for by British government securities, with the shares of British commercial and industrial companies making up another quarter. The remainder consists of shares in banks, oil companies, mines and so on, and in Dominion and foreign stocks. In recent years over three million separate bargains have been concluded each year.

9. Investors. It is probable that three million people own some stocks and shares, but someone in almost every household is an *indirect investor* through membership of a pension fund, trade union, or Friendly Society or by payment of premiums to an insurance company. *Institutional investors*, i.e. insurance companies, banks, investment trusts, pension funds, trade unions and so on, play an increasingly important part in the present day stock market. Together they own one half of all the quoted securities, the biggest single group of investors being the insurance companies.

10. Provincial exchanges. There are several provincial exchanges through which dealings can be conducted and trading floors are in operation at five main regional centres. In March, 1973, the provincial exchanges, together with that of the Republic of Ireland (the Dublin exchange), entered into amalgamation with the London Stock Exchange.

11. Recent changes. The amalgamation of individual firms of brokers and jobbers has changed the nature of the London Stock Exchange to a considerable degree. The new, larger firms are very professional and use the most modern research methods and computerised analysis and record keeping. The changed style of the London stock market is exemplified by the new premises which have replaced the old trading floor and offices. Other examples of the new approach are the introduction of examinations for new members, the agreement that women may become members (since 1973) and the introduction of limited liability, although with careful safeguards for the public.

STOCK EXCHANGE PROCEDURE

12. The trading floor. The heart of any market is the facility which traders have for communicating with each other and this aspect of trading is clearly seen on the floor of the Stock Exchange. At various points around the very large trading floor are communication devices of various kinds, lighted boards for calling members to the telephone, Bank rate indicators, displays showing the sterling/dollar rate and screens on which company or financial news is flashed from time to time. Members of the public are not admitted to the floor of the house and the crowd of people usually to be seen there consists of brokers, jobbers and authorised and unauthorised clerks. So far as the public is concerned, dealing is indirect and is carried out through the brokers.

13. Method of dealing. When a member of the public wishes to buy or sell securities, he will contact his broker, giving precise instructions as to what shares are to be bought or sold. The client's order will be passed to one of the partners or possibly to an authorised clerk who is dealing for them in the House. The floor of the Stock Exchange is divided into a number of "markets" and the broker will know exactly where to find jobbers who deal in the type of share concerned.

Suppose that the client's order is to buy one hundred General Electric £1 ordinary shares. The broker will approach a jobber in the appropriate market and will indicate that he is interested in this particular share without, however, disclosing whether he wishes to buy or sell. There is likely to be a certain amount of fairly good-natured banter in the course of which each of the parties will try to test out the other's bargaining position. The jobber will quote two prices, "141½p to 144p" say. The lower price will be the jobber's buying (or bid) price and the higher his selling (or offer) price. If the price offered is not acceptable, the broker will go to other jobbers in the market in search of a better bargain. If the offer price is satisfactory, the broker will say "I buy one hundred" and the deal will be complete. Both the broker and the jobber will note the particulars in their rough books but there is no exchange of paperwork on the floor of the Stock Exchange; the contract is entirely verbal.

14. Making a price. Although the jobber quotes his bid and offer prices to brokers, he does not fix prices arbitrarily. The prices he quotes are determined by the ease or difficulty of obtaining a particular security. If many people are selling, he will find that he has contracted to buy a great number of shares without having many buyers. To "balance his book" he will have to adjust his prices. A lower bid price will discourage sellers, a lower offer price should encourage buyers. Conversely, if there are many eager buyers, he will find that he has agreed to sell more shares than he possesses. He will have to increase his prices to encourage selling and to discourage buying. Prices have been influenced by the supply of and demand for the security concerned. The jobber has been merely the instrument through which the market forces have worked. Unless he is unfortunate, the difference between his buying and selling prices will have afforded him a profit, but this will not have been won without risk.

15. Marking the deal. The verbal contract made by the broker and jobber on the floor of the House is binding and the client's ownership of the securities is effective from that time. Nevertheless, there is a great deal of "paperwork" to be done before the shares are formally transferred.

Immediately after leaving the jobber the broker usually "marks" the deal by entering the details on a slip and dropping it into one of the boxes provided for this purpose. These markings form the basis of the Stock Exchange Official List of dealings.

16. The contract note. As soon as possible, the broker, or more likely a clerk, will telephone the details of the deal back to the broker's office. There, a *contract note* will be prepared for despatch to the clerk that same night. The contract note will set out:

(*a*) A clear statement that the shares or stock units, have been bought or sold (whichever the case may be).

(*b*) The name of the company concerned and the price of the shares.

(*c*) The total consideration.

(*d*) The broker's commission.

(*e*) The stamp duty on the contract and on the transfer.

(*f*) The total amount due or payable.

In the case of a sale the amount of the transfer stamp will not appear as this is paid by the buyer, as is the small transfer fee which some companies impose. A "bought note" will also show the date of settlement. The buyer's cheque must reach the broker in time to be paid in and cleared by this date.

17. Transfer. On the morning after the bargain, the broker's and the jobber's clerks will meet in the Settling Room of the Stock Exchange to confirm that the details are correct.

It still remains to inform the company concerned that the ownership of the shares has changed. The selling broker will have to ask his client for the share certificate and will require him to sign a transfer form. The buyer does not now have to sign the transfer form as he used to, but his broker will enter the buyer's name and address on the form before sending it to the registration office of the company.

18. "Cum-div" and "ex-div." These expressions are often heard in connexion with the purchase and sale of shares. "Cum-dividend," or "with dividend," merely means that the buyer is entitled to any dividend which may be declared. After a dividend has been declared but before it has been paid, shares are quoted "ex-dividend," or without dividend. When shares are sold "ex-div," the seller retains his right to the next dividend.

19. The Stock Exchange "Account." The Stock Exchange year is divided into twenty-four Accounts, twenty of which are of two weeks' duration and four, covering periods which include public holidays, of three weeks' duration. Business in government and municipal securities and similar stocks is for cash, that is for payment by cheque on the day following the bargain. Other securities are bought "for the Account."

Each *dealing period* is followed by a *settlement period* which ends with Account Day when stocks must be delivered and payments made. On the last two days (Thursday and Friday) of the dealing period bargains may be made for *new time*, that is to say for the next Account. The settlement period begins on the Monday following the end of the dealing period and the seven working days of the settlement period are made up as follows:

Monday	Contango Day	Arrangements made to carry over bargains if necessary.
Tuesday	Making up Day	
Wednesday	Ticket Day	Buying brokers pass to sellers the names of purchasers so that transfers may be arranged.
Thursday *Friday* *Monday*	Intermediate Days	Preparation of transfers etc.
Tuesday	Account Day	Payments made and stock delivered.

While the settlement is going on, dealing is in progress for the new Account, of course, and this dealing period will, in turn, be followed by its settlement period.

20. Buying-in. Should stock not be delivered on Account Day the seller may, after allowing for reasonable delays, have the securities *bought-in* by officials of the Stock Exchange and any expense charged to the seller. Similarly if the seller does not receive a *ticket* (see above) he may have stock *sold out*.

SPECULATION

21. The functions of the speculator. It is usual to consider speculation as wholly bad but a little thought will show that this is not so. Speculators buy when prices are low, that is, when there is little other demand. They therefore tend to raise low prices and by selling when prices are high they depress very high prices. Being ever willing to find a bargain, they are often buying and selling when the market is otherwise inactive, thus making trade possible when it would otherwise cease.

22. "Bulls" and "Bears." A speculator who expects share prices to rise, who is an optimist, is called a *bull*. The pessimist, expecting prices to fall, is known as a *bear*. It is easy to see that a bull can make a profit by buying shares cheaply and selling them at a profit when prices have risen later on. His estimate may be wrong, of course, and if prices fall he will make a loss. The bear, too, can make a profit even though his pessimistic estimate of the market is justified. He can sell shares which he does not possess hoping to acquire them at a lower price at some time before he must make delivery.

23. Using the continuation. A bull, having bought shares without the money to pay for them, may reach the end of an Account and yet be unwilling to sell and so acquire the necessary cash. Even if he has the money, being an optimist, he may expect an even greater appreciation in the value of his shares during the next Account. In these circumstances, a speculator can maintain his position by selling the securities for cash and buying them back for the next Account, the sale and purchase taking place at a fixed price, the *making-up* price. The dealer providing the cash is said to *take-in* the shares and he charges a *contango* for his services.

Speculators who have sold shares which they do not actually possess may find that they reach Account Day without being able to arrange delivery. In that case, they must borrow shares. Bear speculators will use the continuation to obtain the shares they need and there may well be bulls who are only too willing to provide them in order to lay hands on cash. Sometimes there will be more bears eager to obtain stock than bulls who are short of money. In that case, the bear will have to pay a commission, known as a *backwardation*, for the help he receives.

24. Option dealing. An option is a chance, in the Stock Exchange a chance to buy or sell a share at an agreed price and an agreed future time. Options are particularly useful at times of uncertainty, such as the apparently imminent nationalisation of the steel industry in 1965. For some years after the war there was no option market, but in 1958 options were again permitted. The option market does not operate on a very large scale and there are only some half-dozen firms of brokers that act as option dealers.

An option to buy a share is known as a *call option* and an option to sell a share as a *put option*. It is also possible to take an option either to buy or to sell; this is a *put and call option*. The charge for an option is about 10% of the price of the share, plus a commission for "carrying over" the deal. Option dealing adds flexibility to the stock market and makes it possible to "hedge" against falling prices.

PROGRESS TEST 10

1. What are the economic functions of the Stock Exchange? **(1, 3)**

2. What types of person are members of the London Stock Exchange and what are their functions in the work of the stock market? Do you think that recent changes will make them more efficient? **(5, 11, 12)**

3. Explain how a deal is made on the London Stock Exchange. (**13, 15–17**)

4. Write notes on the following:
   (*a*) Contract note. (**16**)
   (*b*) "Cum-div" and "ex-div." (**18**)
   (*c*) Bulls and bears. (**22**)
   (*d*) Contango. (**23**)

5. Write an essay on Stock Exchange speculation. (**21–24**)

PART FOUR

MONEY AND BANKING

CHAPTER XI

MONEY

THE NEED FOR MONEY

The economy that we live in is a money economy. The complex transactions that make up the commercial life of a modern nation would not be possible without money. We are all conscious of this, and yet there are still many misconceptions about the nature of money and of the role it plays in our society.

1. Specialisation and exchange. In the first chapter of this book, the necessity for specialisation and exchange was discussed at some length. If life is not to be poor and meagre, division of labour is necessary and this is only possible if men can exchange the products of their labour.

2. The impracticability of barter. Exchanging the products of one man's labour for those of another can be a tricky business. If goods are bartered directly for goods two problems arise:

(*a*) If we find someone willing to accept the goods we offer, will he have goods that we require? This is the problem of the *double co-incidence of wants.*

(*b*) At what rate should goods of one type be exchanged for goods of another type? How many hand-made chairs should be exchanged for one fat pig? This is the problem of *valuation.*

These problems become more subtle and more difficult to solve if services are exchanged for goods, or services for other services. In addition, there are physical problems of transport and storage. If barter is to be carried on successfully, it is necessary to inspect the goods at the time of exchange and to decide on a ratio of exchange which reflects the quality of the goods offered.

THE DEVELOPMENT OF MONEY

Obviously, any society which depends wholly on barter is very limited in the number and type of exchanges which can be conducted. A solution to the problem is to make exchanges on the basis of some agreed commodity which is generally acceptable. If an exchange of two commodities is made in terms of a third commodity, that commodity is acting as money. The problems of the double co-incidence of wants can be overcome. The first half of the exchange can be made in terms of the money-commodity, and the money-commodity later exchanged for whatever goods are required. If there is a primitive system of prices in being, i.e. some fairly generally recognised set of rates at which various goods can be exchanged for the money-commodity, then the problem of valuation can be solved, too.

3. Early forms of money. Among the commodities used as money in earlier times have been cattle, shells, metal bars, slaves and bronze and copper ornaments and utensils. The adjective "pecuniary," meaning concerned with money, comes from the Latin word *pecunia* (money) which in turn derives from *pecus* (cattle). In recent times, cigarettes were used as money when the official currency had lost its value in Germany in the immediate post-war years.

4. The attributes of a good money material. Although a wide range of commodities were used as money at one time or another, some of them were not very efficient. When only a minority of transactions took place in money terms and many people were peasant-farmers living in isolated and self-sufficient communities, this was not serious, but as soon as a more elaborate commercial life began to develop the drawbacks of cattle or slaves as money would have become apparent. Cattle vary in health and weight, so do slaves, and it must have been difficult to make small purchases in terms of either.

For a commodity to serve as money a number of characteristics are desirable:

(*a*) Whatever material or commodity is selected, it must be *durable*. It is no good keeping your wealth in some form which is going to wear out or deteriorate.

(*b*) The material used must be *acceptable* to other members of the community. It is likely to have come into use as money because of this acceptability.

(*c*) The chosen material should be *divisible*. so that purchases of varying size and value can be made. (You cannot use slaves as money and expect to get half-a-slave in change.)

(*d*) To be practicable the money material should not be too bulky; it should be *portable* so that it can be carried about easily when exchanges are being made.

(*e*) The quality of the money material should be consistent, so that any one unit of it is acceptable in place of any other. The money material should be *homogeneous*.

(*f*) It is also essential that the money-commodity should be easily *identifiable*, so that there is no doubt about the nature of the commodity being offered.

(*g*) If the money-commodity is to retain its value in exchange, it should be reasonably *scarce*.

5. The precious metals as money materials. A consideration of the qualities of the precious metals, and of gold in particular, will show that they have these attributes in a high degree. The system of using a single precious metal as money is known as *mono-metallism*. When two metals, usually gold and silver, are used as money side-by-side, the system is known as bimetallism. Fluctuations in the silver price made this system impracticable.

THE FUNCTIONS OF MONEY

At this point, it would be well to consider the jobs which money does, *i.e.* the *functions* of money.

6. Money as a medium of exchange. This is the simplest of the functions of money. Goods or services are exchanged for money and the money is used to obtain other goods and services. The act of barter is split into two parts. The exchange of goods and services between individuals can be spread over a whole community, so that a complex of exchanges replace a simple person-to-person exchange. The exchange of goods for money may be separated in time from the subsequent use of money to obtain other goods (or services).

7. Money as a measure of value. Since commodities are exchanged through the medium of money, their relative prices determine what one commodity is worth in terms of other commodities. A community's valuation of this commodity or that will change as tastes and fashions change or as the community grows richer. The prices at which goods exchange for money and money exchanges for goods will reflect these changes. Money acts as a measure of value.

8. Money as a store of value. All the early money commodities must have been very inadequate stores of value. Cattle or slaves might sicken and die. Stocks of grain, saved from last year's harvest to be exchanged in the winter and spring, might still become mildewed or eaten by rats. A good money material permits the possession of wealth, the storing of value without loss. Of the modern forms of money, gold is still a very good store of value, but investments of one kind or another may make effective *money substitutes* as stores of value, since they yield an income which may offset the rising prices of other commodities.

9. Money as a unit of account. If a man is in business, it is necessary for him to compute the values of the various stocks of goods that he possesses. These goods will be of a number of different kinds and yet some common unit is needed in which to assess their value. When several people are in business together, some method of computing the profit due to each of them is needed. Money, acting as a unit of account, can serve these purposes.

In both households and businesses, it is necessary to look ahead and to calculate *future* income and expenditure, in short to use a system of budgeting. Again, money is used as a unit of account, although the actual transactions have not yet taken place.

10. A standard of deferred payments. Since money can be used as a unit of account, it permits payments that will be made at a future time to be calculated in the present. Many large-scale enterprises (e.g. building bridges, driving tunnels) are completed over long periods, but contracts can be made on a money basis.

MODERN FORMS OF MONEY

Although gold is still able to fulfil its role as money and is a very important form of international money, the reader will be aware that gold is not used as money in the ordinary course of trade today.

11. Banknotes. Banking began when citizens felt the need to deposit their gold coin or bullion in a safe place, so that marauding armies or bands of robbers could not steal it. One of the best places in which to deposit gold was with the goldsmiths, who worked in the metal and had facilities for its safe-keeping. The goldsmith would issue a receipt which would be surrendered by the holder when the gold was required again. No doubt it was tedious to go to the goldsmith when gold was required to pay a debt, and the practice grew up of transferring the goldsmith's receipt as title to the gold, rather than the gold itself.

By the middle of the seventeenth century goldsmiths' receipts were functioning as banknotes. When the Bank of England was founded in 1694, the issue of notes was one of its major functions and by the beginning of the eighteenth century banknotes had become fully negotiable. Banknotes were at first issued only against bullion in the vaults, and until 1914 Bank of England notes were fully backed by gold except for a very small *fiduciary issue* (*see* XIV, **1, 3**). At the present time, the issue of Bank of England notes is almost entirely fiduciary.

12. Bank deposits. Payment by cheque is far more common among business men than payment by notes or coin. What changes hands is not cash, but the right to cash. Book entries, giving entitlement to cash, pass from account to account. It is bank deposits which change hands and the bank deposit is acting as money. At the present time the volume of bank deposits in the UK is about four times the volume of notes issued. The most important form of money is now *bank deposit money.*

13. Coinage. The stamping of small pieces of precious metal by the authorities, so that they could be freely used as money without the bother of assaying and weighing, was an early development. The coins in use in Britain today, however, are *token coins*, made of cupro-nickel or bronze. They are worth more as coins than as metal. It is merely more convenient to use metal tokens rather than to use banknotes of very low denomination.

14. Legal tender. Token coins are acceptable because they are legal tender; they function as money because the authority of the government is behind them. Legal tender is the form of money which can legally be offered in payment of a debt. By the *Coinage Act*, 1870, *gold* coins issued by the Mint are legal tender up to any amount, as are Bank of England notes in England and Wales. Cupro-nickel (or silver) coins are legal tender up to five pounds only except the 50p coin, which is legal tender up to ten pounds. Bronze coins are legal tender for amounts up to 20p.

NOTE: Bank of England notes of denominations of five pounds and over are not unlimited legal tender in Scotland and Northern Ireland.

15. Decimalisation. After a long period of hesitation, Parliament decided by the *Decimal Currency Act*, 1967, that from 1971 the pound sterling should be divided into one hundred new pence. The change duly took place and from 15th February, 1971 the fully decimal system has been in operation. This system has many advantages. It is more compatible with foreign systems and accounting machines need no modification for sterling use. There are also advantages in calculation since working can be kept in decimals and translated directly into currency.

MONEY AND CREDIT

It has been stated above that bank deposit money is now the principal medium of exchange in this country (*see* **12**). This is an instance of the use of *credit.*

16. The characteristics of credit. The use of credit instruments such as *cheques, bills of exchange* or *promissory notes,* depends on the *confidence* that one person has in another. The ability of a borrower to obtain credit depends on the confidence which potential lenders have in him. An essential aspect of credit is the present use of resources belonging to other people in return for a promise to repay an equivalent amount at some future time, usually with interest. Another feature of credit is, therefore, *time.*

17. The use of credit. The use of credit enables purchasing power or resources to be transferred from those who possess them but have no immediate use for them to those who have urgent need of them and are willing to pay for their use. Credit enables resources which might otherwise be idle to be used to the full.

The volume of credit is flexible and can be adjusted in accordance with the needs of industry or with changes in economic policy (*see* XIV).

THE VALUE OF MONEY

18. Meaning of the value of money. The value of money depends on the command which money gives over other goods and services. When the amount of goods and services obtainable for a given sum of money increases, the value of money is said to rise. If the volume of goods and services obtainable should decrease then the value of money will have fallen. A general *rise* in prices, therefore, will represent a *fall* in the value of money and a *fall* in prices will represent a *rise* in the value of money.

19. Measuring changes in the value of money. The effects of a fall in the value of money have become only too familiar as weekly or monthly pay packets have been found by bitter experience to buy fewer goods and services. Yet there are times when prices seem to be rising faster than ever and at other times prices seem relatively stable. Even when we are most conscious of rising prices, and of the falling value of money, there are likely to be a few prices which are not rising, or even one or two which may be falling. The problem of measuring changes in the value of money is not an easy one.

The device used to measure changes in price is the *index number*. Basically, index numbers are computed by choosing a representative group of goods, finding out their prices at a particular time and then calculating the percentage increase in those prices in subsequent years. A final percentage increase over the *base year* (the starting date) is found by averaging the percentage increases on all the commodities chosen, giving extra importance (weighting) to those that account for a great deal of expenditure and less to those that are purchased to a lesser extent.

Since different groups of people purchase different types of commodities and since all prices do not vary proportionately, one of the problems of index number construction is to choose a suitable "basket of commodities." One of the best known and most useful price indices is the *Retail Price Index*.

20. Causes of changes in the value of money. It has long been observed that prices rose as the quantity of money, of gold bullion for instance, increased. To infer that there was a connection between the two things and that increase in the quantity of money *caused* the rise in prices did not seem unreasonable. This was the *Quantity Theory of Money* in its crude form. A refinement was to introduce the idea of the velocity of circulation, the number of times that a unit of money was used in a given time. An increase in the quantity of money might thus be offset by a decrease in the velocity of circulation or vice versa.

A further development, in the early years of this century, was to introduce the idea of the volume of bank deposits as well as the quantity of "common money," each form of money having its own velocity of circulation and each having an influence on prices.

A more recent view is to consider *real income* and *money income.* Real income can be taken as the flow of goods and services which have become available in a given period of time. If money income increases without any corresponding increase in real income, prices will tend to rise; if real income increases while money income remains stable, prices will tend to fall. Prices are thus the link between money income and real income.

21. Inflation. The phenomenon of *consistently rising prices* is known as *inflation.* Whether a rise in money incomes causes inflation will depend on whether the increased income is spent, Control of consumer demand as well as control of incomes is, therefore, an important part of any attempt to secure stable prices.

PROGRESS TEST 11

1. Write a paragraph on "The impracticability of barter." **(2)**
2. Describe seven desirable characteristics for a good money material. **(4)**
3. What are the functions of money? **(6–10)**
4. What is now the most important form of money in British commercial life? How has this come about? **(11, 12)**
5. Write brief notes on "credit." **(16, 17)**
6. Define "the value of money." Describe the causes and effects of changes in the value of money. **(18–21)**

CHAPTER XII

BILLS OF EXCHANGE, CHEQUES AND CREDIT TRANSFERS

METHODS OF PAYMENT

1. Choice of methods. The easiest way of paying a debt is by the simple presentation of cash in the form of coins or banknotes. There are disadvantages to paying cash, however:

(*a*) If a number of payments are to be made by personal calls, large sums of money have to be carried around, with the consequent risk of loss.

(*b*) Should the creditor carry on his business in another town, it is risky to send cash by post.

(*c*) If banknotes fall into the wrong hands, they are easy to use and hard to recover.

(*d*) They are *negotiable* and anyone accepting a banknote in good faith acquires a valid title to it (*see* **10**).

2. Money orders and postal orders. Money orders and postal orders are not negotiable and they are a convenient way of making small payments. Both these methods are unsuitable for large sums and both involve a certain amount of inconvenience. A call must be made at a Post Office, a form must be completed in the case of a money order and in both cases poundage must be paid. There is a definite gain in security, however, as money orders are payable only to a named person and the payee's name and the paying Office can be entered on a postal order. Both postal orders and money orders can be crossed. More rapid transmission of money can be secured by telegraph money orders.

3. Cheques, credit transfers and bills of exchange. For both individuals and businesses, the use of *cheque payments* has many advantages.

(*a*) There is no need for large sums of money to be carried about or to be at risk while in transit.

(*b*) Cheques can be made out to a definite payee and payment can be restricted by general or special crossings if required.

(*c*) On the other hand, the cheque is a flexible instrument and an open (uncrossed) cheque (*see* **16**) can provide ready access to cash if it is required.

Since 1960, the *credit transfer* has become a popular alternative means of payment. This enables many payments to be made with a single cheque and can be used quite easily even by people who do not have a bank account.

4. Credit cards. In recent years the more traditional means of payment have been supplemented by the use of bank credit and cheque cards. A card is issued to approved customers by the bank and may be presented to traders who are members of the scheme. The issuing bank pays the trader and sends accounts each month to customers who use the scheme. This enables customers not only to pay many small accounts with a single cheque but also offers the opportunity of enjoying an extended period of credit. In addition, the cards act as a form of identification and, to a limited extent, as a guarantee when cheques are drawn.

BILLS OF EXCHANGE

Bills of exchange have their origins in antiquity but are still a useful form of credit instrument. They are not greatly used in the home trade in these days, but they play a large part in overseas trade. The remainder of this chapter is a detailed examination of bills of exchange, cheques and credit transfers.

5. Definition. The *Bills of Exchange Act*, 1882 defines a bill of exchange as "an unconditional order in writing addressed by one person to another, signed by the person giving it, requiring the person to whom it is addressed to pay on demand or at a fixed or determinable future time a sum certain in money to, or to the order of, a specified person, or to bearer."

6. History. The earliest known bills of exchange date from the twelfth century, but there is evidence that instruments which were similar in form were in use in Roman times. The word "bill" comes from the Latin word *bulla* which means a document. The trading cities of Genoa, Venice and Hamburg certainly used bills of exchange during the twelfth and thirteenth centuries and in this country they are mentioned in a Statute of 1379.

The use of bills of exchange continued throughout the middle ages and by the sixteenth and seventeenth centuries there was a definite trend towards increasing negotiability, with the bill sometimes acting as currency when other forms were in short supply. The practice of discounting bills (*see* **11**) developed and as banking institutions grew more efficient the bill became an important means of obtaining credit.

By the nineteenth century bills of exchange had become widely used in international trade and a bill drawn on a London bank was acceptable as payment in most parts of the world (*see* **12**). The increasing use of bills of exchange demanded some codification of the law relating to them and this was achieved in the *Bills of Exchange Act*, 1882.

The twentieth century saw a decline in the use of bills but since the end of the Second World War there has been a revival of their use in international trade.

7. The nature of the bill. A bill of exchange is an order given by one person to another to pay a sum of money. It is usually drawn by a creditor on a debtor; that is to say a creditor, to whom money is owed, orders his debtor to pay up on a certain date. A bill of exchange ordering R. Brown to pay £270 to H. White would look like Fig. 13.

A bill of exchange may also be drawn in such a way as to order one person to pay a sum of money to a named third person. No particular form of words is required by the *Bills of Exchange Act*, but the bill must obviously be drawn clearly and unambiguously.

The act of making out a bill of exchange is known as *drawing* a bill. The person who draws it is the *drawer* and the person to whom a bill is addressed is called the *drawee*.

8. Acceptance. It is easy enough to draw a bill, but it will be meaningless unless the drawee agrees that the sum claimed is due. He will do this by *accepting* the bill, that is by signing his name across the face of the bill to show that he is willing to pay the bill when it matures. Having accepted the bill, the drawee becomes the *acceptor*. An acceptance may be qualified, setting out conditions on which payment will be made.

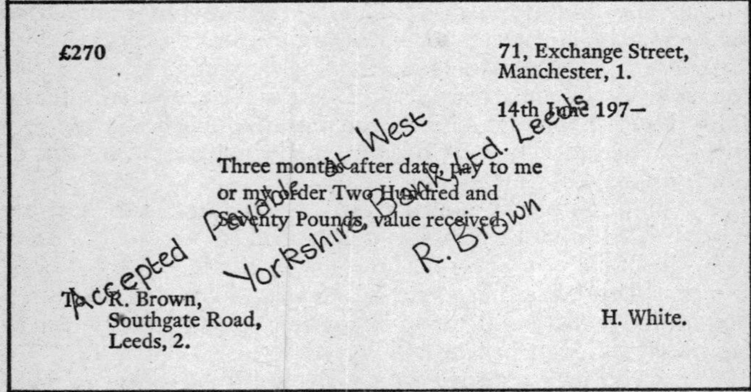
£270

71, Exchange Street,
Manchester, 1.

14th June 197–

Three months after date, pay to me
or my order Two Hundred and
Seventy Pounds, value received.

To R. Brown,
Southgate Road,
Leeds, 2.

H. White.

Fig. 13. A bill of exchange.

9. Period and sight bills. A bill of exchange may be payable: (*a*) *at sight* (on demand) or (*b*) at "*some fixed or determinable period of time*," as the Act says. Sometimes the term *usance* is used to denote the period of time for which a bill is drawn. When the stated period of time has elapsed, the bill is said to *mature* and it can be presented to the acceptor who must honour it. Three *days of grace* are allowed for period bills and a bill which is not paid after this is said to be *dishonoured*.

If the holder wishes to enforce his rights against any other parties who have passed the dishonoured bill to him, he may follow the legal process known as *protesting* the bill in order to obtain formal evidence of its dishonour.

10. The standing of a bill. When a bill has been drawn and accepted, it becomes a potentially valuable security. It is a *negotiable instrument* and anybody who takes it in good faith in payment of a debt acquires a good title to it. Whether a bill of exchange can be given in payment of a debt naturally depends on whether a person receiving it has a good chance of being paid when the bill matures. If the acceptor of a bill is some unknown small tradesman, no one will be willing to take the bill, but if it has been accepted by a reputable business house of known standing, then payment on maturity is virtually certain.

The standing of a bill of exchange depends on the repute of the drawer and acceptor and the nature of the transaction in connection with which the bill was originally drawn. The chances of the bill being honoured on maturity are obviously better if the debtor who accepted the bill incurred his debt in the course of some profitable piece of trading. The drawer may have supplied goods to the drawee on credit and by the time the bill matures the goods will have been sold and funds will have become available. Sometimes details of the transaction concerned are shown on the face of the bill. This is known as *clausing*.

One method of obtaining a bill of good standing is to secure its acceptance by a merchant bank. The standing of the merchant banker is thus substituted for that of the (possibly) unknown drawer. The merchant bank will charge a commission for its services but the bill can be disposed of without difficulty. Merchant banks specialising in the acceptance of bills of exchange are known as *accepting houses*.

11. Discounting a bill. A creditor who holds an accepted bill of exchange may wait until it matures and then present it for payment. Should he require his money before the bill matures, he may sell the bill. Since whoever buys the bill will have to wait for payment in his turn, the purchase price of the bill will be less than its face value. Selling a bill to a bank or to a discount house is known as *discounting* a bill. The discount, deducted from the face value of the bill, will be calculated at an agreed rate per cent per annum for the period that the bill has to run. As the bill approaches maturity, its current worth will become closer and closer to its face value.

12. Using the bill. If the bill of exchange is drawn by a creditor on his debtor, it becomes a means of giving credit to the debtor. Ideally, the bill will be *self-liquidating*, the underlying transaction providing funds just as the bill matures. The creditor may discount the bill and obtain immediate cash or may pass it on in payment of debts which he has incurred. When a holder parts with a bill, having received value of some kind, he *endorses* it by signing on the back. Should the bill be dishonoured, each endorser may be liable in turn, since each of them has passed on the bill in exchange for value, whether that value is goods, services or a money payment.

Bills of exchange may be used to obtain finance and this is particularly important in foreign trade (*see* XXI, **24–27**). The classical method of obtaining bill finance was to draw a bill on a London bank or accepting house and after acceptance to discount it with a London discount house. Bills accepted by London banks or accepting houses are known as *fine bank bills* and command more favourable rate of discount than other bills.

13. Promissory notes. A promissory note is "*an unconditional promise in writing made by one person to another*" to pay a sum of money on demand or at some fixed or determinable future time. They do not require acceptance, being drawn by the person who is to pay. Promissory notes as such are not of very great importance today. Strictly speaking, banknotes are promissory notes issued by a banker and payable on demand.

CHEQUES

14. The nature of the cheque. A cheque is an order to a banker to pay a certain sum of money. The *Bills of Exchange Act*, 1882, defines a cheque as a bill of exchange drawn on a banker and payable on demand. So long as the banker has funds belonging to the customer, he must honour the customer's cheque.

15. Bearer cheques and order cheques. Cheques may be made out to a payee or bearer or order.

(*a*) *A bearer cheque* is paid to whoever presents it at the bank and is not, therefore, a very secure way of transmitting money.

(*b*) *An order cheque* requires endorsement if it is passed on to someone other than the payee and a bank will not accept such a cheque unless the original payee has endorsed it in exactly the same form as it was made out. Cheques paid in to the payee's own account do not require endorsement since the passing of the *Cheques Act*, 1957.

16. Open and crossed cheques.

(*a*) *Open cheques* can be presented at the bank on which they are drawn and cash obtained across the counter.

(*b*) *A crossed cheque* can only be presented to the paying bank by passing it through a bank account.

17. General and special crossings. There are two types of crossing in use.

(*a*) *A general crossing* consists of two parallel lines drawn across the face of the cheque, as shown in Fig. 14. As may be seen, the words "and Co." are sometimes added to the crossing and are a relic of the days when most banks were private firms. The drawer, not knowing the name of his payee's bank would cross the cheque ". . . and Co.," leaving a space for the insertion of the firm's name.

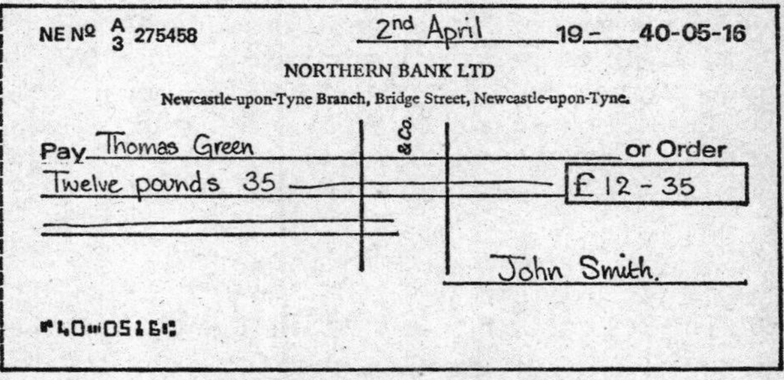

Fig. 14. A crossed cheque.

An additional safeguard is created by adding the words "Not negotiable" to the crossing. Any defects in a holder's title to the cheque are then transmitted to subsequent holders. If the cheque is stolen, therefore, no one accepting the stolen cheque can obtain a valid title to it. The addition of the words "A/c payee only" to the crossing ensures that the cheque is credited only to the account of the named payee.

(b) *Special crossings.* If the cheque is *specially* crossed it bears the name of a particular bank and only that bank will be paid by the paying bank. Some examples of special crossings are as follows:

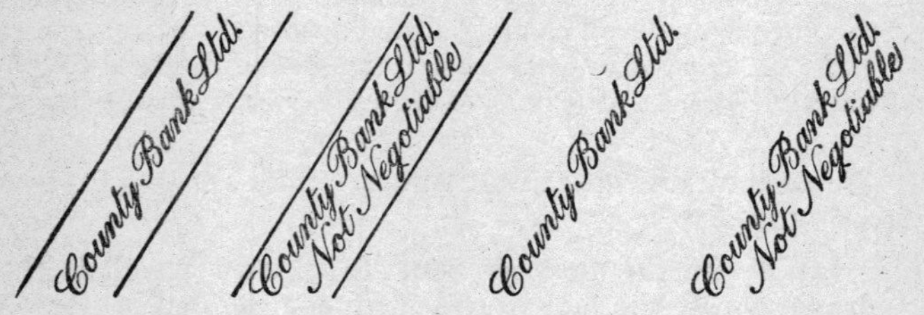

18. Special endorsements. A payee who passes on a cheque to another person may make a special endorsement ordering some named person to be paid.

19. Use of cheques. At one time cheques were accepted with some reluctance. Fewer people had bank accounts than today and payees without accounts passed cheques to other people who had in order to obtain payment. With banking facilities used much more widely, over 95% of all cheques are now paid straight into payees' own accounts.

The increasing use of cheque payments can be seen in the clearings of the *London Bankers' Clearing House* which averaged some £8,000 million each day in 1976.

CREDIT TRANSFERS

20. The General Credit Clearing. In Chapter XIII the way in which the cheque clearing operates is described. The amounts due from each of the banks to the other clearing banks are offset and net amounts due are computed. This is a *debit clearing.* In 1960, the clearing banks set up a General Credit Clearing whereby instructions to *credit* particular accounts could be handled in a similar way. Systems of "traders' credits" and "customers' credits" had been in existence for many years, but the General Credit Clearing brought them into a single clearing system and in 1961 the credit clearing was extended to include credit transfers made by non-customers.

The credit transfer system therefore includes three services:

(*a*) Transfers made on a customer's instructions to the credit of customers either of the same banks or of other banks.

(*b*) Transfers of credits paid in over the counter at other branches or at other banks by customers for their own accounts.

(*c*) Transfers made on behalf of non-customers who pay in cash over the counter to be credited to specified accounts.

(It was the last service which was the real innovation.)

21. The use of credit transfers by business. There has been a strong effort by the banks to encourage business houses to use the credit transfer system for the settlement of accounts and the payment of wages and salaries. A firm using this method would fill in a form for each account to be paid, showing the bank and branch at which the payee's account was kept. A covering schedule, listing the amounts to be credited, would be prepared and sent to the paying firm's bank with the credit transfer forms and a single cheque for the whole sum to be paid. Naturally, the payees' permission to use this system must be obtained.

The advantage of the system is that only one cheque is necessary for many payments and the transfer forms and lists can be prepared by routine office methods. Wages and salary payments can be handled in a similar way.

A further advantage of the system to businesses is that their invoices can incorporate a tear-off credit transfer slip which customers can use when paying, merely taking the credit transfer slip to the bank with the sum due. This method is used by the public utility services and by many private firms with large numbers of accounts.

NOTE: Wages of manual workers can be paid by cheque or credit transfer since the passing of the *Payment of Wages Act*, 1960, provided that the employee has given his consent.

22. Credit transfers and the general public. Members of the general public who have bank accounts can collect credit transfer slips sent to them with firms' invoices and can pay them with a single cheque passed over the bank counter

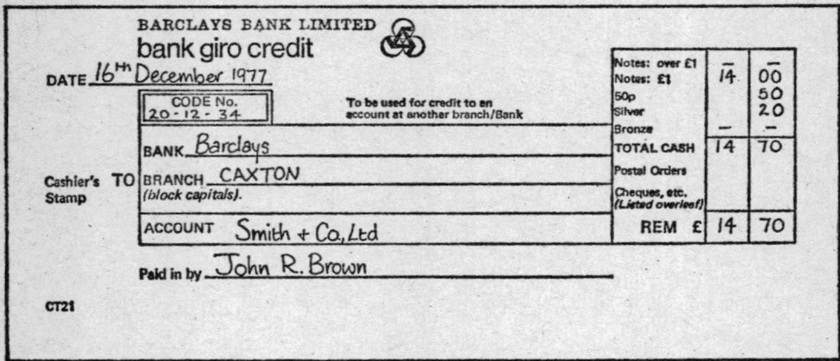

BARCLAYS BANK LIMITED
bank giro credit

DATE 16th December 1977

CODE No. 20-12-34

To be used for credit to an account at another branch/Bank

Cashier's Stamp

TO BANK Barclays
BRANCH CAXTON
(block capitals).
ACCOUNT Smith + Co, Ltd

Notes: over £1	—	—
Notes: £1	14	00
50p		50
Silver		20
Bronze	—	—
TOTAL CASH	14	70
Postal Orders		
Cheques, etc. (Listed overleaf)		
REM £	14	70

Paid in by John R. Brown

CT21

Fig. 15. A credit transfer form.

with a batch of slips. The full value of this service will not become apparent until more of the larger firms, at least, encourage payment by credit transfer and provide slips with their accounts.

A valuable extension of the system is the arrangement by which members of the public who do not have bank accounts can make credit transfers. So long as the creditor agrees, any debt can be paid over the bank counter by filling in a credit transfer form of the type illustrated in Fig. 15 and handing it in with the necessary remittance plus a small fee.

23. The bank giro. In order to emphasise the comprehensive nature of the transfer and payments services which they offer, the principal banks of the United Kingdom have recently introduced the term "bank giro". This term covers cheque and credit transfer services and also the newer method of *direct debiting*. This service enables a payee to claim amounts due to him from customers or others. The paying account is directly debited and there is no chance of accounts being forgotten or of payment being delayed. Naturally, the permission of the paying firm or individual must be obtained before the system can be applied.

24. The Post Office giro. At various times it was suggested that Britain's system of money transfers would be improved if she set up a Post Office giro on the Continental model. Giro systems enable any holder of a numbered giro account to transfer sums to any other account by filling in a form, quoting the appropriate particulars, and sending it to the giro office. In July 1965, the Postmaster-General announced that a form of giro system was to be established.

The giro service came into operation in 1968 and it offers three basic facilities:

(*a*) The general public is able to make cash payments to giro account holders through post offices (although not all post offices offer giro services).

(*b*) Transfers can be made between giro account holders, thus affording a service rather like the banks' credit transfer service.

(*c*) Cash payments can be made from a giro account holder to non-account holders.

A small charge is made for payments into accounts other than the payee's, but no charge is made for account-to-account payments. The Giro Centre at Bootle is highly computerised and offers an extremely fast and efficient service.

PROGRESS TEST 12

1. Make up a definition, in your own words, of a bill of exchange. What is meant by the acceptance of a bill? **(5, 7, 8)**
2. Draw a bill of exchange on B. Jackson, instructing him to pay Smith & Co. £700 in ninety days' time. Make any other assumptions that you need. **(5, 7–9)**
3. What does the standing of a bill of exchange depend on and why is it important? **(10)**
4. What is meant by (*a*) discounting, and (*b*) dishonouring a bill? **(10–12)**

5. Write notes on the following:

(*a*) Period and sight bills. **(9)**
(*b*) Bearer and order cheques. **(15)**
(*c*) General and special crossings. **(17)**

6. Explain what is meant by the credit transfer system. Compare this system with the Post Office giro. **(20–24)**

7. Describe the various ways of paying a debt and indicate the circumstances in which each would be appropriate. **(1–24)**

CHAPTER XIII

THE ENGLISH BANKING SYSTEM: (I)

THE WORK OF THE JOINT-STOCK BANKS

THE ELEMENTS OF THE ENGLISH BANKING SYSTEM

1. The evolution of the banking system. The story of the development of the English banking system is a complex and fascinating one and it cannot be told adequately in a few paragraphs of a general work of this kind. What follows, therefore, is the merest outline, which, it is hoped, will serve to put the later description of present-day banking institutions into historical perspective.

The work of the London goldsmiths in operating an early system of deposit banking was described previously (XI, **11**). When they found that only a proportion of their deposits was required at any one time, they began to lend at interest. So long as their loans were not so great that demands for payment in cash exceeded the coin or bullion available to meet them, all was well.

The middle years of the seventeenth century saw a great expansion of the goldsmith's banking business, so that by the 1670s they were performing many modern banking functions. In addition to lending to merchants, however, they became heavily involved in lending to the Crown. This was remunerative, but in 1672 the Crown suspended repayments. This both weakened the goldsmiths, making them less able to perform banking services, and hardened them against lending to the King.

Although there was thus a clear need for some more powerful banking institution, nothing was done until the *Glorious Revolution*, 1689, which brought William III to the throne. In 1694, the Bank of England was founded and within a few years was given a monopoly of joint-stock banking. The Bank of England was thus the only note-issuing bank apart from individual bankers and partnerships. This situation continued until 1826 when joint-stock banking was permitted outside a sixty-five mile radius from London. After 1833, joint-stock banking was permitted within this radius provided that the banks established did not issue notes.

The long period of its monopoly of joint-stock banking served to confirm the pre-eminence of the Bank of England, and the restriction of the note-issue, both before and after 1833, no doubt encouraged the use of cheques to an extent greater than was the case in other countries.

When the principle of limited liability was extended to joint-stock banks in 1858, the way was open for large-scale banking. A succession of amalgamations followed throughout the nineteenth century and into the present century and one by one the private and country banks which had continued to exist during the Bank of England's monopoly of joint-stock banking were absorbed.

We thus reach the present position, whereby ordinary banking business is carried on by a fairly small number of large, powerful joint-stock banks, operating branches throughout the country. The evolution of the joint-stock banks was paralleled by the gradual adoption of the functions of a modern central bank by the Bank of England.

2. English banking institutions. The banking system consists of those institutions which provide banking services and are concerned with the provision of credit and finance. The relationships between these institutions and the efficiency with which they work are of first-rate importance for the economy of the country.

We can distinguish six different types of institution:

(*a*) The Bank of England, the central bank.

(*b*) The joint-stock banks, or commercial banks, with which the rest of this chapter is largely concerned.

(*c*) The merchant banks.

(*d*) Savings banks.

(*e*) Institutions on the fringe of the banking system, such as the hire-purchase finance houses.

(*f*) The discount houses.

THE JOINT-STOCK BANKS

3. The clearing banks. The joint-stock banks perform banking services for business and for individuals. These are the familiar banks which most of us have used at one time or another. The traditional structure of joint-stock banking dated from the years just after the First World War and at the heart of it were the eleven "clearing banks." After the report by the now abolished Prices and Incomes Board in 1967, it was clear that changes in the traditional structure were likely. A succession of mergers reduced the number of clearing banks:

Barclays	Midland
National Westminster	Williams & Glyns
Lloyds	Coutts

The Co-operative Bank and the Trustee Savings Bank also take part in the clearing. There are also a number of "non-clearing" banks. In addition to the joint-stock banks there are about a dozen private commercial banks performing similar functions.

The *Committee of London Clearing Banks*, consisting of the chairmen of the banks listed above (with the exception of the Co-operative Bank and the T.S.B.), is a very important body in co-ordinating and presenting the views of the joint-stock banks.

It is the body through which the Bank of England transmits official policy to the banks. The work of the *Bankers' Clearing House* is discussed in **16**.

4. Bank mergers. After the Prices and Incomes Board's report on the clearing banks in May 1967, it was apparent that changes in the traditional structure were likely. The initial merger was that between the National Provincial and Westminster banks. This merger produced a unit holding deposits of some £3,500 million and having over three thousand branches. This amalgamation was followed by proposals to merge Barclays, Lloyds and Martins. This merger would have produced a banking unit with deposits of £5,000 million but was reported on adversely by the Monopolies Commission (*see* VI, **19**). Had this merger gone through, the "big five" would have become the "big three," with one of the remaining major units, the Midland, much smaller than the other two.

5. Services rendered by the joint-stock banks. The joint-stock banks exist to make a profit for their shareholders by performing banking services for their customers. During the post-war years, the range of services offered has grown enormously and the banks have made great efforts to brighten their "image" and to appeal to a wider public.

Their services could be summarised as follows:

(*a*) *Deposits.* The banks accept deposits on *current* or on *deposit* accounts. Interest is not generally paid on current accounts and sums may be withdrawn without notice. Interest on deposit accounts is paid according to the individual bank's *base rate* (*see* XIV, 24) and notice is required before withdrawals are made.

(*b*) *Loans and overdrafts.* Making loans to customers on security is one of a bank's most profitable activities. When a *loan* is made, a fixed sum is advanced for a definite period of time and the borrower pays interest on that sum for the agreed period. An *overdraft* is the *right* to borrow up to a given amount. The amount borrowed, and the interest paid, depends on the extent to which the overdraft facilities are used.

(*c*) *Discounting bills of exchange.* This function is one of those offered to businesses by the banks. The bill of exchange is a useful way of arranging finance and payment, but is more used in foreign trade than in the home trade (*see* XXI, 24–27).

(*d*) *Status information and references.* A banker will give an opinion on the standing of a customer if he is asked to do so by another bank. Such information is, of course, completely confidential and is never given direct to outside individuals. Private individuals may sometimes quote a bank as a reference when seeking hire-purchase finance or other form of credit.

(*e*) *Safe custody of valuables.* Customers may deposit documents or valuables with the bank.

(*f*) *Stock Exchange transactions.* A bank will handle customers' investments, making use of the bank's own brokers. The bank does not reckon to give advice on the sale or purchase of investments except in the most general way, but will put a customer in touch with its brokers who will give reports on suitable securities.

(*g*) *Registration of stocks and shares.* A bank will act as registrar for companies or local authorities who issue securities. The bank will handle both the formalities attendant on a new issue and the registration of transfers. It will also look after the payment of dividend and interest warrants.

(*h*) *Executor and trustee services.* Banks will act as executors of wills or as trustees under trust deeds. The banks are impartial and expert and there are many advantages in appointing a bank rather than a private person.

(*i*) *Insurance.* Most banks have insurance departments which, through links with the insurance industry, are able to arrange cover for all the major classes of risk.

(*j*) *Standing orders.* If so instructed, the bank is able to make regular payments of such things as hire-purchase instalments, insurance premiums and subscriptions.

(*k*) *Foreign business.* Each of the joint-stock banks has a specialist branch usually called the Foreign Branch or Overseas Branch. It is a branch located in this country to conduct foreign banking business and to assist businessmen dealing with other countries. The facilities offered would include the provision of *overseas trade information*, reports on *economic conditions* abroad, *status information* regarding foreign clients and *information* concerning *import regulations and trading restrictions* in other countries. Other services would be the handling of *foreign exchange business* and *foreign payments* (*see* XXI).

Although the banks make loans and advances to industry and business, they do not reckon to supply long-term capital to be invested in new plant or other assets. Their object is the temporary provision of additional working capital. If a business requires new long-term capital, it must go to the market or must approach special financing institutions such as the Industrial and Commercial Finance Corporation.

6. Security for loans. When loans or overdraft facilities are given by a bank, security is normally required. The borrower is expected to make available to the bank claims on some kind of property to which the bank can have recourse if the borrower cannot meet his obligations. The security should be readily saleable, stable in value and identifiable as the property of the borrower. Stock Exchange securities, title deeds to real property and life assurance policies are, therefore, suitable forms of security. Alternatively a guarantee may be given by some person of good financial standing.

7. Branch banking. A notable feature of the English banking system is the way in which local banking services are provided by branches of the powerful joint-stock banks. This enables branch managers to keep in touch with local banking needs and yet to have the financial resources of the head office behind them.

THE CREATION OF CREDIT

The way in which the bank deposit functions as money has already been mentioned (*see* XI, **12**). If the banks can create deposits by making loans, it would appear that they are increasing the amount of *bank deposit money* available.

8. Loans create deposits. When a loan is made by a banker, a loan account is opened in the borrower's name and the amount debited to that account is also credited to his current account. The amount loaned is then available in the ordinary way and the borrower can obtain cash or can pay off his creditors by drawing cheques. If he pays debts by cheque, these cheques are paid into other people's accounts and increase the total amount of deposits in that way.

Similarly, when a customer is allowed an overdraft, he may draw cheques on it and the amount of bank deposits will be increased when those cheques are paid in to other banks.

9. The cash ratio. There would seem to be no limit to the banks' power to create new credit money except prudence in keeping an adequate reserve of cash to meet customers' demands. This is not quite true, for there are a number of other checks, but experience has shown that so long as cash is available to the extent of 8% *of deposits*, all will be well.

10. The liquidity ratio. Because convention and experience compel the maintenance of an 8% cash ratio, it is sometimes said that the banks are able to lend up to £12.50p for every £1 deposited. Firstly, this would not in any case be true for technical reasons, and secondly, the *liquidity ratio* is far more important. This is the ratio of *assets readily convertible to cash* to deposits. For many years this was maintained at around 30%, but from 1963 the suggested minimum liquidity ratio was 28%.

11. A new ratio. While the cash and liquidity ratios cannot, in practice, be ignored since they represent an underlying prudence in management, the control of bank lending now rests on a new ratio. In May 1971, the Bank of England issued a paper outlining a number of proposals for the reform of banking practices, one of which was that all banks should hold 12½% of their (sterling) deposit liabilities in specified reserve assets. These assets were:

(*a*) Cash at the Bank of England other than special deposits (*see* XIV, 26).
(*b*) Treasury bills.
(*c*) Money at call with the London money market.
(*d*) British government stocks with less than a year to maturity.
(*e*) Local authority and some eligible commercial bills.

The new *reserve asset ratio* came into force in September 1971 and while these eligible reserves would, in any case, have formed a part of the commercial banks' assets, they are fairly liquid and so are low yielding. When the banks would otherwise improve their profitability by making more loans and advances, the need to maintain the reserve asset ratio is likely to provide a curb on such expansion. A disadvantage of reliance on the new ratio is that heavy issues of Treasury bills might well tend to be reflected in the commercial banks' holdings, so that fresh lending, with a consequent expansion of the money supply, becomes possible.

12. Other checks on bank lending. The banks' ability to lend is limited by the supply of assets suitable for use as security. Ultimately, the banks will only be able to make advances to the extent that the public has property to offer as security. This may be merely an upper limit, but a very definite limit on any one bank's lending is imposed by the need to keep in step with the other banks. A bank which lends excessively will find that it has a great volume of cheques presented against it. As a result of the clearing mechanism described below, meeting these cheques will reduce its cash ratio and so its power to lend.

The authorities have a number of methods of limiting the banks' power to lend. These are described below (XIV), since they are more readily understood in connection with the role of the Bank of England.

13. The balance sheet of a commercial bank. A simplified form of a typical balance sheet of a joint-stock bank is shown in Fig. 16. An actual bank balance sheet is shown for comparison in Fig. 17.

A balance sheet shows the *possessions* of an organisation (its assets) and the *claims* (liabilities) that can be made against those assets (*see* VIII, 24). Many of the items in the bank balance sheet shown are self-explanatory, but the following additional notes may be helpful:

(*a*) *Liabilities*

(*i*) Capital and reserve: claims due to shareholders.

(*ii*) Deposits: claims by depositors, whether their deposits arise directly or by the granting of loans.

(*iii*) Miscellaneous: mostly liabilities arising from bills accepted by the bank.

(*b*) *Assets*

The balance sheet of a bank displays, on the assets side, a tug-of-war between liquidity and profitability. A fair proportion of cash or near cash items are needed to meet depositors' claims, but the more "liquid" the assets are, the less they earn. The items are conventionally arranged in descending order of liquidity.

(*i*) Cash in hand and with the Bank of England: completely liquid but earning no interest.

(*ii*) Cheques in course of collection: nearly as liquid, but again earning nothing.

(*iii*) Money at call and short notice: money lent out at low rates of interest, mostly to the discount market, for very short periods.

LIABILITIES		ASSETS		
	(£ million)			(£ million)
Capital and Reserves	95	Cash in hand and with the Bank of England		181
Deposits	2,175	Cheques in course of collection		120
Miscellaneous	70	Money at Call and Short notice		220
		Bills Discounted (£m)		
		Treasury Bills	175	
		Other Bills	75	
				250
		Investments		300
		Advances		1,129
		Miscellaneous		140
	£2,340			£2,340

Fig. 16. A simplified bank balance sheet.

(*iv*) Bills discounted: Treasury bills and bills of exchange which are held to maturity and will thus become liquid in a comparatively short time.

(*v*) Investments: government securities which *could* be sold to provide cash.

(*vi*) Advances: the least liquid of the major assets but the most profitable.

(*vii*) Other items: customers' liabilities on acceptances, holdings in subsidiary companies and premises and equipment.

(c) *Calculation of ratios*

The ratios mentioned earlier in this chapter can be deduced from the bank balance sheet (Fig. 16) in the way demonstrated below:

Cash ratio:

$$\frac{\text{Cash in hand etc.}}{\text{Deposits}} = \frac{181}{2,175} = 8{\cdot}3\%$$

Liquidity ratio:

		£ million
Liquid items:	Cash in hand etc.	181
	Money at call	220
	Bills discounted	250
		651

$$\frac{\text{Liquid items}}{\text{Deposits}} = \frac{651}{2,175} = 30{\cdot}0\%$$

(d) *Reserve asset ratio*

The balance sheet would require to be shown in considerably more detail for the reserve asset ratio to be calculated in the same way since only *certain* government securities and only some "other bills" come into the approved categories.

BANK CLEARINGS

14. Paying a cheque. When a debt is settled by means of a cheque payment, the debtor draws a cheque on his bank and gives it to his creditor. The cheque is an order to the debtor's bank to pay money to his creditor. In the ordinary way, the creditor, call him Jones, does not take the cheque to the debtor's bank, but pays it in to his own bank, which credits his account. Jones's bank now needs to obtain the money from the debtor's (call him Brown) bank. Brown's account also needs to be debited. The situation is shown diagrammatically in Fig. 18.

15. Local and Provincial Clearings. If Brown and Jones happen to bank at the same branch of the same bank, there

BARCLAYS BANK LIMITED BALANCE SHEET
31 DECEMBER 1975

Liabilities	1975 £000	1975 £000	1974 £000	1974 £000
Deposits and customers' current accounts		6,558,657		6,165,496
Other accounts		201,101		353,161
Balances due to subsidiaries		116,860		240,871
Taxation		44,195		42,287
Proposed dividends		9,465		8,311
		6,930,278		6,810,126
Loan capital				
8¼ per cent Unsecured Loan Stock 1986/93		59,035		59,035
Stockholders' funds				
Share capital:				
Authorised:				
Ordinary shares of £1 each	274,000		229,000	
Staff shares of £1 each	1,000		1,000	
	275,000		230,000	
Issued (converted into stock):				
Ordinary stock	200,319		192,998	
Staff stock	875		875	
	201,194		193,873	
Reserves	384,592		360,652	
		585,786		554,525
		7,575,099		7,423,686

Assets	1975 £000	1975 £000	1974 £000	1974 £000
Cash and short-term funds		1,232,568		1,130,193
Cheques in course of collection		325,380		315,765
Special deposit with the Bank of England		175,840		167,935
Investments		416,964		346,456
Advances to customers and other accounts		4,786,178		5,017,074
Balances due by subsidiaries		142,056		23,854
		7,078,986		7,001,277
Investments in subsidiaries	201,128		175,283	
Investments in associated companies	28,879		24,141	
Other trade investments	418		4,329	
Bank premises, other properties and equipment	265,688		218,656	
		496,113		422,409
		7,575,099		7,423,686

AF Tuke, Chairman [1]TH Bevan, Deputy Chairman RT Pease, Vice-Chairman DE Wilde, Vice-Chairman HUA Lambert, Vice-Chairman DV Weyer, General Manager JPG Wathen, General Manager DM Taylor, General Manager DSG Adam, General Manager R Vine, General Manager JW Dyson, General Manager PE Leslie, General Manager DG Horner, General Manager JG Quinton, General Manager AE Bagley, General Manager DW Garlick, Chief Accountant DH Johnson, Secretary

Fig. 17. Barclays Bank balance sheet as at 31st December 1975.

is no problem. In most cases this will not happen. When claims have to be offset between branches of different banks in the same town, local branches can arrange to work out *net claims* on each other and to offset them by drafts drawn on their head offices.

Where claims are between different banks in different

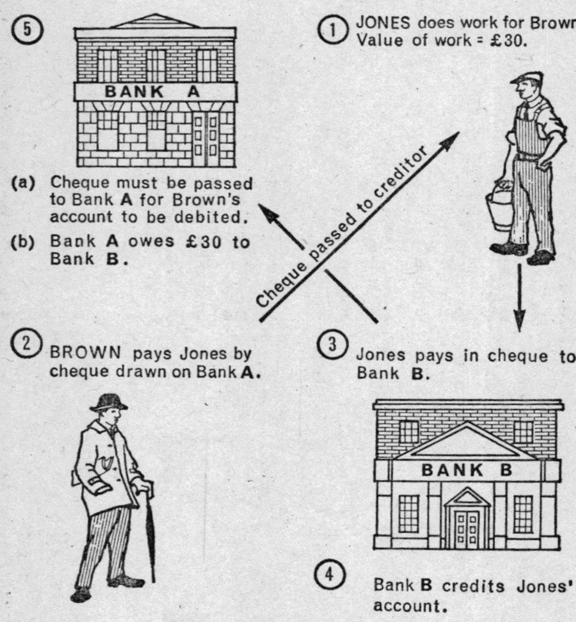

Fig. 18. Paying a cheque.

towns, they may be offset through one of the *Provincial Clearing Houses.* There are twelve Provincial Clearings in major commercial centres such as Manchester, Birmingham and Liverpool. The Provincial Clearings at Birmingham, Bristol, Leeds, Liverpool, Manchester, Newcastle and Southampton use the services of provincial branches of the Bank of England.

16. The London Bankers' Clearing House. Where there is no convenient provincial clearing, cheques drawn on other banks and paid in to a branch bank will be sent to the bank's head office. There they will be sorted into bundles and sent to the London Bankers' Clearing House. At the Clearing House, cheques due to and from each of the clearing banks will be totalled and a balance struck. At the end of the day, some banks will have amounts owing to them and others will have a net amount due from them. Each bank has an account with the Bank of England. Amounts owing and due are offset, through a special account called the Clearing Bankers' Account, so that banks with a net amount owing to them find their Bank of England accounts increased and those with amounts due from them find their accounts diminished.

As a final stage, the cheques are sent back to the branch banks so that the drawers' accounts can be debited. For convenience and efficiency there are separate arrangements for dealing with cheques from City branches (the Town Clearing) and other branches (the General Clearing). It usually takes three days to clear a cheque completely through the General Clearing.

17. Credit Clearing. Since 1960 a General Credit Clearing has been in operation. Credit transfers between banks need to be offset and settled just as cheques do and the arrangements made are similar.

OTHER BANKING INSTITUTIONS

18. The Scottish banks. There are five major Scottish banks, all but one of which have close ties with the English banks. Their activities parallel those of the English banks very closely, but one difference is that three of them retain the right of note issue. These are the Bank of Scotland, the Clydesdale Bank Ltd, and the Royal Bank of Scotland Ltd. Strictly, these notes are not legal tender, but they have equal status, in Scotland, with Bank of England notes. The fiduciary issue of the Scottish Banks is limited to a purely nominal figure but further issues may be made if fully covered by holdings of Bank of England notes. However, the total of Scottish notes in circulation is very small in comparison with the total note issue of the United Kingdom.

Control of the Scottish banks is on rather a different basis from that of the English banks. Asset ratios cannot be applied in quite the same way and there are some other differences in banking practice. However, there is no real difficulty in reconciling the operations of the two banking systems.

19. Savings banks. Savings banks enable people with relatively small sums at their disposal to deposit their savings where they can earn a modest rate of interest and yet be withdrawn at short notice.

Savers who deposit with the Post Office Savings Bank or with the Trustee Savings Banks enjoy the security of the State for the sums deposited and for interest earned. Amounts deposited are placed into funds managed by the National Debt Commissioners who hold government securities sufficient to cover the outstanding liabilities to depositors.

The rate of interest currently payable in the Post Office Savings Bank and the Ordinary Department of the Trustee Savings Bank is 5% (10% for the Investment Account) and 4% respectively.

20. Merchant banks. The merchant banks are substantial business houses most of whom began their careers as merchants and traders, but who became increasingly involved in the financing of trade rather than in trading on their own account. The biggest of them are very well known indeed, Barings, Rothschilds, Kleinworts, Lazards, Schroders and Warburgs being some of the more important.

Their long experience in trade and finance, in some cases stretching back over 150 years, placed them in an ideal position to judge the worth of bills of exchange drawn by other trades. An important part of their business is, therefore, the accepting of bills of exchange, and seventeen of them form the *Accepting Houses Committee*. Bills accepted by a member of the Accepting Houses Committee or by a British bank are "eligible paper" at the Bank of England (*see* XIV, **14–20**).

Another function of many of the merchant banks is the launching of new issues and most of the fifty or so organisations in the City of London that could be called merchant banks are members of the *Issuing Houses Committee.* Other work done by the merchant banks includes foreign exchange business, the provision of loans for industry and acting as trustees and investment advisers. A few of the merchant banks play an important part in London's gold market.

The combination of expertise and special knowledge needed by the merchant banks in carrying out the varied functions described above has made their advice extremely valuable when mergers or take-overs are contemplated. The social and economic implications of this part of their activities have led to publicity and, occasionally, to criticism. A further development in which the accepting houses have played a part is the emergence of *international* money and capital markets.

21. American banks and other institutions. In recent years dollars in the hands of financial institutions outside the U.S.A., being available for lending and borrowing, have become a common international currency. The market for these funds has become known as the "Eurodollar" market and the growth of Eurodollar dealings has been accompanied by the entry of a number of American banks into London. The competition by American banks in London in many fields has become a marked feature of the banking scene in the last few years.

Not only banks, but many other institutions make their money by seeking deposits and making loans. Most notable among these institutions are the finance houses, who apply their money in the provisions of funds for hire purchase. Until recently, the clearing banks had entered this field only indirectly, but the removal of limitations in September 1971, coupled with the imposition of reserve requirements on deposit-taking finance houses, is likely to lead to a much more competitive situation in this field.

22. Competition in banking. In May 1971 the Bank of England issued a consultative document entitled "Competition and Credit Control." Not only did this reflect the more competitive climate which had already come into existence, as evidenced by the emergence of new institutions accepting deposits and making loans, but it also signalled a more open competition between the joint-stock banks themselves. There were no longer to be official ceiling levels on bank lending, collective agreements on interest rates were ended and rates were no longer to be linked to the "Bank rate" of the Bank of England. Bank rate was officially abolished in 1972 and was replaced by *minimum lending rate* (*see* XIV, **24**).

PROGRESS TEST 13

1. Distinguish between:

   (*a*) Current and deposit accounts.
   (*b*) Loans and overdrafts. (**5**)

2. List at least seven services offered by the joint-stock banks. (**5**)

3. What characteristics should property offered as security for a bank loan have? What types of property satisfy the requirements you have mentioned? (**6**)

4. Write brief notes on the following:

   (*a*) The creation of credit. (**8, 9**)
   (*b*) Restrictions on bank lending. (**10–13**)
   (*c*) The London Bankers' Clearing House. (**16**)
   (*d*) Merchant banks. (**20**)

5. Explain the principal items in the balance sheet of a *commercial* bank, showing the significance of each of them. (**13**)

6. To what extent is banking becoming more competitive in the United Kingdom? (**21, 22**)

CHAPTER XIV

THE ENGLISH BANKING SYSTEM: (II)

THE BANK OF ENGLAND AND THE MONEY MARKET

THE BANK OF ENGLAND: ORIGINS AND DEVELOPMENT

1. The origins of the Bank of England. The Bank of England was founded in 1694 with the purpose firstly, of raising money for William III's military expeditions and secondly, of providing a more efficient banking service than the London goldsmiths could. Schemes for such a bank had been canvassed for a number of years and William Paterson, a Scot, and others devised a detailed plan for a bank to accept deposits, issue notes, lend at interest and deal in bills of exchange.

Under the Charter setting up the Bank, the government was to borrow £1,200,000 at 8% interest. The loan was to be raised by public subscription and the subscribers were to be incorporated as the Governor and Company of the Bank of England. The goldsmiths were opposed to the Bank and in 1696 they organised a "run" on it, buying up its notes and presenting them at a time when the coinage was being re-minted and the Bank was short of cash. The run failed and the Bank was subsequently given a monopoly of the right of note-issue among joint-stock banks.

The private banks adopted the practice of depositing their surplus funds with the Bank of England and when joint-stock banking began to flourish after 1862, these new banks also banked with the Bank of England. The Bank had thus begun to acquire another of its major functions, that of being the *bankers' bank*.

During the early years of the nineteenth century, there were several serious financial crises. In order to regulate the note-issue and to try to resolve once and for all the conflict between the Bank's public functions and its private business, the *Bank Charter Act* was passed in 1844. The *Bank Charter Act* permitted the Bank of England to issue £14,000,000 of notes with the backing of first-class securities, but above this "fiduciary issue" every note was to be backed pound-for-pound by gold. At the same time, no new issues by other banks were to be permitted and existing banks of issue were to lose their right of issue if they amalgamated or opened an office in London.

As a further measure of control, the Bank was separated into two departments, the Issue Department and the Banking Department, and a weekly statement of notes in circulation and the backing for them was to be published. As private banks gradually lost their right of issue the Bank of England became effectively the *sole bank of issue*.

NOTE: The last private bank lost its note-issuing powers in 1921 when Fox, Fowler and Co. amalgamated with Lloyds.

Support of other banking institutions at various times of crisis during the nineteenth century eventually led to the Bank's adoption of its role as lender of last resort (*see* **7**).

2. Nationalisation. The gradual acquisition of special powers and responsibilities transformed the Bank of England into a *central bank*. As such it came increasingly under the control of the government and it was recognised as the government's instrument in carrying out monetary policy. During the depression years, however, the Bank's policies came under criticism from some quarters and it was suggested that on occasions it had acted independently and unwisely, putting narrow financial interests before the well-being of the economy as a whole. When the first post-war Labour government came to power in 1945 it was, therefore, determined to nationalise the Bank, and the *Bank of England Act* was passed in 1946.

Nationalisation did not greatly change the nature of the Bank of England, which is still managed by a *Court of Directors* in accordance with its Charter. Shareholders were compensated by an issue of government securities yielding the same gross dividend as in the previous twenty years. The Directors are now appointed by the Crown and the Treasury has the statutory power to give directions to the

Bank, by the *Bank of England Act*, 1946, s. 4. The Bank makes half-yearly contributions to the Treasury in respect of interest payments on the compensation stock.

PRESENT-DAY FUNCTIONS OF THE BANK OF ENGLAND

3. Sole note-issuing bank. The Bank of England is the only note-issuing bank in England and Wales. The value of notes in circulation is now about £6,000 million, of which all but about £300,000 is fiduciary, being backed by securities and not by gold. The size of the fiduciary issue is regulated by the *Currency and Bank Notes Act*, 1954, but this gives the Treasury and the Bank great freedom to vary the note-issue as they think advisable.

4. Banker to the government. Since the Bank had its origins in the government's need for finance, this is the oldest of the Bank's functions. The Bank manages the National Debt, handles the issue of government stocks and superintends the issue of Treasury bills. It is at the Bank of England that the main government accounts are kept and the Bank provides occasional temporary loans to the government by *ways and means advances.*

As the government's banker, the Bank of England is responsible for giving technical advice to the government on monetary and financial policy and expects to be consulted on these matters.

5. The implementation of monetary policy. It is a primary duty of the Bank of England not merely to act as the government's adviser and banker but also to act as its agent in carrying out its monetary policy (*see* **22–29**).

6. The banker's bank. The clearing banks hold part of their liquid assets in the form of balances at the Bank of England. The joint-stock banks' "cash" consists partly of notes and coin and partly of Bank of England balances. Just as an ordinary person can draw on his bank account to obtain notes and coin, so the clearing banks can draw on the

Bank of England accounts. It will also be recalled that it is through the bankers' accounts at the Bank of England that the net positions at the end of the clearings are settled (*see* XIII, **16**).

The Bank's ability to control the size of the clearing banks' deposits is a major source of its power over their lending abilities. The discount houses also bank with the Bank of England.

7. Lender of last resort. The Bank of England does not lend directly to the joint-stock banks. If the banks are short of cash, they are able to call in short-term loans from the discount houses. Should this leave the discount houses short of funds, they can always borrow from the Discount Office at the Bank of England. The rate of interest at which the discount houses must borrow when they are "forced into the bank" is called the *minimum lending rate* (*see* **24**).

8. The Exchange Equalisation Account. Most people are aware that until about forty-six years ago, Britain was "on the gold standard." This meant that banknotes were convertible into gold at a stated rate and that gold could be exported in order to pay for goods bought from abroad. The rate of exchange between sterling and foreign currencies then, as now, depended on many factors, but most important was the demand for sterling by foreigners to buy British goods.

If the value of the pound fell very much in terms of other currencies, it tended to be cheaper to pay foreign creditors in gold rather than in currency. The consequent export of gold led to a reduction in the Bank of England's reserves of gold and consequently in its power to issue notes and in the capacity of the banking system as a whole to lend to the business community. The gold standard system, operated in conjunction with Bank rate policy, formed an ingenious mechanism whereby fluctuations in the rate of exchange were automatically corrected within quite narrow limits.

The form of gold standard which was in operation after the First World War was a much modified one and in 1931 Britain abandoned the gold standard altogether. It was decided, however, that some way of regulating short-term fluctuations in the rate of exchange was necessary now that the self-regulating gold standard system was no longer available. The value of one currency in terms of another depends on the demand for and supply of the currency concerned. The market forces are not fundamentally different from those determining the prices of more ordinary commodities (*see* XV, **22–29**). A new system for the regulation of the rate of exchange had, therefore, to be a system for the buying and selling of currencies.

To do this, a special Treasury account was brought into being. It was to be operated by the Bank of England and its business was to buy and sell sterling so as to keep the value of the pound steady in terms of other currencies. This account was called the *Exchange Equalisation Account*, and in 1939, the greater part of the Bank of England's gold reserve was transferred to it in order to provide additional sums for use in defence of the pound. In the post-war years, the Exchange Equalisation Account has been the repository for the sterling area's gold and convertible currency reserve.

9. The Bank's private customers. As a legacy from former times, the Bank of England still has a very few private customers for whom it conducts banking business in the ordinary way. No new customers are accepted and the Bank's ordinary banking business is a mere vestige which is of no great significance.

THE BANK OF ENGLAND'S ACCOUNTS

10. The form of the return. The *Bank Charter Act*, 1844 required the publication of a weekly return showing the position of Issue and Banking Departments. The return was in the form of a balance sheet for each of the departments, showing the assets possessed and the liabilities standing against them. The return is still published although the size of the fiduciary issue and the proportion of notes in the Banking Department no longer have their former significance.

The week-by-week significance of the return has now

declined and it is more appropriate to discuss the operations of the Bank in terms of its annual accounts, as would be appropriate for any other nationalised concern. It should be remembered, however, that the Bank of England has a very special place in the regulation of economic and monetary policy.

11. The Issue Department. The figures given below are taken from the Issue Department's *Statement of Balances* for the year ended 29th February, 1976.

Position of the Bank of England Issue Department
29th February 1976

Notes issued:

	£ million		£ million
In circulation	6042·3	Government debt	11·0
In Banking Department	7·7	Other government securities	5233·6
		Other securities	805·4
	£6050·0		£6050·0

The note issue, which has doubled in the decade since 1966, is now virtually all fiduciary, that is it is backed only by government securities. It can be seen that the liabilities of the Issue Department consist entirely of notes issued by the Bank. The *notes in circulation* are those in the hands of the general public and of business. The *notes in the Banking Department* are those that have not yet been put into general circulation. All of these notes represent obligations of the Issue Department and the right-hand side of the statement lists the assets held against them. The *government debt* represents loans made to the government by the Bank in the very early days of its existence. The item *government securities* consists of government bonds and Treasury bills and *other securities* includes bank bills and other first-class bills and securities.

12. The Banking Department. The balance sheet of the Banking Department for the same period, in slightly simplified form, is shown on p. 177.

Position of the Banking Department of the Bank of England
29th February 1976

	£ million		£ million
Capital	14·5	Government securities	137·7
Reserves	106·8	Other securities	44·0
Public deposits	84·9	Advances and other accounts	274·0
Special deposits	979·5	Treasury and other bills	1106·1
Bankers' deposits	227·5	Notes and coin	8·0
Other accounts	261·7	Cheques in course of collection	75·1
Other items	7·2	Premises etc.	37·2
	£1682·1		£1682·1

The principal items in the Balance Sheet are set out below, with a brief explanatory note against each of them.

(*a*) *Assets.*

(*i*) *Government securities:* these consist of government stocks, Treasury bills and ways and means advances. In addition, the figure shown includes a very small amount of Local Authority bonds.

(*ii*) *Other securities:* these include other first-class securities and, as well, the share capital (£1,000) of a wholly-owned subsidiary company, the Securities Management Trust Ltd.

(*iii*) *Advances and other accounts:* this item includes the Bank's lending to the discount market. If the market is "in the Bank", this item will increase.

(*iv*) *Notes and coin:* this item includes the unused portion of the note issue, the amount shown as "Notes in the Banking Department" in the accounts of the Issue Department. The coin is obtained by the Bank of England from the Royal Mint, crediting the Exchequer account in payment. The Bank supplies coin to the clearing banks, debiting their accounts as necessary.

(*v*) *Cheques in course of collection:* these are uncleared cheques mostly in respect of public deposits (*see* below).

(b) *Liabilities.*

(i) *Capital:* before 1946, the Bank was a joint-stock company. The only shareholder is now the government but the capital is still shown.

(ii) *Reserves:* this includes the accumulated accounting reserves, including profits retained.

(iii) *Public deposits:* this is the balance standing to the credit of the government account. Payments made by the government will diminish it and payments to the government, for example tax payments, will increase it.

(iv) *Special deposits:* sums deposited by the clearing banks and the Scottish banks at the order of the authorities in order to reduce bank liquidity.

(v) *Bankers' deposits:* these are the clearing banks' ordinary balances. Any action which reduces them will restrict the banks' power to make loans.

(vi) *Other accounts:* balances of Commonwealth and foreign banks are included here as well as the accounts of the Bank's few private customers.

13. The organisation of the Bank. The Issue and Banking "Departments" have no organisational significance, but survive only as an accounting convention. The work of the Bank is under the supervision of the "Court," a body which corresponds to the boards of other nationalised industries. The principal operating departments of the Bank are the Cashier's Department, which employs over a thousand people, the Accountant's Department, which is almost equally large, and the Exchange Control, Overseas and Economic Intelligence Departments. In addition, there are departments concerned with the Bank's internal operations and a printing works. The banking and financial activities which form the best known part of the work of the Bank are carried out by the Cashier's Department and the Cashier is also the Bank's chief executive.

THE BANK OF ENGLAND AND THE MONEY MARKET

14. The money and discount markets. The money and discount markets occupy a key position in the British monetary system. The Bank of England does not lend directly to the commercial banks but is always prepared to make funds available to the London discount market at a price. The effect of the inter-actions between the Bank of England, the discount market and the joint-stock banks is to provide a *pool of liquidity*, the volume of which can be varied at the wish of the authorities.

Before discussing this mechanism in detail, it would be as well to discover exactly what the money and discount markets are.

15. The London discount market. The discount market is a *market in bills*, both Treasury bills and commercial bills. The London discount market consists of the *discount houses* and *bill brokers* who make a living by lending money at higher rates of interest than they borrow it. The twelve biggest discount houses form the London Discount Market Association. There is no one *place* at which the discount market carries on its business, but the discount houses have their offices in the Lombard Street area of the City of London. The three most important discount houses are Union Discount, Alexander's Discount Company and the National Discount Company.

16. The money market. The money market is the *market in short-term loans*. Those involved in the money market are:

(*a*) The discount houses and bill brokers.
(*b*) The English joint-stock banks.
(*c*) The merchant bankers.
(*d*) Various foreign and overseas banks.
(*e*) The Bank of England.

The discount houses require funds for the purchase of bills and short-dated government bonds and the banks have surplus funds which they are prepared to make available to the discount houses. The Bank of England stands prepared to act as lender of last resort, on its own terms.

17. Treasury bills and commercial bills. The nature and functions of bills of exchange was explained previously (*see* XII). A bill of exchange can be held to maturity and then presented for payment or it can be endorsed and used to pay a debt or, alternatively, it can be discounted with a bank or a discount house. The advantages of bill finance appeared to be so great and so obvious that it occurred to the authorities that the government, too, could raise short-term loans in a similar way. Accordingly, the *Treasury bill* was created by an Act of 1877. Essentially, the Treasury bill is a government I.O.U. at three months' date. Since the credit of the government itself is backing the bill, it does not need to be "accepted."

Treasury bills are offered to the market each week in units of £5,000, £10,000 and larger denominations. They are sold by tender and the minimum tender is £50,000. They are also issued directly to government departments that have a temporary surplus of funds, but this issue, known as the "tap," is quite separate from the market issue. Each week, the Bank of England announces the total of Treasury bills to be offered on the following Friday. The bills are sold to the highest bidders and the principal purchasers are overseas banks, non-clearing banks, various industrial companies with cash surpluses and, of course, the discount houses. Tenders from "outside" buyers, at reasonably high, competitive prices, are accepted in full. The discount houses, however, tender as a syndicate and offer a lower price on the understanding that they will take all the bills that remain on offer after the "outside" tenders have been satisfied. The tender made by the discount houses depends on a very careful assessment of probable movements in interest rates over the coming three months. Treasury bills accunt for well over a half of the discount houses' business.

18. Sources of funds for the discount market. The discount houses discount commercial bills and Treasury bills and buy short-dated government bonds. They are able to make a profit by borrowing at low rates of interest for very short periods of time. Banks or business houses that have large sums of money available for short periods can, therefore, find an outlet for their cash that will prevent it from lying idle and yet will give it a high degree of availability. About half the discount market's funds come from the commercial banks. This is the clearing banks' *money at call and short* *notice.* The sums involved are very large and at any one time may amount to some £500 million. Loans from the merchant banks, foreign banks and other lenders account for the remainder.

Although the discount houses' search for funds is now largely conducted over the telephone, the custom of making personal "morning calls" on likely lenders in the City still continues. The total funds controlled by the discount market is of the order of £1,000 million and about £200 million may turn over daily.

19. The discount houses and the clearing banks. The method by which the clearing banks replenish their cash by calling in money from the discount houses has already been mentioned (*see* 7). When the banks do this the discount houses are unlikely to be able to obtain all the cash they require and they will be forced to apply to the Bank of England either to rediscount some of the bills which they hold or to obtain a loan against the security of bills. Since the Bank of England is able to influence the clearing banks' cash holdings, it can force the banks into a position where they are bound to call in money from the discount market and so drive the discount houses into the Bank.

Discount houses buy bills and either hold them to maturity or rediscount them with the joint-stock banks. Naturally, as the bill advances towards maturity it can be discounted for a sum which becomes progressively closer to its face value and there is a profit to be made by holding bills and rediscounting them at a later stage. It is of advantage to the joint-stock banks to hold bills because they can be turned into cash at a rate determined by their maturity dates. The discount houses rediscount bills to the banks in "parcels" which they have arranged in carefully graded order of maturity, so that the banks have an asset which will become completely liquid at a *known*, predetermined rate.

20. The functions of the discount market. The functions of the discount market can be summarised as follows:

(*a*) The discount market provides funds for business by discounting commercial bills and for the government by holding Treasury bills and short-dated bonds.

(*b*) The authorities dislike using ways and means advances and the discount market's willingness to cover the tender makes an important contribution to government finance.

(*c*) The skill of the discount market in assessing the appropriate rate at which to tender has repercussions on other interest rates.

(*d*) Standing between the clearing banks and the Bank of England, the discount market makes possible a flexible money market which can adjust smoothly to changing conditions.

21. Parallel money markets. During the past fifteen years, other markets in short-term funds have grown up to parallel that operated by the discount houses. Much of the lending and borrowing in these markets takes place between banks, although the clearing banks do not take part but still rely on the discount houses. The impetus behind the newer money markets has to a large extent come from the needs of local authorities for large sums.

THE BANK OF ENGLAND AND MONETARY POLICY

22. The methods of the Bank of England. Now that the principal institutions have been described, it is possible to see how the Bank of England is able to control them. The weapons available to the Bank are:

(*a*) Variation of the minimum lending rate policy (but *see* 24).

(*b*) Open market operations.

(*c*) Special deposits.

(*d*) Directives.

23. Bank rate. Bank rate was the minimum rate at which the Bank of England would discount bills of approved quality or would lend against suitable security.

In September 1972 the government introduced a policy of competition and credit control, and it was thought that the Bank rate, at that time 6%, should no longer have a strong influence on the rates charged by the banks on overdrafts, and those offered on deposits. In October, the Bank of England, with the approval of the Chancellor of the Exchequer, decided to abolish Bank rate and replace it with a new rate related more directly to the money market. By this means, more emphasis has been put on market competition as a means of regulating the cost of money.

24. Minimum lending rate (MLR). The new rate which replaced Bank rate was intended to be more flexible in operation and to be responsive to market conditions. It is therefore linked to the Treasury bill rate, which in turn depends on the supply of bills offered by the Bank and the size of the tender (*see* **17**).

The important rates for industry now are the clearing banks' base rates, which are determined by the individual banks. The Bank of England will retain its position as lender of last resort, and this rate will be fixed at one half per cent above the Treasury bill rate.

Although the rate is intended to be automatically fixed by the Treasury bill formula, the Bank of England is still able to fix an independent rate if it wishes to give a general lead to interest rates. Otherwise, the rate is announced every Friday afternoon.

A rise in Bank rate signified that money was scarce and interest rates high. It signified an attempt to check inflation, and U.K. businessmen would know that expansion would be difficult. A fall in the rate would have the opposite effect. While the MLR is not intended to be used in the same way as Bank rate, there are signs that it may be employed in a very similar way, whenever the authorities wish to give a strong lead to the markets.

25. Open market operations. If the Bank of England sells securities in the market, the buyers will pay for them with cheques drawn on the ordinary commercial banks. When these cheques are paid in, the clearing house operations will show the commercial banks as indebted to the Bank of England. This position will be corrected by a reduction in the banks' deposits at the Bank of England. Since deposits at the Bank of England are effectively cash, the commercial banks' cash ratios will be reduced and they will be forced to call in money from the discount market, thus forcing the discount houses into the Bank.

Conversely, if the Bank of England buys securities it will *increase* the commercial banks' deposits. Although this will increase their cash ratios, making it easier for them to lend, they will not necessarily do so.

The Bank may conduct open market operations in both Treasury bills and in government bonds. In either case, the Bank does not operate in its own name. Treasury bills are bought and sold in the market through a firm of discount brokers whose representative is known as the *special buyer*. When gilt-edged securities are sold in the market, operations are conducted through a firm of stockbrokers, their representative being known as *the government broker*. Needless to say, operations in the market are readily identified by all concerned as being on behalf of the Bank. Open market operations may be conducted on their own as a means of reducing credit, or in conjunction with a rise in the Bank's penal lending rate, to force the market into the Bank and so make the increase effective. Sales of Treasury bills, while reducing commercial banks' deposits at the Bank of England, will also tend to increase their holdings of eligible assets and so are likely to be self-defeating as a means of reducing the money supply.

26. Special deposits. In 1958, doubt about the effectiveness of existing powers led the government to introduce the *special deposit scheme* which gave the government, through the Bank of England, power to influence the banks' liquidity directly.

This scheme gives the authorities the power to direct the London clearing banks and the Scottish banks to place on deposit with the Bank of England an amount equal to a given percentage of their deposits. These special deposits bear interest but are not available as liquid resources. A call for special deposits restricts the lending powers of the banks.

27. Directives. The *Bank of England Act*, 1946 gave the Treasury power to issue directives to the Bank of England

and gave the Bank similar powers over the commercial banks. So far, neither set of powers has been used, discussion and informal advice having proved adequate and effective.

28. Recent developments. The Bank of England's attempts to control the money supply have been much impaired by two things:

(*a*) The development of institutions which accepted deposits and made loans but which were not subject to control in the way that banks were.

(*b*) The willingness of the Bank of England to buy gilt-edged stocks whenever they were offered, which meant that the banks could always sell gilt-edged and so maintain their liquidity position even when the Bank of England was trying to restrict credit.

These obstacles to effective monetary control have been removed by the following four measures:

(*a*) The Bank no longer being always prepared to buy gilt-edged stock except when it has a year or less to go to maturity.

(*b*) Requiring banks to hold 12½ per cent of their liabilities in specified reserve assets which include gilts with under a year to run but exclude those with longer to go to maturity.

(*c*) Requiring all except the smallest deposit-taking finance houses to cover 10 per cent of their liabilities in the same way.

(*d*) Calling for special deposits on a more regular and flexible basis.

These new requirements should be considered in conjunction with the measures to improve competition in banking which were mentioned in the previous chapter. The whole package of measures constitutes a considerable change in British banking and monetary control.

29. Motives for changes in monetary policy. Monetary policy is largely concerned with controlling the volume of spending power. The actual policies pursued are partly politically and partly economically determined. Responsibility for monetary policy in Britain is divided between the Chancellor of the Exchequer, the Treasury and the Bank of England. Collectively these are known as *the authorities.*

The objectives of monetary policy may be to control rising prices, to maintain demand and prevent unemployment, to restrain home demand and so reduce the demand for imports, or to restore foreign confidence in Britain's ability to correct an adverse balance of payments.

PROGRESS TEST 14

1. Write brief notes on "The functions of the Bank of England." (3–9)
2. Explain the part played by the discount market in the English banking system. (14–20)
3. How do Treasury bills differ from commercial bills? (17)
4. What was Bank rate and why was it abolished in October 1972? (23, 24)
5. Discuss the ways in which the Bank of England may influence the volume of credit available in the country. (22–29)

PART FIVE

THE HOME TRADE

CHAPTER XV

BUYING AND SELLING

LEGAL CONSIDERATIONS

1. Commercial relationships. A great deal of commercial life is concerned with buying and selling. When goods are bought and sold, the buyer and seller enter into an agreement. Such agreements are called contracts and they are legally binding.

2. The nature of a contract. There are many technicalities involved in the making of contracts. These are best left to lawyers. For our purposes, it is sufficient to understand that a contract exists where the two parties come to an agreement for the supply of goods or the carrying out of services, that whatever is to be done is done for gain, and that although some contracts must be in a special form, many may be merely verbal or may be implied from the behaviour of the people concerned.

3. "Caveat emptor." The law assumes that buyers are alert, intelligent and capable of making good judgments. The legal motto *caveat emptor* means "*let the buyer beware*" and it emphasises that the law will take no heed of the buyer's weakness, ignorance or gullibility. He is assumed to have entered into the contract with his eyes open. This underlying principle has been considerably modified by the operation of the *Trade Descriptions Acts* of 1968 and 1972, which offer protection from misleading descriptions and from false claims about prices.

4. Sale of Goods Act, 1893. This is the most important piece of legislation concerned with the sale of goods. It is not concerned with work done or services performed. Among its many provisions it is worth noting that:

(*a*) Goods supplied must be of "merchantable" quality (s. 14) if they are sold by someone who normally deals in them.

(*b*) The buyer should be able to enjoy quiet possession of the goods and the goods should be free of any third-party rights of which the buyer is unaware (s. 12).

(*c*) When the buyer has made known to the seller any particular purpose for which the goods are required and has made it clear that he is relying on the seller's skill and judgment, the goods should be reasonably fit for that purpose (s. 14).

5. The Supply of Goods (Implied Terms) Act, 1973. There was nothing to prevent a buyer and seller from making a contract which excluded the provisions of the *Sale of Goods Act*. This was because the contract was a purely private affair between the two parties concerned. However, the clause excluding the provisions of the Act was often included without the buyer's attention being drawn to it and frequently it was hidden in the small print of the "guarantee" forms when household appliances or other equipment were purchased. The *Supply of Goods (Implied Terms) Act* strengthened the requirement that goods should be of "merchantable quality" by requiring that they be suitable for the purposes of the buyer when the buyer had made that purpose known to the seller. The Act made exclusion clauses in guarantees, such as those discussed above, invalid. The Act does not apply to services, however, nor does it cover private sales, auctions or certain other excluded transactions.

PROBLEMS OF PURCHASING

6. Everyday contracts. Buying a bus ticket in the morning or calling at the butcher's to purchase the weekend joint are very ordinary occurrences, but in each case the people concerned have entered into contracts. The subject matter of such contracts is usually so simple that there is little room for mistake. It is only when something goes badly wrong that the implications of the contracts become apparent.

7. Purchasing for a business. Care is necessary when entering into contracts as an individual, but in business the subject matter is more complex and the sums of money concerned are greater, and so additional caution is necessary. Carelessness in specifying delivery dates, qualities of materials to be supplied or methods of transport to be used could cause disastrous delays or wastages. Bad judgment in assessing the price or time at which to buy could be equally damaging to the business. The task of obtaining supplies for a business is usually placed in the hands of a specialist purchasing officer or purchasing agent.

8. Purchasing methods. The policy adopted by the purchasing officer will vary with the business and with the type of commodity concerned. A large business will deal with scores of suppliers and will buy hundreds or even thousands of lines. A manufacturing business may buy both raw materials and finished or semi-finished components. Among the methods used would be:

(*a*) *Contract purchasing.* A firm may enter into long-term contracts with suppliers for large quantities to be supplied at regular intervals, usually at advantageous prices.

(*b*) *Scheduled purchasing.* Without giving the supplier a definite contract, a firm may indicate the quantities that it estimates to be needed over a period. The supplier can then plan his production with greater confidence.

(*c*) *Period purchasing.* Where requirements are regular but not large, ordering may be on a month-to-month basis.

(*d*) *By requirement.* Orders may be given as required for occasional or emergency purchases.

(*e*) *Market purchasing.* The purchasing officer, while taking note of production requirements, will try to stock up when prices are low and to buy less when prices are high.

(*f*) *Speculative purchasing.* Buying policy may be guided by price changes rather than by production needs, so that over-buying when prices are low with a view to later selling at a profit is the rule. There is an element of risk in such a policy, but it may be a major source of profit at times. Non-ferrous metals and wool are sometimes bought and sold by manufacturing firms in this way.

9. Choosing suppliers. In the selection of suppliers, the purchasing officer has a number of possible strategies. He may split his orders among a number of suppliers if goods are in short supply or he may choose local firms to ensure quick delivery and close personal contact. The reputation of a supplier for high quality goods or, if machines are concerned, for a good after-sales service may influence the purchasing officer's choice, as, of course, will the price, and the discounts and period of credit offered.

10. Purchasing by consumers. Purchases by businesses are usually made by experts who bargain with their suppliers on more or less equal terms. Purchases by consumers are made by individuals who cannot hope to be experts in the qualities of all the goods they buy and who often lack any real knowledge of business procedures. There is, therefore, some need for *consumer education* and *consumer protection.*

THE CONSUMER MOVEMENT

11. Need for consumer protection. People have more money to spend than ever before. A bewildering variety of goods and services is offered to them, and many new products are made by industrial processes of extreme complexity. The business of choosing between products is made more complicated by the competing claims of persuasive and skilful advertisers and by the impersonal nature of modern retailing methods. There is a need for information and advice to help consumers to make intelligent and informed choices so that they can obtain value for their money.

In 1963 the government of the day set up the *Consumer*

Council to look after consumers' interests, but by 1971 this was thought to have outlived its usefulness and it was abolished. Many people thought this move premature. More recently a *National Consumers Council* has been set up to make representations on consumer affairs.

12. The Consumers' Association. The Consumers' Association is a body of quite a different kind. It tests goods and investigates services offered to the public and publishes the results in a monthly magazine called *Which?* A *Research Institute for Consumer Affairs* has been established to undertake research into services.

13. Consumer groups. In many parts of the country consumer groups have been started to investigate goods and services available in their localities. There is a *Federation of Consumer Groups* which co-ordinates the work of local groups. There has been criticism by retailers of the work of some consumer groups.

14. The British Standards Institution. This organisation, principally concerned with standards of size and quality in industry, also tests consumer goods. Products that conform to B.S.I. standards are awarded the *kite mark*, the Institution's certification trade mark.

15. Consumer Consultative Committees. The interests of consumers of services provided by the nationalised industries are protected by Consumer Consultative Committees. These representative bodies advise the nationalised Boards on matters that affect consumers and also inquire into complaints. On the whole their work is insufficiently publicised and consumers do not make adequate use of them.

16. Consumer legislation. Further protection is provided for consumers by the *Fair Trading Act*, 1973. This established the post of *Director-General of Fair Trading*, an official who has the responsibility of collecting information and advising his minister on activities concerned with the supply of goods and services to consumers. The Director is assisted by a *Consumer Protection Advisory Committee*. He may publish information about current practices, may offer advice to consumers and has additional responsibilities concerning the control of monopolies.

HIRE-PURCHASE AND CREDIT SALES

17. Need for consumer credit. People often want things which they cannot afford to pay for immediately. When the goods concerned are household necessities the need for the extension of credit to consumers is obvious and urgent. Often, though, the goods required are "conventional necessities," which only appear to be essential. Nevertheless, the availability of hire-purchase or other credit facilities makes it possible to acquire goods at once and to pay for them out of income over a period of time.

18. Distinction between hire-purchase and credit sales. Under both hire-purchase and credit sale agreements a deposit is paid and the balance is paid off by instalments. Both forms of agreement are legally binding contracts (*see* 2, 3). Under a *hire-purchase* agreement the goods do not become the customer's property until the last instalment has been paid. Under *credit sale* arrangements, the goods belong to the customer from the start, just as in an ordinary purchase of goods for cash.

19. Other forms of credit trading. A considerable volume of credit trading is concerned with purchases which, individually, are for fairly small sums, payment being made by weekly instalments and formalities kept to a minimum. *Check trading*, *credit drapery* and *clothing clubs* are variants of this type of trade. Written agreements are not required when the total purchase price is less than £30 and sometimes the only documentation is a payment card entered up when weekly payments are made.

Some of these traditional methods of meeting the needs of working class consumers are being superseded by large-scale *mail order trading*, which also offers credit terms.

Many department stores now offer *budget accounts* which enable customers to enjoy credit facilities up to a given limit in exchange for a fixed monthly payment.

20. Legislation on consumer credit and hire-purchase. There is a danger that consumers may be persuaded into hire-purchase commitments which they cannot afford, or that a single failure to meet an instalment when it becomes due might lead to forfeiture of the goods. The *Hire-Purchase Acts*, 1938 and 1964 were intended to prevent such abuses, their essential provisions being:

1938 Act

(*a*) There must be a written agreement signed by the parties concerned, showing the cash price and the hire-purchase price.

(*b*) The hirer (customer) has the right to terminate the agreement, but must bring the payments up to one-half the hire-purchase price.

(*c*) After the customer has paid one-third of the hire-purchase price, the goods can only be taken back under a court order.

1964 Act

(*a*) When agreements are signed at home, a second copy must be sent by post and the customer has a three-day period after this in which to repudiate the agreement.

(*b*) The "ceiling" for goods covered by the Acts was raised to £2,000.

Consumer credit plays such an important part in the home trade and in many people's lives that it was felt that the whole of this area of trading, and the complex legislation which surrounds it, should be investigated. As a result, the Crowther Report of 1971 proposed that the whole tangle of old legislation should be swept away and replaced by comprehensive new laws. At the time of writing, the *Consumer Credit Act*, 1974, is being brought into force. This Act, which applies to transactions of less than £5,000 for the most part, re-enacts the provisions of the *Hire-Purchase Acts* but covers as well a far wider field of consumer credit. When the provisions of the Act are fully implemented, a wide variety of agencies offering credit facilities, credit references and many related activities will be subject to close regulation.

21. Finance houses and hire-purchase. In many cases, retailers do not finance hire-purchase transactions from their own funds, but pass the debts to a finance house under a *block discount* arrangement. The retailer then receives an advance from the finance house equal to a proportion of the face value of the agreements concerned. Alternatively, the customer may find that his agreement is not with the retailer but with the finance house itself, which is thus the true owner of the goods until all the instalments are paid.

THE DETERMINATION OF PRICE

22. Market forces. When a market is competitive there are many buyers and many sellers, so that no buyer or seller can dictate the prices at which deals are made. If one seller tries to force the price up, buyers will go elsewhere. If a buyer tries to keep prices down, sellers can find plenty of other customers. In these circumstances, prices are determined by supply and demand.

23. Demand. Demand can be defined as:

The quantity of a commodity that buyers will be willing to take at a given price over a given period of time.

Demand is not the same as the need or desire for a commodity. Market prices are only affected when customers back up their desire by being willing to offer money for the commodity.

24. Supply. Supply can be defined as:

The quantity of a commodity that suppliers will be willing to offer on the market at a given price over a given period of time.

Supply is not the same as the *stocks* of a commodity in existence at any one time. Only when suppliers are offered enough money to induce them to sell are market prices affected.

25. Other conditions for a competitive market. If market forces are to have complete freedom, it is necessary for all concerned to know what prices are ruling in the market, otherwise they may make bad bargains through sheer ignorance. They must also be well informed about the technicalities of the products being bought and sold. The market will not be competitive unless everyone is free to buy or sell to anyone he chooses. Restrictions preventing some people from entering the trade will prevent the market from being truly competitive. The Stock Exchange and the commodity markets (*see* X and XX) are examples of highly competitive markets.

26. Perfect competition. If there are many buyers and many sellers, and the conditions outlined above are in force, perfect competition will exist. Whether this would be a good thing for the economy is a matter for discussion; it never has existed and is unlikely to do so now. Perfect competition is a theoretical concept, useful as a starting point for economic analysis but not to be found in the real world.

27. Imperfect competition. Buying and selling always takes place in conditions that are less than perfectly competitive. Perhaps a quarter of British industry sells its products in conditions that are highly, although not perfectly, competitive. In all other cases, the major suppliers are able to determine prices to some extent.

28. The working of supply and demand. The way in which supply and demand influence price can be seen from the following hypothetical example.

Suppose that we are considering the market for wheat. At some particular time, we are able to find out what buyers would be willing to purchase at a range of prices over a given period. We make a schedule of these prices:

Demand schedule for wheat

Price (£ per ton)	*Quantity demanded* (thousand tons)
75	100
78	98
81	90
84	75
87	65
90	50
93	45
96	40

Similarly, we could make a schedule of quantities that suppliers were willing to offer at the same range of prices:

Supply schedule for wheat

Price (£ per ton)	*Quantity supplied* (thousand tons)
75	35
78	50
81	60
84	75
87	90
90	95
93	100
96	120

At a price of £84 per ton, buyers would take all the wheat offered. At lower prices, demand would exceed supply and prices would be forced up. At prices above £84 per ton, more wheat would be offered on the market than buyers would take at these high rates. Prices would tend to fall. In the circumstances given by the schedules, the *equilibrium price* would be £84 per ton.

In real market situations, buyers and sellers do not know the demand and supply schedules for the product. They try to infer what the demand and supply conditions are and in what ways prices are likely to move (*see* XX). Whether the schedules are known or not, the forces of demand and supply are still at work.

29. Consumer demand under imperfect competition. It may appear, from everyday experience, that large suppliers can ignore consumer demand and charge what they please. Even monopolists cannot do this, however. They may set prices and these prices may be marked on goods in the shops, but if the prices are too high, consumers will not buy, goods will remain on the shelves and the monopoly producer will have to cut back production. An alternative would be to try to increase the demand by energetic advertising, so that he could continue to charge the old high price, but this would increase his costs.

PROGRESS TEST 15

1. What legal principles or statutes should a prospective buyer or seller have in mind? How would they affect him? (3–5)

2. Write brief notes on the purchasing policy of a business. (6–9)

3. How far is there a need for special legislation or special organisations to protect consumers? **(10–16)**

4. Why is special legislation needed to protect those who buy goods on hire-purchase terms? What are the main types of protection given? **(18–20)**

5. What are the advantages and disadvantages of hire-purchase and other forms of credit trading? Does recent legislation offer sufficient protection to consumers? **(17–20)**

6. Describe the way in which the price of a commodity is determined in a competitive market. **(22–29)**

CHAPTER XVI

THE RETAIL TRADE

THE FUNCTIONS OF THE RETAILER

1. Functions of retailers. The retailer is the last link in the chain of distribution. We expect him to be able to supply all the many goods that we need from day to day and we are usually a little annoyed if he is unable to produce precisely the goods that we require in the right quantity and at the right time. An important part of the retailer's task is to *maintain continuity of supply.* It is essential to remember that the process of production is not complete until the goods are in the hands of the final consumers. If the retailer does not carry out his part of the process efficiently, the efforts of workers in the factories, in transport and in the wholesale trade are frustrated.

2. The retailer's task. The exact nature of the retailer's task can be understood more easily if we consider his functions one by one.

(*a*) *Anticipation of consumer demand.* Since customers do not usually give their orders in advance but expect the retailer to have their requirements on his shelves, the retailer must *anticipate* demand. He is therefore involved in the expense of buying goods in advance of sales and in the risk of anticipating customers' wants incorrectly.

(*b*) *Knowledge of customers' wants.* Successful anticipation of demand is only possible if the retailer is in close touch with his customers and is really familiar with their buying trends.

(*c*) *Storage.* Ordinary families and individuals do not carry large stocks of consumable goods in their larders and store-cupboards. Without an efficient retail trade they would have to do so. Because the retailer stores goods, he takes the risk of deterioration and damage and bears the costs of storage.

(*d*) *Buying large, selling small.* Whether the retailer is supplied directly by the manufacturer or through a wholesaler, he buys in fairly large quantities and sells in the smaller quantities that are convenient for consumers' use.

(*e*) *Grading, packing and sorting.* Buying in large quantities and selling in smaller quantities may sometimes involve the retailer in grading, packing or sorting commodities. In these days of processed and prepacked goods this is less often the case than in former times, but butchers, fruiterers, tailors and other retail trades are still concerned in their various ways with grading and preparing their goods.

(*f*) *Selection, recommendation and advice.* Consumers rely on the advice of their retailers when buying many goods, both those which are technically complex, such as television sets or motor-mowers, and also such apparently simple goods as packaged foods and dress materials.

The efficient retailer has a responsibility not only to advise on goods that are already established in the market, but to inform his customers of new lines as they become available and to stock them if he believes that they will be required.

(*g*) *Credit.* The shopkeeper is often expected to give credit to his customers. This applies particularly to small shops in working-class areas and to stores catering for a prosperous middle-class clientele.

(*h*) *Delivery.* Many retailers offer delivery as an additional service. Where goods are too bulky to be taken away by customers delivery services are, of course, essential.

The retailer's functions might be summarised as knowing the customers' needs and maintaining continuity of supply. This is true whether the retail organisation is a small shop relying on personal contact or a large-scale concern using market research techniques. The extent to which *all* the retail functions are carried out depends on the type of goods sold and the nature of the retail establishment concerned.

TYPES OF RETAIL ORGANISATION

Retail trade has tended to become more competitive in recent years. New types of retail shop have appeared on the scene and an increasingly significant proportion of retail trade is successfully carried on without conventional shops. The various types of retail establishment met with in Britain are listed below. It is interesting to reflect on which of them carry out *all* the retail functions, which functions each of them performs and why this is so.

3. Types of retailer.

(*a*) Costermongers and hawkers.
(*b*) Mobile shops.
(*c*) Unit shops.
(*d*) Multiple stores.
(*e*) Variety chain stores.
(*f*) Department stores.
(*g*) Supermarkets and self-service stores.
(*h*) Discount stores.
(*i*) Tied shops.
(*j*) Hypermarkets.
(*k*) Leased shops.
(*l*) Voluntary groups and chains.
(*m*) Mail order.
(*n*) Automatic selling.

Each of these types of retail organisation is considered in detail below.

4. Costermongers and hawkers. Although these represent the simplest form of retailing, there is a great deal of difference between the itinerant hawker with a suitcase of tawdry odds-and-ends and the established stall holder who has occupied a particular site in a recognised market for many years. Between the two extremes are a variety of "barrow-boys" and casual traders. All have in common a minimum outlay on premises and equipment and flexibility in the commodities they sell. Many of them share a forceful and sometimes flamboyant selling technique.

5. Mobile shops. The development of housing estates far from town centres during the fifties and sixties led to a great increase in the sale of foodstuffs and household goods from travelling vans. For a time this was one of the fastest growing sectors of the retail trade, with specially designed vehicles being used and the retail co-operative societies taking a lead in developing this type of trade. The spread of car ownership and the rise of more attractive and efficient forms of retailing halted the growth of selling from mobile shops, but recently the dairy trades, exploiting the existence of well-established delivery networks, have revived house-to-house selling by widening the range of goods offered by the familiar milk vans.

6. Unit shops. The unit shop, the single shop operated by one man, is also a very flexible form of organisation. The main advantage of the independent retailer is that he is in personal touch with his customers and can have an intimate knowledge of their wants. His market is necessarily a small one, the stocks that he carries are relatively small and he relies on his suppliers being willing to fulfil his small but regular orders. Although the independent retailer may be forced to give credit to retain his customers, he will be reluctant to do so as his working capital is likely to be very limited. The spread of branding and nation-wide advertising to cover an increasing range of goods has tended to reduce the individuality and character of the unit shop and competition from larger retail organisations has made life increasingly competitive for the small shopkeeper. There are about half a million unit shops in Britain and of these 200,000 are very small, having weekly turnovers of less than £200.

7. Multiple stores. The standard shopfronts of the multiples are familiar in every suburb and provincial town. The names of the principal multiple stores are household words: *Boots*, *Burtons*, *Richard Shops*, *Freeman*, *Hardy & Willis* are examples. Their common characteristic is the sale of a narrow range of goods by efficient, controlled, standardised methods. The names of the shops and the goods associated with them will recall the sections of the retail trade in which the multiples are most active: pharmaceuticals, clothing, food, shoes. The multiple store is frequently part of an integrated wholesale-retail group. The average multiple has about fifty branches, but the larger chains may have many more than this; Boots, for example, has 1,300 branches.

Bulk-buying, low operating costs, large turnover and standardised selling methods, with limited discretion for local management, have led to the outstanding success of the multiples in the post-war retail trade. They supply goods of reliable quality and although they give few additional services their stores are pleasant and are briskly and efficiently run.

8. Variety chain stores. Examples of variety chain stores are *Woolworths*, *Marks and Spencer*, *British Home Stores* and *Littlewoods*. Their names are as much a part of everyday life as those of the multiples. Originally, the variety chain stores sold goods with a very low price limit. This limit has gradually been raised and the range of goods sold has been extended. The modern variety chain store, in order to maintain its competitiveness in a more affluent world, has endeavoured to improve its image and to widen its appeal. Most variety chains now sell men's and women's clothing of reasonable quality, records, radios, stereo equipment and foodstuffs and it would be difficult to put an upper limit to the price range of goods offered. They also accept cheques and credit cards and sometimes offer extended credit and hire-purchase facilities. The variety chain stores retain their characteristics of open display of goods, with prices clearly marked, and of low prices maintained by bulk-buying and quick turnover. The sales of the variety chains are so large that they are able to have goods manufactured to their special requirements and to lay down detailed design specifications and delivery dates. The low prices and improved quality of the goods sold by variety chain stores now appeal to a middle-class as well as to a working-class public and so provide powerful competition for the department stores.

9. Department stores. The aim of the department store is to provide a complete range of shopping services under one roof. To induce the customer to make as many purchases as possible within the store, shopping is made as pleasant as possible. Services such as restaurants and hairdressing salons are often available on the premises and there are usually many small touches of luxury throughout the store. The high level of services provided leads to heavy overheads, which can only be covered by a high turnover. The need to maintain sales at a high rate coupled with the wide range of goods stocked puts a premium on the economical use of floor space, every square foot of which must make its contribution to the profits of the store.

The precise range of goods sold varies form store to store, but normally includes drapery, soft furnishings, clothing, furniture, hardware and foodstuffs. Each department specialises in a particular line of goods and is under the control of a buyer whose greatest asset is a flair for knowing exactly what will sell, and must therefore be stocked, at a given time. Examples of large department stores are *Harrods*, *Selfridges* and *John Lewis*, but most sizeable provincial towns boast at least one such store.

Since the war, the department stores have failed to maintain their share of consumers' expenditure. Much of their trade has been captured by the multiples and the variety chain stores. Single department stores without any wider organisation to support them have found it difficult to survive. Groups of stores, however, sharing central administrative services and having the advantages of bulk-buying and a group wholesaling organisation have been able to compete. More than half the department stores in this country are now members of large groups.

10. Supermarkets and self-service stores. In the last fifteen years, there have been many changes in retailing methods, but the most obvious to the casual observer have been the conversion of many grocers' shops into self-service stores and the opening of bright, glossy supermarkets in the main shopping streets of most towns. The first self-service store in Britain was opened in 1942 by the London Co-operative Society. By 1950, there were only five hundred such stores, but in recent years well over a hundred new self-service shops, many of them conversions of existing shops, have appeared each week. At first independent retailers were slow to convert, but increasing competition from the multiples, the collapse of resale price maintenance (*see* 22) and the influence of the voluntary chains (*see* 15) have led to an accelerating rate of conversions to the self-service principle. The self-service store provides speed and convenience for customers and can reduce labour costs, but lack of capital makes conversion difficult for the small shopkeeper, and if his site is away from the main shopping centre he may not be able to achieve the higher turnover which would make conversion worthwhile.

Supermarkets are distinguished from self-service stores by the greater range of goods sold and by the greater floor space employed, usually more than 250 square metres. A central site is essential for the supermarket. The supermarket chains employ managers of high calibre and take great trouble to ensure that they are thoroughly trained.

Wage costs in supermarkets have been reduced to some 5% of sales and there is greater scope for the employment of specialised staff. Both buying and selling are carried out on a scientific basis and the larger supermarket chains have carried out much research into consumer motivation and buying habits.

11. Discount stores. Stores selling an even wider range of goods than the supermarkets with a minimum of service and in rather austere premises have become known as discount stores. By cutting overheads to the bone they are able to offer a variety of goods, including consumer durables such as refrigerators and washing machines, at heavy discounts.

Discount stores were slow to gain a foothold in this country, but the last few years have seen a rapid growth in specialist discount stores selling furniture, household durable goods and building and decorating supplies at low prices.

12. Tied shops. Tied shops accept restrictions in the way in which they trade or in the goods which they sell and in return receive assistance from the manufacturers concerned. In the case of the well-known Wimpy Bars, the operators agreed to purchase hamburger steaks from Pleasure Foods Ltd., and receive griddles and toasters on free loan. The premises are inspected to ensure that the site is suitable and can provide an adequate turnover and the standard decor must be used. In return the operator receives advice and help with the operation of the business as well as considerable publicity.

13. Hypermarkets. A hypermarket is a very large store with a selling area of at least 2,500 square metres, that is at least twice the size of a large supermarket. Hypermarkets sell a wide range of foodstuffs plus a fairly large range of other goods. They are entirely self-service stores, with the selling area on one level. Usually situated on the edge of towns, hypermarkets are geared to the needs of the car-owning consumer. Their advantages are low costs, and therefore prices, greater convenience and relief of town centre congestion. Hypermarkets have been slow to develop in Britain, but they are expected to open in increasing numbers in the next few years. A reservation sometimes expressed is that they may take too much trade away from town centres, leaving them depressed and, eventually, run down.

14. Leased shops. Mention has already been made of the importance of proper utilisation of floor space in department stores. One way of doing this is to lease floor space to a manufacturer of a nationally known product of first-class quality. The leased area is operated by the manufacturer and the retail store provides necessary services such as telephones, lighting and heating. Precise arrangements vary, but a common arrangement is for the store to receive some 10–15% of the turnover as well as benefiting from the prestige, and increased custom, which comes from having the leased "shop" on the premises.

15. Voluntary groups and chains. Voluntary chains are intended to improve the efficiency of independent retailers so that they can compete with the multiples and supermarkets. Collectively, the small shopkeepers are a very important group of customers for the wholesale trade.

Supermarket chains, multiple stores and grouped department stores have their own wholesale organisations and it is therefore in the interests of the independent wholesale trade to help to support the unit shop.

The voluntary chain operates by means of agreements between a wholesale firm and individual shopkeepers trading with it. The retailer agrees to place a minimum weekly order and to accept deliveries at specified times. He also agrees to conform to standards of service and hygiene and to display the chain insignia. In return the retailer obtains supplies at concession prices and may in addition be able to obtain financial assistance and help with self-service conversions. Most of the chains provide collective publicity including posters, press advertising and television commercials. At the time of writing, over 30% of independent grocers belong to voluntary chains.

16. Mail order. The total value of mail order sales in the United Kingdom is around £2,000 million per annum. Although there are several hundred mail order firms, twenty large firms account for 80% of mail order business. There are, in fact, two distinct types of mail order business:

(*a*) Mail order trading in a single line or a narrow range of goods.

(*b*) Large-scale mail order trade through part-time agents.

Firms conducting mail order business of the first type are, for the most part, small. Their advertisements are familiar from certain magazines and from the "small ads" in the newspapers.

The second type of mail order firm bases its business on a network of part-time agents, selling a wide range of goods on credit from an elaborate and lavishly illustrated catalogue. The catalogues, which are expensive to produce, are sent only to the firm's agents and are revised in the spring and autumn of each year. The agent, usually a housewife, is expected to work up a group of customers among her acquaintances and relations and is rewarded by a commission of about 10%. Credit arrangements vary a little from firm to firm, but basically require payment by twenty instalments each of 5p in the pound of the price of the goods. There is a rapid turnover of agents and since the maintenance of a force of agents is essential, recruiting is energetic and continuous.

The larger firms trading on this basis are well known from their catalogues and from press advertisement. They include *Great Universal Stores*, *Littlewoods*, *Grattans*, *Freemans and Furness*. Large-scale mail order trading is carried out with great efficiency. In recent years there has been very thorough investigation into packaging, in order to ensure safe delivery, and a great deal of skilled market research to determine what goods should be included in the catalogues.

17. Automatic selling. The number of automatic vending machines in use in this country is probably approaching five hundred thousand. They have two advantages over conventional selling methods:

(*a*) They are available for twenty-four hours a day.

(*b*) No labour is required other than that necessary to recharge and maintain them.

Simple vending machines have been familiar for many years, but those now being installed are much more complex. Some machines offer a variety of products, others incorporate refrigeration machinery or devices to supply hot drinks. The cost of the more elaborate machines is considerable and may be of the order of £1,500, excluding installation. Many operators choose to rent vending machines.

RECENT TRENDS IN RETAILING

18. Summary of factors affecting the retail trade. In order to understand what has happened in retail trade over the past ten or fifteen years, it is necessary to be aware of the underlying causes that have been at work. The more important of these are:

(*a*) Rising affluence among large sections of the population.

(*b*) The lowering of social class barriers.

(*c*) High labour costs.

(*d*) Greater mobility.

(*e*) Changes in spending patterns.

(*f*) The increased use of branded, prepacked, nationally advertised goods.

(*g*) New advertising and sales promotion techniques.

(*h*) New techniques of management and control.

(*i*) Improved accounting and communications equipment.

(*j*) New materials for display and shopfittings.

A full discussion of these factors is out of place in a work of this kind, but most people are conscious of them in a general way.

19. Effects on retail organisation. Many of the factors listed favour the development of the larger type of retail organisation. High labour costs, branded goods, prepackaging, more adaptable counters and displays, better cash registers, improved management and a more prosperous buying public have all played a part in the success of the supermarket chains. The trend has been for the supermarkets, multiples and variety chains to increase their share of consumers' spending and for the department stores and independent retailers to have a reduced share. "High Street shopping" has prospered at the expense of local shopping, so that the big shops in the main centres have increased their trade and the trade of shops in side streets has decreased.

Another very important trend has been the growth of "shopping without shops." Both mail order, including direct selling by manufacturers, and automatic selling have increased, particularly in the last three or four years. The success of mobile shops is also indicative of the tendency not to want to make a shopping expedition for small or mid-week purchases.

Independent shopkeepers have responded to competition by joining voluntary chains and by converting to self-service where this is possible (*see* **15**). There is little doubt that retail trading is more competitive and lively than it has been for a long time.

20. Trading stamps. Many retailers have attempted to preserve the loyalty of their customers and to increase their sales by issuing trading stamps. The usual method is to issue to customers one trading stamp for each $2\frac{1}{2}$ pence spent. The customer collects the stamps, sticks them in the official "saver's book" issued by the stamp company and exchanges them for goods either by sending the completed book to the company or by presenting it at one of the company's redemption centres. The goods given in exchange can be chosen from an illustrated catalogue, rather similar to a mail order catalogue, though much smaller and with the items "priced" in terms of completed books.

The retailers buy the stamps from the stamp company, paying about £3.50 for a pad of 5,000 stamps. The stamp company receives income from the retailers' cash purchases of stamps and from investment of surplus funds in the period between the sale of the stamps and their redemption by the customers. Bulk-buying enables the stamp company to obtain goods at heavy discounts to give in exchange for stamps.

Although there are almost a score of trading stamp companies operating in Britain, more than 80% of the business is in the hands of the *Green Shield Trading Stamp Company* and *Sperry & Hutchinson.* It has been estimated that if stamp trading is to benefit the retailer, he must be able to increase his turnover by 10%. Benefit to the consumer depends on the retailer being able to absorb the cost of the stamps without putting up prices. In addition to the stamp companies' tokens, the co-operative societies have now largely replaced their traditional dividends by stamp schemes and in all some 10% of retail sales are now covered by stamp schemes of one kind or another.

In spite of the undoubted success of trading stamp promotions, there are signs that the recent recession in the retail trade is forcing traders to re-examine both the costs and benefits to them of stamp schemes.

21. Branding and compound trading. The idea of branding is very old and can be traced back to medieval times. It is essentially a device to distinguish a particular product and to gain for the maker or manufacturer some of the goodwill which would otherwise go entirely to the retailer. It also gives the consumer some protection against his own lack of knowledge and gives some assurance that standards of quality will be maintained.

Branding is only effective if it is allied to effective advertising; a brand that no one knows about is unlikely to benefit producers, distributors or consumers.

Although branding itself is very old, the post-war years have seen its extension to an ever-widening range of goods. National advertising of branded goods has become more powerful and has been more scientifically employed. With the extension of branding and advertising has gone the development of more efficient and distinctive packaging that has had the effect both of giving better protection to the goods and of reinforcing the brand-image. When goods are packed ready for sale to a public that wants named brands, the need for the traditional division of retailing into exclusive trades, grocers, butchers, stationers and so on, disappears. There has been an increasing trend, therefore, towards *compound trading*, with grocers selling confectionery and butchers selling frozen vegetables.

22. Resale price maintenance. Many manufacturers of branded goods prefer to have their goods sold to the public at fixed prices. In some trades the desire to enforce fixed minimum prices was so strong that collective agreements, compelling trades to observe agreed prices, were rigorously enforced by the trade associations concerned.

Collective resale price maintenance was prohibited by the *Restrictive Trade Practices Act*, 1956. Individual resale price maintenance, enforced by manufacturers through terms in their contracts with wholesalers or retailers, continued without restriction until the *Resale Prices Act*, 1964. This Act prohibits the enforcing of minimum prices except in those cases where agreements have been registered with the Registrar of Restrictive Practices, who has power to bring such agreements to the attention of the Restrictive Practices Court. Suppliers who wish to enforce minimum selling prices must show that the ending of resale price maintenance would be to the detriment of consumers by causing:

(*a*) a substantial reduction in the variety or quality of goods; or

(*b*) a reduction in the number of retail outlets; or

(*c*) a reduction in necessary after-sales services; or

(*d*) danger to health by reason of a lowering of standards or the employment of unqualified staff due to price cutting; or

(*e*) a general and long-run increase in prices.

The Act also gives manufacturers a limited right to withhold supplies from retailers who use their goods as "loss-leaders," that is as "bait" sold at cost price or less to lure customers in, while other goods are sold at the full retail price or more. In addition to meeting these detailed requirements, suppliers seeking to impose resale price maintenance must show that the gain to the public by permitting fixed prices outweighs any disadvantage.

Although the *Resale Prices Act* was rather slow to take effect, the expense of fighting a case before the Restrictive Practices Court has led many manufacturers to allow agreements to lapse and there is now little overt support for resale price maintenance. The arguments of the supporters of resale price maintenance have been that maintained minimum prices protect small traders, that abolition will lead to the domination of retail trade by the larger units and that fluctuating prices will make it difficult to plan production. Although the battle against RPM is all but won, the practice of *recommending* retail prices has continued in some trades.

23. Value added tax. Until 1973, various goods sold in the shops attracted "purchase tax." With entry to the European Economic Community, it was necessary to move to a uniform system of indirect taxation and purchase tax and selective employment tax (SET) were replaced by value added tax (VAT). The principle of this form of taxation is that the value added to the goods at each stage in production bears tax at a given percentage rate. At the next stage of production, the manufacturer deducts the VAT already charged on the inputs purchased (the "input tax"), calculates the total tax due (the "output tax") and remits the difference, the VAT due on his own value added, to the Customs and Excise. Since the final price includes *all* the VAT passed on at each stage, the eventual customer bears the whole of the tax. Value added tax applies to services as well as to goods, but in this case the tax is effectively on the labour costs and profit added by the company or person providing the service. The labour involved in calculating total VAT, deducting VAT already included at earlier stages in the process and accounting for all deductions and payments is considerable and is by no means a negligible burden, particularly to the smaller business.

PROGRESS TEST 16

1. Compare the multiple store with the department store. Which has been the most successful in recent years and why? **(7, 9, 18, 19)**

2. In what way does a supermarket differ from a self-service store? How do you account for the success of both types of store since 1950? **(10, 18, 19)**

3. Describe the layout and methods of a typical variety chain store. What changes have taken place in the methods of stores of this type in recent years? **(8)**

4. Write notes on the following:

   (*a*) Leased and tied shops. **(12, 14)**
   (*b*) Voluntary chains. **(15)**
   (*c*) Mail order. **(16)**
   (*d*) Automatic vending. **(17)**

5. Write brief notes on "Recent changes in retailing methods." **(18–22)**

6. Compare any two modern retailing methods. To what extent does each of them fulfil the traditional functions of the retailer? **(1–22)**

CHAPTER XVII

THE WHOLESALE TRADE

THE WHOLESALE FUNCTION

1. Is the wholesaler necessary? The notion of reducing costs and prices by "cutting out the middle-man" seems so simple that many people would give a wholehearted "no" to this question. Before we can say whether the wholesaler is necessary or not, however, it seems reasonable to find out just what he does and then to ask two further questions. Is the job being done efficiently? Is the independent wholesale firm the right organisation to do it?

2. The development of wholesaling. In medieval times there was little need for the wholesaler or for wholesaling as a separate function. Goods were either bought at fairs from travelling merchants or directly from the craftsmen who had made them. When the craftsman and his customers were in such close touch, there was no need for an intermediary.

As the scale of production grew, manufacturing processes became more elaborate and a much longer period of time elapsed between the start of a process and its completion. When this happened it became necessary for someone to anticipate demand and to give orders many months before the eventual sale of the goods. With improved transport, wider markets and a more varied supply of goods, both wholesaling and retailing emerged as separate functions. With many small retailers who had limited capital and limited knowledge of sources of supply, some organisation had to bridge the gap between the manufacturer and the retail shop.

By the mid-nineteenth century the distributive process could not have continued without the wholesaler. We need not accept unreservedly, however, the suggestion that this is so today, when transport and communications have improved so much.

3. The services of the wholesaler. At this stage it is possible to see that the wholesaler does give services to both the manufacturer and the retailer. These services may conveniently be classified as follows:

(*a*) *Warehousing.* Neither manufacturers nor retailers are equipped to hold large stocks, nor do they want the expense and trouble of doing so.

(*b*) *Buying in advance of demand.* The wholesale trade must anticipate what customers will be buying in the coming months. This means accepting the risk of being wrong. Buying ahead also provides a steady market for manufacturers.

(*c*) *Finance.* The wholesaler helps to finance trade by buying from manufacturers and so keeping their resources liquid and by giving generous trade credit to retailers.

(*d*) *Expert buying and selling.* As an expert buyer, the wholesaler will try to buy when prices are low, storing goods until they are less plentiful and selling at a profit. This will help to even out supplies between glut and shortage (*see* XV, **22–29**). As an expert seller he will be on the lookout for new products and new markets.

(*e*) *Knowledge.* Following on from the previous point, the wholesaler is in an ideal position to know of markets for the manufacturers' products and of sources of supply for the retailer.

(*f*) *Preparation.* In some trades, the wholesaler grades, sorts, packs or prepares goods. He may sell goods under his own brand name.

(*g*) *Information.* Since the wholesaler is in touch with both retailers and manufacturers, he is in an ideal position to pass back information about what products are selling and what criticisms are being made. This will also be reflected in the wholesaler's orders to the manufacturer, of course.

(*h*) *Delivery.* Wholesale firms hold a key position in the delivery of goods.

4. Summary of the wholesale function. *The wholesaler forms a link between producers and retailers.* If it were not for the wholesaler, retailers would have to place innumerable small orders with manufacturers, who would have to make up great numbers of packages to be delivered over long distances. By dealing through the wholesaler, distribution is reduced to an orderly pattern.

By holding stocks the wholesaler, in effect, provides a "pool" of goods from which retailers, who prefer small stocks but a wide range, can draw. This conserves resources and results in fewer goods being "in the pipeline" at any one time. By giving large orders to manufacturers and making prompt payments, the wholesaler provides a steady market and makes orderly continuous production easier to sustain.

THE PLACE OF THE WHOLESALER

5. Necessity for the wholesale function. The services given by the wholesaler should lead to more efficient distribution and lower costs. Only if these economies are achieved is the wholesaler's place in the distributive process justified. It should be clearly understood, however, that *some* organisation must perform the services listed in the last section. In some trades they are carried out by separate wholesale firms in the traditional way, in others by wholesale organisations working for multiple stores or supermarket chains and in others again they are performed by the larger manufacturers. The wholesale function does not disappear even when the independent wholesaler is superseded.

6. The need for the independent wholesaler. There is likely to be more scope for the independent wholesaler where retail outlets are small and numerous, where the manufacturing unit is small, where manufacturers and retailers are geographically scattered or where trade is seasonal. It is in these circumstances, too, that the financing services of the wholesaler are most likely to be needed. Since the scale of production has tended to increase in very many industries and new methods of large-scale retailing have become more common, it is not surprising that the independent wholesaler has been almost eliminated from the chain of distribution in a number of trades.

7. Alternative methods of distribution. Among the ways in which the wholesaler has been displaced are:

(*a*) *direct selling from manufacturer to consumer,*
(*b*) *direct selling from manufacturer to retailer,* and
(*c*) *selling by manufacturers through their own retail shops.*

Direct sales by manufacturers to consumers may be by mail order or through door-to-door calls by salesmen. Goods sold directly by producers include office equipment and accounting machines at one level and such things as domestic appliances, brushes and cosmetics at another. Sales by manufacturers to retailers have become even more common as the scale of production has increased.

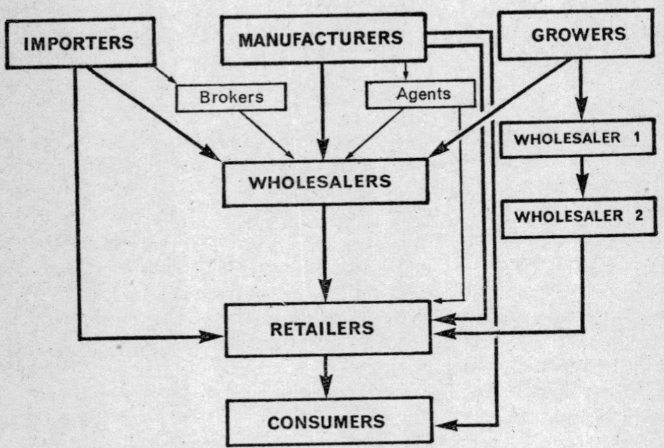

Fig. 19. Some methods of distribution.

Manufacturers usually prefer to use their own salesmen and representatives and their own distribution network if the volume of business warrants it. If production is on a very large scale, manufacturers may be able to operate their own retail shops. Producers' own shops are familiar in a number of retail fields, including boots and shoes, pharmaceuticals and dairy produce. Fig. 19 shows some of the ways in which goods may reach consumers.

THE STRUCTURE OF THE WHOLESALE TRADE

8. Workers and establishments. There are about three-quarters of a million workers employed in the wholesale trade. They are employed by some 40,000 organisations operating 55,000 separate establishments. Nine-tenths of these workers are engaged in the distribution of goods to the home trade. About a quarter of all wholesaling establishments are concerned with the food trades in some way.

9. Types of wholesaler. The pattern of wholesaling in any particular trade depends on the number and size of producing or manufacturing units, the type and number of retail outlets and the nature of the commodity concerned. If there are a great number of small and scattered producers and the product is one with many different grades and varieties, there may be a need for two wholesale stages:

(*a*) *Primary wholesalers* will specialise in collecting together fairly small quantities from suppliers and will sell in bulk to:

(*b*) *Secondary wholesalers* who will, in turn, sell to the retail trade.

The distribution of horticultural produce is largely carried out in this way.

The biggest units in the wholesale trade are *general wholesalers*. Stocks carried by a large, general wholesaler may well be valued at several million pounds and such a firm will dispatch thousands of consignments every day. A concern of this type, dealing with a range of non-perishable goods, will be organised into a number of departments each under the supervision of an expert buyer. Although in many cases traders may visit the wholesale warehouse to give their orders, it is becoming more frequent for the "house trade" to be conducted from modern showrooms, where customers can place orders after inspecting samples. A large wholesale firm will also have its own outside sales force calling on retailers. *Specialist wholesalers* operate on a smaller scale and offer a greater selection of goods over a narrower range.

Wholesale firms can also be categorised as *national*, *regional* or *local* wholesalers. Large general wholesalers operate on a nation-wide basis as do many of the larger specialist firms. Other wholesalers serve a particular region of the country and have their trade concentrated in, for instance, the eastern counties. In most towns there are also small specialist wholesalers supplying retail shops in the town and the countryside round about.

Recent developments include "*cash-and-carry*" *wholesaling*, enabling small retailers to buy goods at lower prices. No credit or other services are given and the trade is largely confined to low-priced, quick-selling goods such as toys, household goods and packaged foodstuffs. Small retailers have also attempted to improve the competitiveness of their buying by getting together to form retail buying groups.

10. Agents and other intermediaries. Most of the forty thousand wholesale organisations hold stocks of goods, but some intermediaries merely acquire legal title to goods and transfer them without any handling, storing or processing. Such intermediaries may well be serving a useful purpose if other sections of the trade lack knowledge of sources of supply or of outlets, but some would not be necessary if other traders were as efficient and knowledgeable as they should be.

Manufacturers may employ *agents* to sell goods for them. The agent will try to obtain orders from wholesalers or from the central purchasing offices of multiple stores or variety chains. Some agents, although self-employed, will sell in the manufacturer's name, but others will sell in their own names. Agents of both these types do not come into possession of the goods, but merely work for a percentage commission on the business they handle. *Factors*, although selling for manufacturers or producers, take legal possession of the goods and sell as if on their own behalf, invoicing customers directly.

11. The Co-operative Wholesale Society. The largest single unit in the wholesale trade is the C.W.S. (*see* V). It manufactures many lines of its own, has establishments overseas and owns its own ships.

THE FUTURE OF THE WHOLESALE TRADE

12. Wholesalers and the large-scale retailers. Earlier sections of this chapter have mentioned the tendency for multiple stores, supermarkets and variety chains to by-pass the wholesaler. It has been estimated that costs at the wholesale level incurred by a multiple store group, providing its own central wholesaling services, are little more than half those which would be incurred by trading through outside wholesalers. Department store groups have also been able to reduce costs by providing central buying and warehousing services. The increased use of branded, nationally advertised goods has tended to emphasize the role of the manufacturer, who no longer relies on the wholesaler to find markets for his products.

13. Wholesalers and the small retailers. It appears that the continued existence of the independent wholesaler is closely linked with the welfare of the smaller retail shop. The wholesale trade already does much to support the small retailer by providing trade credit, but propping-up the less efficient retailers is not going to provide the prosperous outlets that are needed. The organisation of voluntary groups among retailers is a more positive step and combines aid to the retailer with incentives to increased efficiency.

Other suggestions towards strengthening the links between wholesalers and retailers have stressed the advantages of *selective distribution*, with individual wholesalers concentrating their efforts on a small number of retailers. These chosen retailers could receive help with sales promotion, staff training and other aspects of their work so that the wholesaler would be sure of a limited number of secure and expanding outlets.

14. Structure and management. There is still room for a great deal of rationalisation in the wholesale trade. Although there have been amalgamations, these have not always led to a reorganisation of facilities and potential economies of scale have not been realised. It is probably true that many firms are still much too small to operate efficiently. Even in today's harsher economic climate, there is still too little sense of urgency and a great deal of complacency. Management is too often untrained and labour tends to be poorly paid. However, there has been progress in the use of mechanical handling equipment and the computerised processing of orders.

PROGRESS TEST 17

1. Describe the wholesaler's function. What effects would it have if wholesaling were abolished? **(1–7)**

2. Is there still a place for the independent wholesaler? Can other organisations carry out the wholesale function? **(6, 7)**

3. Write notes on each of the following:

   (*a*) Primary and secondary wholesalers.
   (*b*) General and specialist wholesalers.
   (*c*) Agents and other intermediaries. **(9, 10)**

4. In what ways can the wholesale trade be modernised? **(12–14)**

PART SIX

INTERNATIONAL TRADE

CHAPTER XVIII

FOREIGN TRADE AND THE ECONOMY

THE ADVANTAGES OF INTERNATIONAL TRADE

Just as individuals find that they can enjoy higher standards of living by specialising and exchanging the products of their specialisation, so nations can provide better living standards for their people by concentrating on the type of production for which their resources best suit them. International specialisation obviously cannot be carried so far as the division of labour among individuals. A degree of self-sufficiency is necessary for national security. Also the diversity of resources that many nations possess, the many skills of their people and the variety of industries that have developed over the years all preclude absolute specialisation.

1. International trade. Trade between nations benefits all concerned in various ways:

(*a*) It enables nations to enjoy products which they could not produce within their own borders, e.g. Britain imports bananas, coffee, cocoa and other tropical products.

(*b*) It makes it possible for nations to obtain goods more cheaply than they could produce them themselves, e.g. European countries import British tractors.

(*c*) It provides a greater variety of commodities and gives a wider choice of designs and styles, e.g. Italian clothes or West German office machinery in Britain.

(*d*) As has already been said, it permits countries to specialise in the production of goods and services for which their particular pattern of resources makes them best suited.

A vigorous and active international economy promotes better living standards all over the world.

2. Bi-lateral and multi-lateral trade. When economic or political convenience leads two countries to concentrate a great deal of their international commerce between themselves, this is known as bi-lateral trade. Sometimes bi-lateral treaties are concluded in respect of particular commodities, but when bi-lateral trade is extensive between two nations, it is likely to lead to distortion of their economies and to exclusion from the full benefits of international trade.

The trade of a nation which deals not with two but with many other countries is said to be multi-lateral. A policy of multi-lateral trade is likely to bring the maximum advantage from foreign trade.

DANGERS IN FOREIGN TRADE

3. Examples. While international trade brings considerable advantages to the world as a whole, particular countries may sometimes suffer as a result of it. International trade has sometimes led to excessive specialisation. Sugar accounts for 99% of the exports of Mauritius and tea for 66% of Sri Lanka's exports. In these circumstances, fluctuations in demand and price may have devastating effects on a country's economy.

When a particular industry in a country is greatly dependent on exports, that industry may suffer if demand for its product falls, even though foreign trade benefits the country as a whole.

Occasionally, producers in one country may use another country as a ready market for excess produce which is sold at very low prices. This is known as "dumping." Home industries may be damaged by such practices.

4. Restrictions on trade. In order to protect home industry, most nations impose restrictions on trade with other countries. Such policies may be justified if they are used to protect growing industries which will be low-cost producers when they are fully developed, or to prevent disastrous unemployment in home industry. In many cases, however, they merely serve to inhibit the growth of trade and to protect the home economy from necessary competition and change.

Import duties are imposed in order to restrict imports by making them more expensive. *Quotas* limit imports by restricting the total quantities of designated commodities that may be imported.

THE PATTERN OF BRITAIN'S FOREIGN TRADE

The 56 million inhabitants of the United Kingdom rely on overseas suppliers for about one-half of their foodstuffs. The industries of the United Kingdom consume great quantities of basic materials such as raw cotton, iron ore, rubber and timber. Many billion gallons of fuel oil are consumed in the United Kingdom each year. The traditional role of the United Kingdom was to export manufactured goods and to import food and raw material. In recent years, however, other countries' manufacturing industries have been developing faster than Britain's, and her import bill now includes large sums for manufactures and semi-manufactures.

Importing on such a large scale would not be possible unless it was balanced by a large export trade. The diagrams in Fig. 20 show the scale and pattern of Britain's overseas trade in commodities in 1975.

BALANCE OF PAYMENTS AND BALANCE OF TRADE

In many of the post-war years the total value of exports was less than that of Britain's imports. The difference is known as the *balance of trade* or *crude trade gap*.

5. Invisible exports and imports. If this were the whole story, Britain's trading position would be bad indeed, but in addition to commodities, *services* are both bought and sold internationally. These services include *shipping*, *air transport*, *tourism*, *banking* and *insurance*. Overseas expenditure is also incurred in maintaining armed forces overseas and in maintaining diplomatic and other personnel in foreign countries. These purchases and sales of services are known as *invisible* exports and imports. There is normally a favourable balance on the invisible account.

6. Balance of payments on current account. The visible and invisible accounts together form the *current account* of the balance of payments statement, as shown below for the year 1975.

BALANCE OF PAYMENTS 1975, CURRENT ACCOUNT

Visible Trade	
	£ million
Exports	18,768
Imports	21,972
Adverse balance	3,204
Invisible Trade	
	£ million
Services provided and dividends, etc, received	11,038
Services received and dividends, etc. paid	9,507
Favourable balance on invisibles	1,531
Adverse net current balance	£1,673 m

7. Flows of capital. In addition to the trading figures shown, British businessmen invest abroad and this requires foreign currency. The government, too, lends overseas. On the other hand, foreign firms invest in the United Kingdom. These capital inflows and outflows must be taken into account when determining the final balance of payments position. In some years, the capital inflows have been adequate to finance a current account deficit, but in 1975

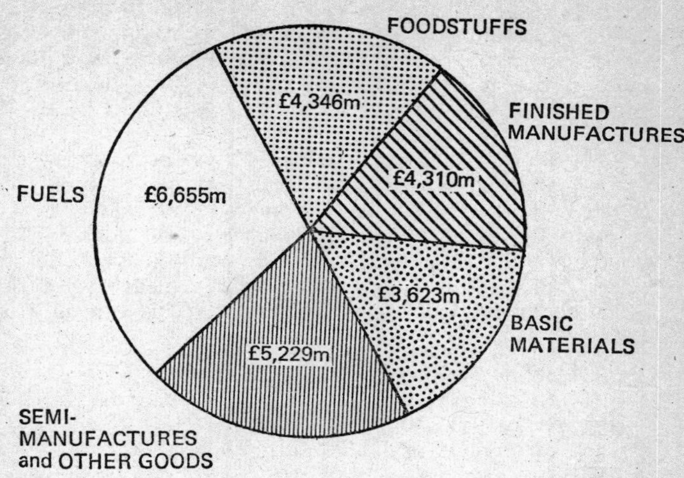

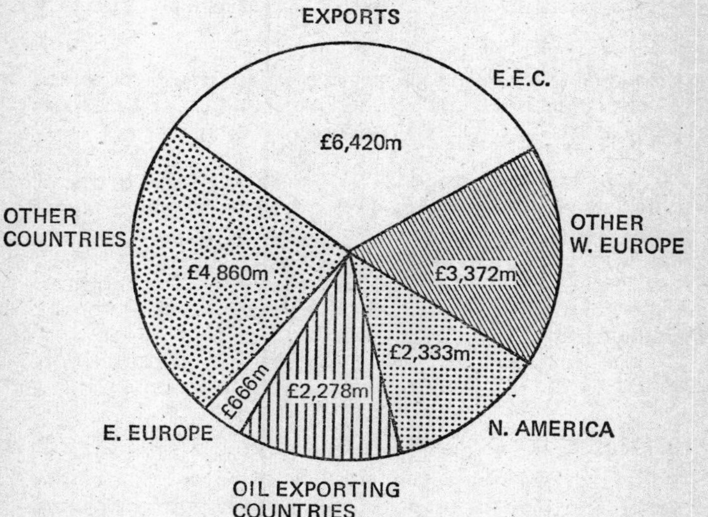

Fig. 20. The foreign trade of the UK 1975, showing exports (£19,929 million) and imports (£24,163 million).

the sum of £1,673 million was far too large to be covered in this way. In that year, investment by foreign companies and other private capital inflows amounted to £194 million, while public sector borrowing overseas brought in £387 million.

8. Meeting an adverse balance. In years in which the current and capital accounts together give a favourable balance, reserves may be augmented or assets can be accumulated overseas. In 1975, however, the considerable sum of £1,092 million remained to be financed even after all capital inflows had been accounted for. In such years the residual adverse balance must be met. This can only be done by:

(*a*) Selling assets overseas.

(*b*) Running down Britain's gold and convertible currency reserves.

(*c*) Accumulating debts in other countries.

(*d*) Drawing on credit facilities provided by international institutions such as the International Monetary Fund.

None of these means of meeting an adverse balance can be used indefinitely. The only real solution is to export sufficient to "pay for" UK imports.

9. The terms of trade. The expression "the terms of trade" refers to a comparison between import and export prices. When export prices rise relative to import prices so that a given volume of exports can pay for an increased volume of imports, the terms of trade are said to improve. A rise in import prices would signify a deterioration in the terms of trade.

An improvement in the terms of trade tends to make it easier to achieve a favourable balance of payments.

BRITAIN AND THE EUROPEAN COMMUNITY

10. Trade and the economy. The overseas trade of the United Kingdom interacts in many ways with the home economy. Whether the balance of payments is adverse or favourable determines the extent to which the government is able to follow policies which permit economic growth. Competition from imported goods affects the sales of articles produced in Britain and therefore the level of activity and employment in the industries concerned. Similarly, costs in British industry determine whether our goods are able to compete in foreign markets and so influence the balance of payments position.

All too often in recent years, British industry has not been competitive. Consequently, it has been difficult to maintain a favourable balance of payments and therefore also difficult to maintain steady economic growth. Lack of growth has sapped business confidence and has prevented industry from enjoying many of the economies that would come from modernisation and a larger scale of production.

11. The Common Market as a solution. There is an obvious need for some solution which would enable Britain to break away from the situation in which every attempt at expansion leads to a balance of payments crisis and a favourable overseas payments position can only be achieved under conditions of stagnation and unemployment. To many people, entry into the Common Market seemed just such a solution; it promised access to a market of over 200 million people and would provide the competition which would shake industry out of its lethargy and stagnation. There were risks, but also opportunities.

This point of view still has its critics and the disadvantages of "going into Europe" will be examined when the structure and purposes of the European Economic Community have been explained.

12. A customs union. There are a number of ways of establishing an international trading area. The technical name for the form used for the European Economic Community is a *customs union*. This means that while tariff barriers and import quotas are abolished between the countries concerned, a common *external* tariff is applied to give protection against goods entering from countries outside the union. In fact, the E.E.C. is more than a customs union, since labour, capital and enterprise are permitted to move freely within the Community. It is this which makes the union a "Common Market."

If the removal of internal barriers to trade is to be effective it is necessary to ensure that "non-tariff" barriers to trade are not allowed to continue. In order to make the Community truly a common market, it is necessary to have an agreed policy concerning taxation, state aid to industry and monopolies. Progress is being made towards the harmonisation of taxes and laws and some effects of this policy have already been felt.

13. The Treaty of Rome. The original six countries forming the E.E.C. signed the Treaty of Rome on 25th March 1957. These countries were:

France	The Netherlands
West Germany	Belgium
Italy	Luxembourg

The treaty came into force on 1st January 1958. The operation of the Treaty and, indeed, the nature of the Common Market is most clearly exemplified by Article 3 which provides for:

(*a*) The elimination, between member states, of customs duties and quotas.

(*b*) The establishment of a common external tariff and a common commercial policy towards other countries.

(*c*) The abolition, within the Community, of obstacles to freedom of movement for persons, services and capital.

(*d*) The establishment of a common agricultural policy.

(*e*) The adoption of a common transport policy.

(*f*) The establishment of a system to ensure that there is no distortion of competition.

(*g*) The establishment of procedures to co-ordinate economic policies.

(*h*) The co-ordination of the laws of the member states to ensure the proper functioning of the Common Market.

(*i*) The creation of a European Social Fund.

(*j*) The establishment of a European Investment Bank.

There was also a provision that overseas countries could become *associated* with the Community without being given full member status.

The various provisions of the Treaty did not come into force at once, but were introduced gradually, some being still in the course of implementation. The abolition of internal trade barriers, however, was completed by 1968.

14. The institutions of the E.E.C. The major institutions set up by the Treaty of Rome are as follows.

(*a*) *The Council of Ministers.* This is the top decision-making body of the E.E.C.

(*b*) *The Commission.* The Commission is the executive body charged with the implementation of policies decided on by the Council of Ministers. It can draw up proposals of its own, but they must be agreed by the Council. The Commission has a large "civil service" and is an extremely powerful body.

(*c*) *The Court of Justice.* The Court consists of judges drawn from each of the member states and supervises the application of the Community rules.

(*d*) *The Economic and Social Committee.* This body, which includes representatives of labour, employers and the professions, has a consultative role.

(*e*) *The European Parliament.* The Parliament has had very limited power so far, but in the last resort it may dismiss the Commission.

15. Britain's entry into the Community. The *Treaty of Accession to the European Communities* was signed on 22nd January 1972 and finally came into force on 1st January 1973, the necessary legislation having been placed before Parliament during the intervening year. Under the Treaty of Accession, Britain agreed not only to be bound by the Treaty of Rome but also to join the *European Atomic Energy Community* and the *European Coal and Steel Community.* The adoption of the common external tariff was allowed to take place gradually and was effectively completed by July, 1977.

TRADE AND PAYMENTS AFTER ENTRY

16. The enlarged Community. Denmark and the Irish Republic joined the E.E.C. with Britain in 1973. This makes an economic grouping of nine countries with a total population of over 246 million. The enlarged Community has a greater population, produces more steel and has a larger merchant fleet than either the Soviet Union or the U.S.A. A block of this size can negotiate preferential trading agreements much more successfully than a single nation. The Norwegian government also negotiated terms for entry, but in September 1972 a popular referendum was held, and by a large majority the decision to join the E.E.C. was overruled.

17. The agricultural question. Britain's agriculture is extremely modern and efficient; that of some of her European partners is not. Consequently, the application of the *Common Agricultural Policy* (CAP) is likely to work to the disadvantage of the United Kingdom. The CAP is financed by levies on food imports, by the payments into the common budget of customs duties on imported industrial goods and by the allocation of a proportion of the receipts from VAT. The CAP is intended to stabilise the prices of agricultural products in the Community and to protect farm incomes. It was not expected that the CAP would prove advantageous to the UK's very efficient agricultural sector, but a temporary advantage is currently being gained owing to the effect of the low external value of the pound sterling, which is not yet adjusted for (1976) when calculating payments due to Britain from the Community Agricultural Fund.

18. The impact on industry. The common external tariff is lower than Britain's existing tariff on manufactured goods, consequently entry into the E.E.C., while opening up the European market, will also expose British industry to increased competition from other countries as well as from her Common Market partners. While the long-term effect should be good, since there will be no barriers to British firms exporting to Europe, the short-term impact may be very severe for some sections of the engineering industry, for manufacturers of domestic appliances and perhaps even for the motor industry. On the other hand, some industries will experience a definite gain from both the economies of scale offered by the larger market and from the change from high levels of purchase tax to a lower rate of value-added tax.

19. Summary. There are many other arguments concerning the advantages and disadvantages of joining the Common Market and some of the most important concern constitutional issues and questions of sovereignty. Here, we are concerned only with trading advantages and disadvantages. These may be summarised as:

Advantages:

(*a*) British industry will have access to a very large European "home" market without any barriers to trade.

(*b*) Competition and economies of large-scale production should make industry more efficient.

(*c*) Increased trade should give a greater variety of goods in British shops.

(*d*) Both Britain and the other European countries should be able to concentrate on the manufactures to which they are most suited, thus making production more efficient.

(*e*) The countries of the E.E.C. have experienced rapid economic growth and close association with the European economy should help to promote British growth.

(*f*) Britain's lead in technologically advanced industries, such as aerospace and electronics, should bring trading advantages.

Disadvantages:

(*a*) Britain's contribution to the Community budget, estimated as at least £200 million at current price levels, is likely to impose an additional balance of payments burden.

(*b*) The removal of tariff barriers and quotas will expose British markets to competition from powerful competitors.

(*c*) The common external tariff is lower than Britain's present import duties, on the whole, and will expose

British manufacturers to additional competition from non-E.E.C. countries.

(*d*) Economic growth in Europe has shown some signs of slowing down and to this extent advantages may not be realised.

(*e*) Community policy may inhibit monetary flexibility so that we would not be able to vary exchange rates in accordance with changing trading conditions.

(*f*) Food prices are likely to rise under the CAP and to stimulate wage demands, thus making it difficult to keep prices competitive in export markets.

Mitigating factors:

(*a*) Industrial tariffs between the E.E.C. countries and Britain are to be abolished gradually.

(*b*) Adoption of the common external tariff will also be gradual.

(*c*) Special provisions have been made with respect to certain commodities and materials imported from Commonwealth countries.

(*d*) The contribution to the Community budget will not reach its full extent until 1977.

PROGRESS TEST 18

1. Describe and illustrate the advantages of international trade. (**1**)

2. What is the difference between bi-lateral and multi-lateral trade? Towards which of the two should a nation's trading policy tend? Give reasons. (**2**)

3. If international trade is advantageous, why do nations impose restrictions on it? (**1–4**)

4. Why is there so much concern in Britain over an adverse balance of payments? (**3–9**)

5. Write concise notes on the following:

   (*a*) Balance of trade.
   (*b*) Balance of payments.
   (*c*) Invisible exports. (**5–9**)

6. Discuss the extent to which entry into the E.E.C. has either fulfilled or disappointed the hopes of those who proposed it. (**10, 11**)

7. Describe the main objectives, policies and institutions of the European Economic Community. (**12–14**).

8. What do you consider to be the main effects on the U.K. economy of joining the Common Market? (**15–19**)

9. Assess the advantages and disadvantages to Britain's balance of payments of joining the European Economic Community. (**18–20**)

CHAPTER XIX

THE IMPORT TRADE OF THE UNITED KINGDOM

CHANNELS OF IMPORT TRADING

The previous section gave figures of the broad categories of commodities imported into the United Kingdom. The quantities of foodstuffs and raw materials entering the country each day are very large and must find their way into the wholesale trade without delay. Since overseas suppliers are not likely to have a detailed knowledge of the British home trade, it is frequently necessary to use *intermediaries*.

Sellers must find buyers for consignments and in view of the very large quantities involved, prices must be satisfactory to both parties. Where goods can be graded, described or sold by specification, therefore, *organised markets and exchanges* are important.

The problem of routing imported commodities quickly into the home trade may be solved in a number of ways, but in most cases the services of specialist importers with an intimate knowledge of their own branch of the trade are used.

1. Choice of methods. The methods used will depend on the nature of the goods, the extent of commercial development in the exporting country and the scale on which the British importer operates.

Staple commodities are usually sold by standard specification or by sample and intermediaries are normally used. *Manufactured goods* are not so easily purchased through intermediaries since technical details are important and accurate general descriptions are not possible.

2. Direct importing. A manufacturer who uses very large quantities of imported materials may find it convenient and economical to set up his own importing organisation. Where manufacturing operations are carried out on a very large scale, the need to safeguard supplies of raw materials in order to avoid any interruption of production acts as a strong incentive towards direct importing. Some of the well-known multiple stores have their own import departments and the C.W.S. imports directly on a very large scale.

3. Foreign exporters' UK branch. Just as large importers may prefer to operate their own import departments, foreign firms that have a regular export trade with Britain sometimes set up their own branch offices in the UK, usually at one of the major ports. Occasionally foreign firms will operate their own retail shops in Britain.

4. The influence of multi-nationals. A more extreme version of the use of UK subsidiaries occurs when multinational corporations are involved. The large multinationals process materials, produce partly finished components or final manufactured goods wherever local conditions make it profitable to do so. Under such a policy of "global resourcing" not only the flows of trade, but also the prices at which goods are passed from one subsidiary company to another may depend on whether or not it is prudent to show a profit in the UK company or in a subsidiary company registered in the exporting foreign country. Situations in which both ends of an international transaction are effectively under the same control occur in both the import and export trades of this country.

INTERMEDIARIES IN THE IMPORT TRADE

5. Import merchants. The import merchant trades on his own account and not as an agent. He buys goods or produce from overseas suppliers and sells to manufacturers or the wholesale trade. Because he holds stocks of goods, buyers can inspect them easily and can obtain immediate delivery. The import merchant often helps to finance the trade and also carries much of the risk, since he buys in anticipation of home demand and has a great deal of capital tied up in stocks.

A large proportion of the trade in staple produce is dealt with in this way, as is some trade in partly manufactured goods. Most import merchants tend to specialise in particular types of commodity or in trade with particular areas.

6. Agents and brokers. When goods are not sold through an import merchant, all but the largest foreign exporters need the services of an intermediary who has an intimate knowledge of the British market for the commodity concerned. This role is filled by the *import commission agent.*

The import commission agent sells on behalf of the foreign exporter. Goods are sent to the agent who finds a market for them, selling at the best price he can and paying all the expenses involved. He will then remit the proceeds to his foreign principal after deducting an agreed commission. If an agent not only finds a market for the goods but also guarantees that payment will be made, he is known as a *del credere* agent and demands a correspondingly higher commission.

One of the fundamental problems of foreign trade is for a seller to find customers in a foreign country and for buyers requiring imported goods to know which foreign suppliers in which countries can provide the right commodities at favourable prices. An intermediary whose function is to bring buyers and sellers together is known as a *broker.*

Import brokers have great experience in dealing and have a wide knowledge of the technicalities of the products in which they deal, of the markets concerned and of the prices ruling in them. For their services they are paid a commission or *brokerage.*

7. Links with the export trade. It should be remembered that contact with foreign firms and a knowledge of trading practices builds up connections that may be useful in both the import and export trades, and that merchants and agents may find profitable business in both importing and exporting.

PROCEDURES AND FORMALITIES IN THE IMPORT TRADE

The importation of goods from abroad necessarily involves a certain amount of detailed regulation, which the individual importer, and the foreign exporter, must consider. The *documentation* relating to a consignment of goods is best dealt with from the point of view of the exporter (*see* XXI, **14–23**). Of special importance in the import trade, however, are *import licensing, exchange control* and *Customs procedure.*

8. Import licensing. All imports of goods into this country must be covered by an *import licence* issued by the Department of Trade. The apparent severity of this regulation is modified by the fact that very many goods are covered by an *open general licence* allowing unrestricted import of goods listed on schedules which the Department of Trade amends periodically. Sometimes a trader may obtain permission to import unrestricted quantities of a commodity. An *open individual licence* is then issued in his favour. In the great majority of cases, though, a *specific licence* must be obtained for goods not covered by the open general licence. Specific licences always refer to a particular type of goods, to be imported in specific quantities and to a given value. They are valid for a strictly limited period, usually from six to twelve months.

The purpose of the licensing system is to preserve a balance between imports and exports. The Department of Trade works closely with the Bank of England and import licensing is closely co-ordinated with exchange control, so that the issuing of a licence ensures access to the necessary foreign exchange.

9. Exchange control. The exchange control regulations are intended to conserve Britain's reserves of foreign currency and the system is operated by the Bank of England, working closely with the commercial banks. No special permission is needed to make payments to residents in the "scheduled territories" (the sterling area) and so long as the necessary import licence has been issued, there are few formalities for payments outside the sterling area when a payment is part of a contract of which the total value is not more than £5,000. For larger contracts, the appropriate procedure must be followed before the Bank will authorise payment.

10. Customs procedure. Goods imported into this country must be cleared through Customs and may be subject to duty. Customs duties were originally levied to provide revenue, but now serve the purpose of protecting home industry and of helping the balance of payments. Customs duties may be *specific* or *ad valorem.*

Specific duties are charged at a certain sum per quantity of the commodity imported.

Ad valorem duties are charged at a percentage rate of the value of the commodity imported.

11. Customs entry forms. Goods must be entered for clearance on Customs forms, which are known as "entries." These are required both for statistical purposes and so that imported goods can be examined and the correct duties paid.

A variety of entry forms are in use, but the two main classes are those

(*a*) for goods free of duty and
(*b*) for dutiable goods.

Within each of these two classes there are entry forms for *goods for home use*, for *goods entered for warehousing*, for goods intended for *re-export* or for *trans-shipment.*

Customs entries are normally completed in triplicate, with possibly an additional copy for exchange control purposes. Two copies are presented to the Customs authorities who will check the goods against entries, and will return one copy to the importer when the duties have been paid. This copy, together with the *bill of lading*, will be presented to the shipping company in order to obtain possession of the consignment.

If the entry cannot be completed because the supporting documents are not to hand, a *bill of sight* must be made out. This serves as a provisional authority to unload the goods.

12. Drawback. When goods on which duty has been paid are incorporated in a manufactured article which is subsequently exported, a refund of duty may be claimed. This refund is known as a "drawback."

13. Bonded warehouses. It is sometimes the case that an importer does not wish to take delivery of goods immediately, where the duty on such goods is heavy; immediate payment would be an unwelcome expense and would result in a completely unproductive tying-up of working capital. In these circumstances, the importer will find it convenient to place the goods in a *bonded warehouse.*

This is a warehouse owned by a company which has given a bond to the government that should the goods stored be dealt with other than in a lawful manner, a considerable sum of money will be forfeit. The importer pays a charge for the use of the warehouse facilities and goods can only be removed from the warehouse in the presence of a Customs officer and on payment of the duty. An advantage to the importer is that the goods may be worked on, repacked or samples taken from them while they are in bond. Large importers of goods subject to heavy duty may own their own bonded warehouses.

PROGRESS TEST 19

1. Discuss the reasons why intermediaries are so often used in the import trade. Is there any difference in practice between the importing of commodities and the importing of manufactured goods? **(1–4)**

2. Describe the various methods by which imported goods may be brought to the British home market and outline the roles of the various traders who may be involved. **(1–7)**

3. Explain how agents and brokers are paid. What is meant by the term *del credere* applied to an agent? **(6)**

4. Explain how the import licensing system works. **(8)**

5. Write notes on the following:

   (*a*) Exchange control and the import trade. **(8, 9)**
   (*b*) Customs entries. **(11)**
   (*c*) Bonded warehouses. **(13)**

CHAPTER XX

THE COMMODITY MARKETS

THE NATURE OF THE MARKETS

The magnitude of the quantities of raw materials and foodstuffs imported into the United Kingdom has already been stressed. These very large quantities of commodities must be channelled efficiently into the home trade and it is therefore necessary that buyers should be found without delay and deals completed at prices that are acceptable to both buyers and sellers. This result has been achieved by the establishment of highly centralised, organised markets.

1. General characteristics of these markets.

(*a*) The markets have a world reputation for efficient, fair competitive dealing.

(*b*) They are composed of expert dealers who have a very high degree of knowledge of prices, technicalities and market conditions.

(*c*) Dealings are on a private treaty basis and are carried on a wholesale level.

(*d*) In most of the markets, the commodities can be so accurately graded and described that inspection of actual consignments is not necessary.

(*e*) Dealings can be made for *future* delivery as well as for present or prompt delivery.

(*f*) The efficiency of the market mechanism and in particular the existence of "futures" dealings makes informed speculation possible.

(*g*) The British commodity markets are important centres in the world markets for commodities.

2. Auctions. When it is not possible to grade and describe a commodity accurately, and quality varies greatly from one consignment to another, buyers must have the chance to inspect and assess the commodity. Sales by auction are an effective way of ensuring fairness and a high degree of competition in these circumstances. London auctions in tea, wool and fur are world famous.

SPECULATION

There is an element of speculation in much buying and selling. Prices vary over time and merchants who buy for stock are always aware of the possibility of gains from rises in price and of losses from falls in price. There is a speculative element present whenever a trader buys with the intention of making such gains.

Speculation is often regarded as anti-social, but if speculators are well informed and skilful, it may have a number of useful functions.

3. Advantages of speculation.

(*a*) Since speculators buy when prices are low and sell when prices are high, they tend to raise excessively low prices and to depress excessively high prices. *Their activities tend to even out price fluctuations.*

(*b*) Speculators buy at low prices when there is a glut and sell at high prices when there is a shortage. *Skilful speculation tends to even out fluctuation in supply.*

(*c*) Speculators act as *professional risk-bearers*, leaving the ordinary trader free to buy commodities for use in his business without undue worry about the risk of price fluctuations.

Ill-informed speculation and the "rigging" of markets have none of these good effects and are entirely harmful.

4. Spot and futures markets. When a contract is concluded for immediate or prompt delivery, it is said to be a *spot contract* and the price agreed is called a *spot* price. On the other hand, commodities may be quoted for delivery some months ahead at a price agreed *now*. Such a contract for *forward* delivery is known as a *futures contract* and the price as a *futures* price.

For major commodities, the markets quote a number of

prices, varying according to the delivery date. Markets which deal in futures are often known as *terminal* markets. Futures markets can only operate when the commodity can be accurately graded and specified. Futures prices tend to be higher than spot prices, because of the risk of unforeseen price changes, the cost of storage, insurance cover and the interest on borrowed capital.

5. Factors influencing prices. Among the things which may affect commodity prices are:

(*a*) Increased acreage of a crop under cultivation.
(*b*) New discoveries of minerals.
(*c*) New uses of a raw material.
(*d*) Effect of weather, storms, drought, etc. on crops.
(*e*) Good or bad harvests.
(*f*) The occurrence of crop diseases.
(*g*) Strikes, revolutions or government action.
(*h*) Stockpiling or releases from stockpiles.
(*i*) Changes in demand due to increases or decreases in industrial or economic activity.

In the markets all these factors are carefully studied and interest rates are watched. All the facts and forecasts are taken together and on this information, and the market's reaction to it, futures prices are based.

6. "Hedging." Although speculation and the use of futures contracts tend to stabilise prices, dealers would be exposed to the full risks of market fluctuations if their forecasts proved wrong. When large quantities are involved even small price differences are important and to avoid risks from unforeseeable price fluctuations, a procedure known as "hedging" is used.

7. Example of hedging. A simplified example based on the market in wheat, the futures market for which is held in the Baltic Exchange (*see* **11**), may help to clarify the principle. Trade can be agreed for delivery in the months of September, November, March and May and prices are quoted in pounds sterling per tonne, with a minimum trading fluctuation of 5p. As mentioned earlier, the grade of wheat must be exactly specified for futures trading to take place and there are precise E.E.C. standards regarding the quality of wheat to be supplied.

Suppose that in January a merchant has contracted to deliver wheat, which he holds in store, in March. If the price should fall, he will make a loss. He can hedge against this by selling *March futures*. The deal might proceed as follows:

The merchant sells 200 tons at a March futures price of £86·00 per ton. The yield from the futures sale will be	200 × £86 = £17,200
In March, the spot price falls to £86·00 per ton. The futures contract must now be covered by buying in at this, lower, price. Cost of "buying in" is	200 × £83 = £16,600
Profit on futures contract =	£ 600

The fall in price would have led to a loss on the sale of the actual wheat, but this would have been compensated for by the profit on the futures contract.

Had the price have *risen*, there would have been a loss on the futures contract, since it would still have been necessary to buy in to cover the delivery contracted for, but a greater profit would have been made on the physical sale.

The result has been that the merchant has a *known* profit, whether the price rises or falls, and that the speculator who buys or sells futures, without intending to accept delivery of the physical commodity, has taken the risk.

8. Trading on margin. Another interesting point is that much speculative trading is carried out *on margin*, a deposit only, usually 10% of the price, being paid. This deposit is maintained intact by calling for the payment of *differences* as the price changes.

FUNCTIONS OF THE COMMODITY MARKETS

9. The functions of the commodity markets. These may be summarised as follows:

(*a*) They provide an organised trade in commodities, particularly in imported foodstuffs and raw materials.

(*b*) They provide a means for handling a considerable part of Britain's "entrepôt" or re-export trade.

(*c*) They provide international centres for trade between importing and exporting countries even when the commodities are not landed at British ports.

(*d*) The futures markets provide a means for speculation and for hedging against price fluctuations.

(*e*) The futures markets provide the means of linking the world's spot markets.

THE LONDON EXCHANGES AND MARKETS

London has a long history as a centre for the buying and selling of primary products. Like Lloyd's and the Stock Exchange, many of the commodity markets began in coffee houses and moved to more exclusive and permanent premises as trade grew.

10. London exchanges and markets. There are many active commodity markets in London, some trading in the physical commodities only while others have specialist facilities for futures trading. Some of these markets are well known while others, such as those for shellac or for essential oils used in perfumes and flavourings, are very much the concern of specialists in the particular trade. The City of London retains its traditional geographical separation of commercial activities to some extent and commodity trading is still based on the area in the south-east of the City's square mile. Some of the principal exchanges are:

The Baltic Exchange, St. Mary Axe.
The London Metal Exchange, Whittington Avenue.
The Rubber Exchange, Plantation House, Mincing Lane.
The London Corn Exchange, Mark Lane.
The London Commodity Exchange, Plantation House, Mincing Lane.
The Diamond Market, Hatton Garden.

In recent years, there has been a good deal of re-organisation and an increase in the level of sophistication with which dealings are conducted, and while the bald description of trading may still sound very traditional, the handling and presentation of information about prices and quantities traded in most markets employs up-to-date and technically advanced methods.

Among the markets in which trading is necessarily based on the actual commodity, and in which dealing is conducted through auctions, are those for *tea* and for *furs*.

11. The Baltic Exchange. The full name of this Exchange, the "Baltic Mercantile and Shipping Exchange," comes from the fact that the commodities originally dealt in were those which came from the Baltic countries. It is organised as a joint-stock company and its members include shipowners, merchants and millers.

The Exchange deals in four classes of business:

(*a*) The chartering of ships and cargo space.
(*b*) The chartering of aircraft and space in aircraft.
(*c*) The purchase and sale of grains.
(*d*) The purchase and sale of oil seeds and vegetable oils.

NOTE

(*i*) Dealings are confined to members of whom there are some 2,500.

(*ii*) The greater part of the very extensive trading floor is given over to the market in *shipping space*. This is an international market and shipping brokers and representatives negotiate on behalf of shipowners of many nationalities.

(*iii*) The trade in *commodities* is transacted on the basis of description and no samples are produced. Payment is for cash against shipping documents. The *grain futures markets* take place at certain times only, the members concerned congregating around the "ring" and calling their bids.

12. The London Commodity Exchange. The various markets which make up the London Commodity Exchange moved into Plantation House after the London Commercial

Sale rooms were destroyed in 1941. The Exchange is controlled by the London Commodity Exchange Co. Ltd. The trades represented include *cocoa*, *coffee*, *ivory*, *shellac*, *sugar*, *copra* and *spices*. Dealing is through *members only* and contracts made with non-members are subject to the rules of the appropriate association. Each trade has its own association, with its own rules and organisation. The commodity associations establish standard contracts, provide for arbitration and act for their members in exchange control negotiations with the authorities.

13. The rubber market. The foregoing remarks apply to the rubber market which meets in Plantation House, but which is here dealt with in more detail.

London is one of a number of centres at which rubber is bought and sold. Other overseas markets are New York, Colombo, Singapore, Djakarta, Amsterdam and Hamburg. Singapore is primarily a sellers' market and New York a buyers' market, but the special importance of London is that it has no bias as between buyers and sellers.

The market consists of members of the Rubber Trade Association of London, which represents three mutually exclusive classes: *producers* (or their agents), *brokers* and *dealers*. Contracts may be verbal on the floor of the London Commodity Exchange or may be made by telephone or in brokers' offices. Contracts must be made through brokers, who may not trade on their own account. Verbal contracts are confirmed by brokers sending both parties identical contracts, which are signed by buyer and seller, counterfoils being returned in confirmation. The broker is remunerated by brokerage on a recognised scale.

Contracts are normally for "standard ribbed smoked sheet" (R.S.S.) or "Standard Malaysian Rubbers" (S.M.R.s) and certificates of quality are issued after inspection of samples. Contracts are also made against advice that the rubber has been shipped and in these cases, payment is made against shipping documents.

Producers may sell forward for three, six, nine, or twelve month periods. Until recently, contracts for future delivery were made on "Settlement House" terms, but in 1974 the London Rubber Terminal Market Association was established and contracts are now based on International Commodities Clearing House terms. The standard grade for hedging contracts is "R.S.S. 1."

14. London Metal Exchange. Official dealings on the London Metal Exchange are in *copper*, *tin*, *lead* and *zinc*. There are some six hundred members, some of whom are individuals and others member firms. Only a minority of members may take part in dealings in the Exchange, other members having to deal through the *ring dealings* members.

Dealings take place daily from Monday to Friday, commencing at twelve noon and continuing until 1.05 p.m. An "unofficial" afternoon session starts at 3.45 p.m. and continues until 4.40 p.m. The method of dealing at each session is for each metal to be taken in turn, dealing by "outcry" continuing for five minutes, after which time the next metal is taken. After 4.30 p.m. "kerb" dealing continues for another ten minutes. Contracts are concluded in multiples of 25 tons for copper, lead and zinc and for multiples of 5 tons in the case of tin.

All four metals can be dealt in for both spot and forward delivery, but the tendency in recent years has been for the market to be used for forward sales and purchases and for spot sales for the larger quantities used in manufacturing industry to be made in dealer's offices outside the market.

15. Wool markets. The importance of London as a spot market for wool has much declined in recent years, the principal wool sales in the United Kingdom, although conducted by the Committee of London Wool Brokers, now being held at Bradford (*see* **18**).

It is not possible to grade and describe wool sufficiently accurately for wool sales to be on a basis of standard specification or standard sample. Sale is therefore by *auctions* which are conducted by the Committee of London Wool Brokers. There are eight series of sales each year, the duration of each series being about two weeks. Most bargains are made on the basis of samples, the wool being inspected both by buyers and by the selling brokers. The purchase price must be paid in full by the *prompt* day, which is the Friday fourteen days after the week in which the sale was made.

There is a separate *Wool Futures Market* which was set up in 1953, when it was realised that protection against price fluctuations was needed. The futures market is controlled by the London Wool Terminal Market Association and offers brokers the opportunity to buy or sell wool tops up to eighteen months ahead. The London futures contract had, for twenty years, been on the basis of a grade of wool known as "Bradford 64's B top," but in 1974 the contract was revised in line with the Sydney market. Trading is, therefore, currently based on "Australian CWC, Type 78 of 64's quality." Competition from synthetic fibres has recently led to a fall in the volume of trading in wool futures.

16. London tea auctions. Most of the tea imported into Britain is sold at auctions held at the new Tea Trade Centre under the auspices of the Tea Brokers' Association of London.

Three sales are held each week, each day being devoted to the sale of tea from a particular area. Tea is classified in the growing country and consigned to the producers' London agents in full or half chests. On arrival in London, selling brokers draw samples which are valued by expert tasters. On the basis of this assessment, catalogues are drawn up and prices at which the various lots, or "breaks," can be offered are fixed. The catalogues show the quantity of tea offered by each broker, the estates where the tea was grown and the warehouses where the tea now lies and can be sampled. Wholesalers, exporters and firms of tea blenders are represented at the auctions and there are arrangements for arbitration in the case of dispute.

17. The London diamond market. Hatton Garden is the centre of the London diamond market which deals with the greater part of the world's output of stones. Many dealers in precious stones have their premises in this part of London. Diamond "sights" are held ten times a year at the London offices of the Diamond Trading Company and cutters, brokers and dealers who are notified of the sights submit their requirements and specify the amount they are prepared to spend. Parcels of stones containing both fine quality stones and stones of lesser value are allocated to buyers on the basis of the specifications which they have submitted. At the sights the buyers have the opportunity of inspecting the stones allocated and of accepting or rejecting the parcel. The mixed parcels of stones bought at the sight are later broken up and sent to the smaller dealers and cutters who do not buy direct at the sights.

18. Provincial exchanges. While there are a number of smaller exchanges at which trading in physical commodities, particularly in grains and the produce of local agriculture, can take place, the great provincial exchanges such as those of Liverpool and Manchester have declined. The *Liverpool Cotton Exchange* still exists but futures trading in cotton has ceased since intervention by the government trading agencies of the major powers put an end to the free play of market forces in this trade. The *Liverpool Corn Exchange*, controlled by the Liverpool Corn Trade Association, still functions and there is trading on both spot and futures markets. The other great general provincial exchange at Manchester closed as a trading floor in 1976. Bradford is still the centre of the British wool trade and periodic sales of wool are held at the *Bradford Wool Exchange*.

PROGRESS TEST 20

1. Describe the general characteristics of the British commodity market. Why are some commodities auctioned, rather than dealt in by private treaty on the floor of an exchange? (**1, 2**)

2. To what extent and in what respects is speculation (*a*) harmful, (*b*) beneficial? (**3–8**)

3. Explain carefully what is meant by a "spot" price. Explain the various factors which might affect the spot price of a commodity. (**4, 5**)

4. How can a producer use a "selling hedge" to protect himself against a fall in prices before he can sell his crop? (**6, 7**)

5. Describe the organisation and trading methods of one of the commodity markets. (**10–18**)

CHAPTER XXI

THE EXPORT TRADE OF THE UNITED KINGDOM

PROBLEMS OF THE EXPORT TRADE

The importance of the export trade to the UK economy hardly needs further emphasis, but while exporting may be a matter of high policy for the nation as a whole, it must also be profitable for the individual firms involved.

1. Special difficulties of the export trade. If trading in overseas markets is to be successful a number of difficulties must be overcome:

(*a*) There is the problem of finding the most suitable markets.

(*b*) Costs of production must be low enough for prices to be competitive even when transport costs and import duties have been added.

(*c*) The exporter's sales policy is unlikely to be effective unless the appropriate members of his staff are familiar with the language of the buying country.

(*d*) Advertising and display must be suitable for the foreign market.

(*e*) There may be special technical requirements in the importing country.

(*f*) The product may require modification to meet climatic conditions in the importing country.

(*g*) Packing must be robust enough for the journey.

(*h*) Local trading customs may be different from those in the home trade.

(*i*) It may not be easy to find suitable overseas agents to handle the product.

(*j*) Foreign currencies are involved.

(*k*) Documentation and procedures are more complicated than in the home trade.

(*l*) Foreign governments frequently impose restrictions on the imports of certain goods.

2. Special risks of the export trade. Arising from these difficulties are a number of special risks:

(*a*) *The rate of exchange.* If payment is made in the currency of the importing country, there is a risk that the rate of exchange will have changed between the time that the price was quoted and the time that payment is made.

(*b*) *Default of the overseas buyer.* Assessing the creditworthiness of a customer in the United Kingdom is often difficult; assessing the standing of a foreign buyer is even more so.

(*c*) *Overseas government regulations.* There may be changes in regulations controlling the import of various goods or foreign countries may impose exchange control regulations which prevent the receipt of payment by the British exporter.

(*d*) *Political changes.* Changes of government, including revolutionary changes, may frustrate contracts with foreign importers.

AID TO EXPORTERS

3. The Export Credits Guarantee Department. The Export Credits Guarantee Department is a government department which provides insurance against export risks on a commercial basis. Cover can be provided against risks such as:

(*a*) The insolvency of the buyer.

(*b*) The failure of the buyer to pay for goods which he has accepted.

(*c*) A buyer's default on a contract before acceptance of the goods but after they have been shipped.

(*d*) Action by a foreign government which prevents the receipt of payment.

(*e*) The imposition of import restrictions.

(*f*) Civil disturbance in the importing country.

(*g*) War between the importing country and the United Kingdom.

The Department requires exporters to carry a small percentage of any loss and in most cases the cover is limited to 85% of losses caused by insolvency or delay in paying and up to 95% for other losses. There are special policies covering transactions involving large-scale capital projects and also for small exporters.

4. E.C.G.D. financial guarantees. For longer-term projects, where the period of credit that exporters can offer to their overseas customers may be of vital importance, the E.C.G.D. will offer guarantees for loans provided by the joint-stock banks.

Early in 1965, the terms under which E.C.G.D. guarantees would be given were widened to include all kinds of manufactures and the lower limit for loans guaranteed was reduced to £50,000. At the same time, the rates at which the banks would provide loans were improved.

5. Other government aid to exporters. The government department most closely concerned with helping exporters is the Department of Trade. The *export services division* can give information regarding markets, overseas agents, tariffs, quotas and import regulations. A number of export officers are employed who will give help and advice to exporters. Specific aid to British exporters through market research, promotions at trade fairs and assistance to UK firms operating overseas is organised through the *British Overseas Trade Board*, an official body consisting of representatives of industry, of the Department of Trade and of the Foreign and Commonwealth Office.

The official journal *Trade and Industry* provides a record of changes in regulations and carries articles on markets and other topics of interest to exporters. Exporters may also subscribe to the *Export Services Bulletin*, which is published daily. The Department of Trade publishes booklets giving information on various markets and the Stationery Office publishes *Economic Surveys* relating to a number of areas.

6. Non-government aid to exporters. The joint-stock banks and merchant banks have extensive overseas connect ions and are able to give much information to exporters. The *Chambers of Commerce*, which are voluntary bodies on which small business men as well as large firms are represented, work closely with the Department of Trade and provide a means of rapid and effective liaison.

Most industries have set up trade associations which help member firms, and national organisations, such as the *Confederation of British Industry*, can offer their considerable experience and resources to exporters and prospective exporters.

EXPORT CHANNELS

Having taken advantage of the extensive aid now available, the exporter must decide whether to use the resources of his own organisation to overcome the various problems of the export trade or whether he should sell to an export merchant. Even if he decides to export on his own account he will probably need to use agents or intermediaries at some stage or other.

7. Direct export. A firm that attempts to carry out all the work connected with the export of its products must be prepared to tackle the tasks of:

(*a*) export sales promotion and market research;

(*b*) dealing with orders and correspondence from foreign customers;

(*c*) technical modification of designs to suit export markets;

(*d*) packing goods in ways suitable for transport overseas and for display in foreign markets;

(*e*) arranging for shipping and proper documentation of export consignments;

(*f*) setting up adequate credit control and payments systems; and

(*g*) ensuring that local (foreign) regulations are complied with in the manufacture, packing, etc., of the product.

Probably all exporting firms perform some of these functions, but only the larger ones, with large and stable export markets, will find it necessary or possible to employ the specialist staff required to carry out all of them. Very large exporters may set up overseas branches in some markets, possibly incorporating them as companies registered in the foreign country.

8. Export groups. Smaller firms, wishing to enter the export trade but lacking the resources and experience to do so alone, may find it possible to join with other firms in the formation of an *export group*. Such a group is able to handle the marketing, shipping and credit control problems of member firms. The British government has recommended the setting-up of export groups.

9. Export merchants. Selling to an export merchant is a most convenient way of entering foreign markets, since it avoids most of the complexities associated with the export trade. The export merchant buys from British suppliers goods which he judges to have an export potential and sells them in appropriate foreign markets. He buys and sells on his own account, not as an agent.

The export merchant tends to specialise and will hold stocks in this country and sometimes in the countries where his main customers are to be found. The British manufacturer who sells to an export merchant is relieved of all anxiety about the credit-worthiness of foreign customers and receives payment promptly in sterling. All the problems of marketing, shipping, finance and payment are left to the export merchant. The export merchant deals directly with principals both here and overseas and his reputation with suppliers and customers is, along with his knowledge of export markets, a major asset.

10. Foreign buyer's commission agent. *Export commission houses*, acting on behalf of foreign importers, play a significant part in the British export trade. Their job is to execute the orders of their foreign principals, finding goods as requested and placing orders with British manufacturers.

Requests from foreign buyers are known as *indents* and

may be *open* indents, giving the agent discretion in finding sources of supply and in placing the order where he thinks fit, or *closed* indents, specifying exactly the goods required and the firm which is to supply them. In the latter case the agent is often known as a *confirming house* and is merely concerned to place a firm order and attend to the necessary formalities.

The more progressive export commission agents are concerned to bring new British products to the notice of their foreign clients and so to increase the trade passing through their hands.

11. Manufacturers' export agent. Exporters who deal directly with their foreign customers, but who are not handling a sufficient volume of trade to warrant the setting up of a full-scale export department, may use the services of a manufacturers' export agent who will attend to marketing and shipping problems for them.

12. Forwarding agents. Even suppliers who maintain their own shipping departments frequently find it convenient to use forwarding agents. The forwarding agent's familiarity with shipping matters and the fact that he will have a representative at the docks offer distinct advantages. In addition many agents offer a *groupage* service whereby small parcels may be grouped with those of other manufacturers, thus minimising charges.

13. Overseas agents. If overseas selling is to be effective it is essential to have some sort of representation in the country concerned. The most general way of securing this is by the appointment of an overseas agent. The agent may be a *buying* agent, purchasing goods from the manufacturer in bulk at a fixed price less commission or at an agreed low price. Alternatively, he may be a *commission* agent, accepting and transmitting orders for an agreed rate of commission. Finding reliable agents, who do not already hold competing agencies for the products of rival firms, is a major problem for prospective exporters. Most of the sources of help mentioned above can assist in finding suitable agents (*see* **5**).

EXPORT FORMALITIES

In addition to the risks and expenses of the home trade, overseas trade has the further difficulties involved in conveying and safeguarding consignments over great distances, arranging payment in foreign currencies and complying with restrictions imposed by the governments of both importing and exporting countries.

14. Export licences. Basically there are few restrictions on exports from the United Kingdom. Export licences are required, however, for a limited range of goods of "*strategic*" importance and for *works of art*, *antiques* and *articles of historical value.* The actual list of goods requiring export licences changes from time to time.

15. Shipping documents. The transporting of exported goods to their destinations will involve:

(*a*) the chartering of a ship; or
(*b*) the chartering of cargo space in a ship or an aircraft; or
(*c*) the sending of single packages or a few packages.

A contract for chartering a ship is known as a *charterparty*, a contract for chartering cargo space is called a *contract of affreightment.* If single parcels, perhaps wooden crates of some commodity, are to be sent overseas a document known as a *parcel ticket* is used.

16. Shipping notes. When goods are forwarded to the docks, a shipping note must be prepared, notifying the wharfinger of details of the shipment. When goods are sent to the docks by rail, the railway authorities may prepare the shipping note from details given on the rail consignment note.

17. Invoices. Commercial invoices must be prepared as for the home trade. They should not show cash discounts but should give the terms of sale and should quote the packing specifications, the vessel on which the goods are consigned, the import licences issued by the importing country and the export licences, if any. If the details are too lengthy to be conveniently shown on a single invoice form, a supplementary *weight note* may be used.

In order that the correct duties may be charged and the goods described in a way acceptable to their Customs authorities, some countries require special forms of invoice to be used. *Consular invoices* are required by a number of countries, including many South American republics. These invoices are made out on a prescribed form, frequently in the language of the country concerned and must be "legalised" by the country's consulate, a service for which there is usually a fee.

Commonwealth countries normally require a *certificate of origin and value* to be prepared and some other countries require commercial invoices to be certified by a recognised authority such as a Chamber of Commerce.

18. Price quotations in foreign trade. It is important that the price quoted should be quite explicit as to the delivery terms intended. Not only is it essential to avoid misunderstanding, but the delivery terms quoted will affect the liability of the parties should loss or damage occur.

The most common delivery terms and their meanings are given below.

Ex works: Goods sold at a price which requires the buyer to take delivery at the works.

Loco: Delivery within a limited area which must be defined, *e.g.* "loco Manchester."

f.o.r.: Free on rail. The seller is responsible until goods are placed on public railway.

f.a.s.: Free alongside ship.

f.a.q.: Free alongside quay.

Delivered docks: The port or docks concerned should be specified.

f.o.b.: Free on board. This term is used very frequently. The place at which the goods are to be placed free on board must be specified.

c. & f.: Cost and freight. A term used where the seller is to attend to shipment but not to provide insurance cover.

c.i.f.: Cost, insurance and freight. The price includes freight and insurance to the final port which should be named, *e.g.* "c.i.f. Bombay."

Franco: All charges paid to the point named.

19. Bills of lading. The bill of lading is a receipt for goods shipped or received for shipment. In addition it is used as a document of "title" to the goods and it also embodies the terms of the contract of carriage.

Although bills of lading are not negotiable, their use as documents of title enables the goods to be controlled over the period of the voyage and, if necessary, until payment is made. Every bill of lading issued in this country has as its first clause the *Clause Paramount* which ensures that the provisions of the *Carriage of Goods by Sea Act*, 1924 are not evaded.

Should a bill of lading not be available when the goods are taken on board, a *mate's receipt* will be issued, to be surrendered in due course against the bill of lading.

When the goods are loaded at the docks, a comprehensive record of the number of packages, their weights, marks, measurement and condition is made by the tally clerk and any damage or deficiencies are noted on the docks returns and are subsequently recorded on the bill of lading. A bill of lading without any note of damage or deficiency is called a *clean bill.* It is frequently necessary to tender a clean bill of lading in order to obtain payment.

20. Certificates of inspection and health certificates. Sometimes the contract under which the goods are shipped will require certificates as to the condition of the goods. The regulations of the importing country may also require such certificates.

21. Insurance policies. Goods in transit must be adequately covered by insurance and if the exporter is responsible for arranging insurance cover, either the policy or a certificate of insurance must accompany the bill of lading.

22. Exchange control. In order to ensure that payment is received in this country, a Form C.D. 6 must be completed in respect of consignments valued at more than £5,000, f.o.b., exported to countries outside the sterling area. The form is in two parts, one of which is handed to the Customs authorities and the other handed to a bank for transmission to the authorities when payment is actually received.

23. Customs entries. H.M. Customs & Excise must be notified when goods are exported, both in order to maintain statistical records and to ensure that the proper export licences have been obtained. "Pre-entry" is required only when goods are exported under licence; in other cases the entries may be completed within six days of sailing.

EXPORT PAYMENTS

The problems involved in export payments are the security of the means of payment, the length of credit required and the convenience of the buyer and seller. In a buyers' market, the convenience of the buyer and the provision of a lengthy period of credit may be paramount, whereas the seller may have to sacrifice some element of security and risk the possibility of default by the buyer.

If he can, the exporter will try to retain control over the goods until he is sure of payment. Some methods of payment will not ensure this. Payment by the importer's own cheque, for example, against the documents of title to the goods, would leave the exporter unprotected if the cheque was not met. To some extent such difficulties can be overcome if the importer and exporter deal through their respective banks, so that the amount due is transmitted to the exporter's bank by telegraphic transfer or by mail.

24. Documentary credits. Arrangements are made by the importer for his bank to send a letter to the exporter informing him that a credit has been opened in his favour at a correspondent British bank or perhaps at a UK branch of the foreign bank. The exporter is able to draw on this credit as soon as the goods are despatched and the relevant documents presented. The documents concerned might include:

(*a*) A full set of "clean bills of lading."
(*b*) Invoice.

(*c*) Insurance policy.
(*d*) A consular invoice.
(*e*) A bill of exchange drawn on the bank.

The documents must be exactly as specified in the letter of credit and will be forwarded to the importer's bank by air mail, thus arriving in the foreign country before the goods. The documents will be released to the importer when he puts his bank in funds or as agreed with his banker. The credit may be *irrevocable*, so that the obligations of the parties, once entered into, cannot be revoked. Such a credit may be *confirmed* by a London bank, in which case it will be a confirmed, irrevocable credit. A *revocable* credit, on the other hand, can be cancelled by the buyer.

25. The acceptance credit. Instead of receiving payment direct from the bank on presentation of the documents, the exporter may draw a bill of exchange on the bank; the bank will accept the bill and return it to the exporter who may then discount it. The buyer will not be required to pay his bank until the accepted bill matures.

26. Documentary bill drawn on importer. A bill of exchange with the documents relating to the transaction attached is known as a documentary bill. Bills may be drawn on the overseas importer and sent, with the documents, through the exporter's bank, to the importer for acceptance. If the bill is drawn at sight (*see* XII, **9**), the documents will only be handed to the importer against payment. The abbreviation D/P, documents against payment, is often used in this connection. If the bill is a *usance* bill, drawn for payment at some future date, the documents may be deliverable against acceptance. D/A is the abbreviation used here. If documents are surrendered against acceptance of the bill, control of the goods is lost before payment is received, but this method is frequently used where the parties are known to each other or the code of the importing country requires it.

The finance needed by the exporter over the period until the bill is paid and the proceeds remitted to him may be provided by his bank giving him overdraft facilities, or the bank may discount the accepted bill. Alternatively it may "negotiate" the bill for him, paying him the amount of the bill, less interest, on the understanding that it may have recourse to him in the event of default.

27. Accepting houses and export finance. If the exporter is of good standing, he will find that there are a number of accepting houses that will help with the finance of export transactions. For a commission, the accepting house will agree to accept bills drawn on them to a certain sum and the bills may then be discounted. The accepting house will normally require security.

28. Export factoring. The exporter can avoid all the risks of non-payment by selling his debts to a *factor*. The factor pays the exporter, who thus obtains prompt payment, and then collects the debts from the overseas customers. There are several variants of this scheme.

PROGRESS TEST 21

1. In what ways is export trading more risky than selling in the home market? What part does the Export Credit Guarantee Department play in relation to the special risks of the export trade? **(1–4)**
2. Describe the main sources of information and help, both official (government) and private, which are available to the export trader. **(3–6)**
3. How are the export methods of the large-scale organisation likely to differ from those of the small exporter? **(7–13)**
4. Write brief notes on "Export merchants and commission agents." **(9, 10, 13)**
5. Write brief notes on "Invoices and price quotations in foreign trade." **(17, 18)**
6. What is a "bill of lading?" What part does it play in the despatch of an export consignment? **(19)**
7. Describe the main formalities and documents involved in preparing a consignment of goods for export. **(14–23)**
8. It has been said that some two hundred large firms account for about one-half of the British export trade. What factors, do you think, account for this? What steps might smaller firms take to improve their export performance? **(1–28)**

PART SEVEN

ADVERTISING, TRANSPORT AND INSURANCE

CHAPTER XXII

ADVERTISING AND MARKET RESEARCH

ADVERTISING IN MODERN BRITAIN

1. The pervasiveness of advertising. It is not possible to live in Britain, or in any modern western country, and remain unaware of advertising. In the streets, in buses and trains, even, with commercial television, in the privacy of our own homes, the advertisers thrust their claims upon us. The level of artistic and technical skill displayed in advertisements is often very high. The use of colour and design is so forceful and has such impact that it influences serious painters whose "pop-art" pictures are exhibited and criticised with the same solemnity as more academic work. Advertising is an important social force and in discussing its commercial and economic aspects, the wider implications should not be forgotten.

2. Advertising and public relations. Public relations officers (P.R.O.s) and public relations counsellors help both corporations and individuals who are in the public eye to maintain acceptable and attractive "images." They perform a valuable service for their employers and sometimes for the public, especially when they ensure that attitudes or statements are not misunderstood. Public relations activities will not be considered as advertising, however, and will not be discussed further in this book. There is also a great deal of unpaid "advertising" in aid of charitable or voluntary work. This is also outside our field.

3. The function of advertising. Advertising affects the consumer in the following ways:

(*a*) *Information.* A distinction is often made between informative and persuasive advertising. Informative advertising announces a product and gives potential buyers the details they need. Much advertising in the technical press is informative since it is directed at an expert, trained readership. If consumers are to exercise freedom of choice, informative advertising is necessary so that they can know what goods are available and where they can be bought.

(*b*) *Persuasion.* Human memory is short and fallible and repetition is necessary to keep customers aware of a product. Excessive repetition, however, is intended to persuade, not to inform. The borderline is indefinable and all advertisements contain both persuasive and informative elements. The advertising of many consumer goods is almost entirely persuasive in character. The information given is small, but all possible pressure is put on the consumer to buy the advertised product rather than other goods.

(*c*) *Maintenance of demand.* It is arguable that advertising is necessary to maintain demand at a sufficiently high level to provide full employment. Without the prodding of the advertisers, consumers would settle for a lower standard of living and far less energy would be put into the task of increasing material well-being.

(*d*) *Creating mass markets.* The use of mass-production methods often results in lower unit costs (*see* VI). Large-scale production requires large markets, however, and forceful advertising and sales promotion can provide those markets, thus permitting large-scale production, lower costs and eventually lower prices.

(*e*) *Quality.* The fact that a good has been widely advertised may compel a manufacturer to maintain high standards of quality.

4. Advertising and competition. Advertising may be used as a weapon of competition, particularly in a situation where there are only a few sellers, each of whom is trying to increase his share of the market. It may also serve to reduce competition and to confer a degree of monopoly power. Advertisements that try to persuade consumers that there is no substitute for their product are attempting to create a sub-market in which they will be free from competitive pressures.

THE CHOICE OF ADVERTISING MEDIA

5. Planned advertising. Advertising today is not carried out in a haphazard, hit-or-miss way. An advertising campaign is planned with a certain market in mind. If the product is one which is most likely to be sold to young married people in the 25–35 age group, then the campaign will be directed towards that group, using methods that will come to the notice of the group and appealing to instincts and emotions that are dominant within it.

The means through which the advertisement is purveyed to the public is known as the *advertising medium* (plural *media*). A campaign is normally based not on a single medium, but on a selection of media. The choice of appropriate media is the subject of careful study and analysis and their use is carefully synchronised to achieve the maximum effect.

6. Appeal in advertising. The combination of the product to be advertised and the market at which the campaign is to be directed will determine the "appeal" which is to be used. Different appeals will be appropriate for different products. If foodstuffs are being advertised, the appeal will probably be to the appetite and illustrations will show attractively prepared, hotly-steaming meals. For other products, the appeal may be through the emotions of parental love, social aspiration, sex or fear.

7. The advertising media available. An advertising campaign will be designed to make a specific appeal to some particular section of the public through carefully chosen media. The main advertising media are:

(*a*) *The press:* national and local newspapers, general magazines, specialist magazines, trade press.

(*b*) *Television and radio.*

(*c*) *Outdoor and transport advertising* (posters): public places, trains, buses, underground trains.

(*d*) *Window and point-of-sale display.*
(*e*) *Exhibitions and trade fairs.*
(*f*) *Direct mail advertising* (circulars and catalogues).
(*g*) *Cinema.*

8. The choice of media. The final choice of media used in a campaign will depend on:

(*a*) *The social class* (socio-economic group) to which the medium appeals.
(*b*) *The age group* to which the medium appeals.
(*c*) *The geographical area* covered by the medium.
(*d*) *The cost* of using a particular medium.
(*e*) *The number of people* reached by the chosen medium.

CHARACTERISTICS OF VARIOUS ADVERTISING MEDIA

9. Press advertising. More money is spent on press advertising than on any other medium.

(*a*) *Newspapers:* Advertising in *national newspapers* carries all the immediacy and urgency of the national news. A product which is advertised in the national press is brought to the notice of great numbers of people. Rates charged will depend on the circulation of the paper concerned and the position of the advertisement in the paper. The *Daily Mirror* and the *Sun* have average daily circulation figures of around four million and can charge appropriately high rates. The *quality* of readership also counts and *The Times*, with a circulation of about 250,000, can also quote very high rates. The *local press* has a much smaller coverage and rates are consequently lower.

(*b*) *Magazines:* These may be general or specialist. *General magazines* appeal to a variety of people and may be used to advertise goods that interest a wide range of consumers. *Specialist magazines* are intended to cater for particular groups, such as motorists, fishermen, yachtsmen, stamp collectors and so on. Magazines of this sort are best used to advertise goods that appeal to the specialist readers. Women's magazines form a very important group, since the greater part of family spending power is controlled by women. The two magazines *Woman* and *Woman's Own* have almost two-thirds of the market in this group. Whichever section of the press is used, it is important to bring the product to the notice of the retail trade. Advertisements in the national press and the major general magazines will do this, but it is also important to advertise in the *retail trade press*.

(*c*) *Use of press advertising:* Newspapers are read with a sense of urgency; magazines tend to be read in a more leisurely fashion and to be passed on from one person to another, the total *readership* of a weekly magazine being built up over three weeks or more. The *Radio Times* and *TV Times* are special cases in this respect, and both enjoy a fairly sustained readership over the week covered in addition to having large circulation figures. With magazines, as with newspapers, the position of the advertisement affects the cost. A press campaign introducing a new product might use the national newspapers, the women's magazines and the radio and television periodicals. The daily press would give forceful, urgent impact, bringing the product to the public's notice, the women's magazines would give more detailed information combined with luxurious presentation, and a sustained background and support would be provided by the programme papers.

10. Television and radio. The 1954 *Television Act* allowed the insertion of advertising material into television programmes. The first television commercial was broadcast in September 1955 to an audience of about a quarter of a million. In 1975, a one minute commercial put out on all the channels might be seen by some twenty million viewers and cost its sponsors over £7,000.

Because of the relaxation and intimacy of the domestic situation in which viewing takes place, television advertising is especially potent. For this reason and also because of the mixed family audience involved, it is important that there should be some supervision of the material used and the manner in which the advertising message is "put over." In the early days this function was discharged by the Independent Television Authority, which was established in 1954. With the coming of commercial radio, the duties of this body were extended to cover both the nineteen local commercial radio stations and the fifteen television programme companies, the new controlling body being known as the Independent Broadcasting Authority (I.B.A.).

11. Outdoor and transport advertising. Posters have a wide coverage and an advertisement displayed at a central site in a medium-sized town will be seen by about three-quarters of the town's inhabitants. The people who see a poster will be on the move, however, and so its message must be simple. Large posters on central sites can be used to echo the main theme of an advertising campaign in which press and television deal with the message in a more extended fashion. Outdoor sites are usually owned by billposting companies who rent the space to advertisers. The use of outdoor advertising is subject to control under the *Town and Country Planning Act*, 1947.

Transport advertising includes posters on stations, cards in buses and underground trains, cards on escalators and in lifts, side-streamers and front and back posters on buses and sidepanels on vans. In the larger cities, public transport is used by very large numbers of people. Commuters tend to be relatively young and middle-class and they form a valuable market.

12. Window and point-of-sale display. Window displays play a considerable part in brightening our towns. Great skill and artistry are often shown in their design and they are important because they present goods to the consumer at the point where the chain of distribution finally reaches him. Window displays and manufacturers' displays in shops persuade the consumer to make his purchase and to choose from among competing lines. Window and point-of-sale display clinches the work done by press and poster campaigns.

13. Exhibitions and trade fairs. Many specialist exhibitions are organised in the course of the year as well as the better-known ones such as the Motor Show or the Business

Efficiency Exhibition. Exhibitions are usually organised by the appropriate trade association and serve to enhance the industry's prestige and to improve contacts with potential customers. Trade fairs are more specialist in their appeal and are organised with the intention of doing business rather than merely of improving public relations, although considerations of prestige will not be forgotten, especially if the fair is an international one.

14. Direct mail advertising. Sending circulars or other advertising matter direct to potential customers is a method which is growing in importance. Specialist agencies able to supply classified lists of names and addresses help with direct mail advertising in some trades. One firm specialising in the distribution of free samples and unaddressed sales literature has a full-time and part-time staff of some 10,000 people.

15. Cinema. Regular cinema-goers tend to be between 16 and 35 years of age and form a young and affluent audience. Surveys have shown that it is an audience which does not watch television regularly so that this medium tends to complement rather than compete with commercial television.

THE ADVERTISING INDUSTRY

16. Why an "industry?" Total expenditure on advertising amounts to more than £1,500 million a year. This is over £4 million every day. It is only the revenue from advertising that permits the publication of newspapers and magazines of the size and type to which we have become accustomed, or that makes commercial television possible. The external appearance of our towns and cities is, for good or ill, shaped by advertising to a considerable extent.

Advertising employs many thousands of people, directly and indirectly, and a variety of skills, artistic and technical, are utilised in the production of advertising material. We are quite justified in referring to advertising as an industry, although it may be a rather unusual one. Like other industries, it has its own typical structure and organisations.

17. The structure of the advertising industry. The advertising industry may be considered as consisting of:

(*a*) *The advertisers;* the firms with goods or services to sell and who need to advertise them.

(*b*) *The media owners;* the owners of newspapers, magazines or other press media, television programme companies and others who own or control advertising media.

(*c*) *The agencies;* the organisations which act as intermediaries between the advertisers and the media owners and which play a key role in planning and implementing most advertising campaigns.

18. The work of the agencies. While the activities of advertisers and media owners need little further explanation, the work of the agencies does require some amplification. The part played by the agency in advertising is not unlike that of the wholesaler in distribution. Without the agency, media owners would have to contact each advertiser who used their particular medium. This would mean dealing with very many separate advertisers instead of with a relatively small number of agencies.

From the point of view of the advertiser, the advantage of using an agency is that the agency can supply the expert staff necessary to devise and launch an effective advertising campaign. Few trading or manufacturing businesses could hope to do this without outside help and even the largest companies use the services of advertising agencies. A large agency employs copywriters, artists and design staff and can also provide market research and other services.

A major part of the work of an agency is the booking of space for its clients' advertisements. About two-thirds of all British advertising is placed by agencies, and this includes practically all television and press advertising. Displays, exhibitions and so on are not usually arranged by the agencies. Although the agency works directly for its client, the advertiser, commission is paid by the media owners, the usual rate being 15%. A typical advertising agency employs between two and three hundred people, although the larger agencies, such as the London Press Exchange, have staffs of up to a thousand.

19. Principal representative bodies. The representative organisation for advertising agencies is the Institute of Practitioners in Advertising, which has about 250 agency members. Members of the I.P.A. must have no connection with advertising media.

Media owners are represented by the Advertising Association, which has some 1,200 member companies. In 1962, the Advertising Association was instrumental in setting up the Advertising Standards Authority, an independent body intended to maintain high standards in advertising.

The interests of advertisers are the concern of the Incorporated Society of British Advertisers.

MARKET RESEARCH

20. Need for market research. With the growth of mass markets and of large-scale production methods, there is little room for miscalculations. Mistakes are costly and it is absolutely necessary to know the market. The problem is to know as precisely as possible how consumers will react to a new product or how they are already reacting to a product on the market.

21. Internal research. Market research may be carried out by analysing a firm's own past records. This will involve comparisons of sales by area, or from one period to another or in relation to changing economic conditions.

22. Product testing. Many factors determine whether or not a product will sell. In addition to the characteristics of the product when in use, the type and design of package, the brand name and many other details of presentation will be important. In order to assess the effect of all these things test batches are made up and housewives or other potential customers are asked to use the product and report on it. Ideally, each small test batch will differ in one particular only, so that the effect of each factor can be isolated when the reports are compared.

23. Area retail tests. When design details have been settled, an area which is considered to be representative of the market as a whole can be selected for a retail test. An advertising campaign on a small scale, limited to the test area, precedes the issue of the product to selected retailers. Sales results and reactions are analysed to judge the probable results of a national campaign.

24. Consumer surveys. A consumer survey is a check of a cross-section of the buying public. The members of the public who are to take part in the survey are selected by various sampling techniques. If the sampling procedure is to be statistically valid, every possible member of the "population" which is to be sampled must have an equal chance of being selected. Note that this is a technical use of the word "population" and means all the units from which a sample is to be chosen. It does not mean the population of the country. Such a sample is known as a *random sample.* Random sampling would often be expensive and impracticable in actual situations and variants known as quasi-random, multi-stage, cluster, stratified and quota-sampling are used. Interviewers call on the *respondent* and ask them to reply to a questionnaire. The success of the survey depends on the soundness of the sampling method, the skill in drafting the questionnaire and the patience and integrity of the interviewer.

25. Market research and advertising. An important aspect of market research is in assessing the effectiveness of an advertising campaign or of advertising media. Methods used include readership surveys, audience measurement and copy-testing. Advertisement testing of this last type may include prepublication and post-publication research. The usual way of carrying out pre-publication research is to show members of the public a selection of advertisements, including those to be used in a forthcoming campaign, and then to test the impact of the advertisement by seeing how much the respondent can remember about it. Post-publication research is based on surveys of readers of the publication in question and the level of recall is graded according to the amount of detail remembered.

26. Motivational research. The effectiveness of market research depends on the truthfulness with which respondents answer questions put to them. Often people give the answers which they feel to be expected rather than those which are true. A further complication is that consumers respond to unconscious motives, of which they cannot, by definition, be aware. Motivational research seeks, by means of a battery of sophisticated psychological techniques, to expose these hidden motives so that product design, advertising and display can take account of them.

PROGRESS TEST 22

1. Distinguish between informative and persuasive advertising. Explain briefly what you think "competitive advertising" means. **(3, 4)**

2. Explain how advertising may help to reduce production costs. **(3, 4)**

3. What is meant by "appeal" in advertising? **(6)**

4. List six different advertising media. Which is the most important in terms of money spent by advertisers? **(7, 9)**

5. Write brief notes on "outdoor advertising." **(11)**

6. Discuss briefly the factors that influence an advertiser and his advisers in the choice of media. **(5–8)**

7. Describe the role of the advertising agency. **(16–19)**

8. List the various methods of market research. How does market research differ from motivational research? **(20–26)**

9. You are planning a campaign to launch a new domestic kitchen appliance. Describe the part that press and magazine advertising might play in your campaign. **(3–9)**

10. "Nearly £5 million is spent on advertising every day. This is an unjustifiable waste of resources." Discuss. **(1–26)**

CHAPTER XXIII

TRANSPORT

ECONOMIC CONSIDERATIONS

1. The importance of transport. An efficient system of transport is essential both for the individual trade or manufacturer and for the economy of the country. A good transport system lowers distribution costs, thus permitting wider markets and larger-scale production. By facilitating the movement of goods and workers, efficient transport offers industrial firms a wider choice of locations, enabling them to select districts which give the best balance of economic advantages. With the wider distribution of commodities, a greater choice of goods is available for consumers. Efficient, low-cost transport makes improved living standards possible.

2. United Kingdom internal transport. The main forms of transport within the United Kingdom are:

(*a*) Road.
(*b*) Rail.
(*c*) Internal air services.
(*d*) Pipelines.
(*e*) Inland waterways.

Of these, road transport is by far the most important in terms of the volume of freight carried. In 1974, this means of transport accounted for 65% of the 85 thousand million ton-miles of total freight movements (*see* **14**). In addition to the forms of transport listed above, *coastal shipping* also plays a significant part, almost 15% of freight movements within the United Kingdom using this mode of transport.

3. Ports, docks and airports. The importance of foreign trade to the British economy hardly needs further emphasis and in the early seventies shipping arrivals and departures at UK ports were averaging 200 million net tons a year. In addition, British civil airports were handling nearly $1\frac{1}{2}$ million aircraft movements each year, although only about half of these movements were of commercial importance. The effective international movement of goods and passengers on this scale depends as much on efficient and rapid turn-round at ports and airports as on the actual means of transport employed.

4. The choice of transport. If the choice of transport is left to the individual trader he will be influenced by the comparative costs per mile, by the incidental expenses involved and by the speed and convenience of the various alternatives. Choices made on the basis of cost to the individual transport used will not necessarily lead to a balance of transport services that is acceptable to the whole community. Transport has long been a matter of public policy in Britain and the long and costly process of modernising and reshaping the railways, the restricted nature of competition in road transport and the social costs of congestion on the roads all tend to make price competition an inadequate measure of efficiency in transport.

THE ORGANISATION OF INLAND TRANSPORT

5. Inter-war development. The present organisation of transport services in Britain is a development of trends that began to be important between the two World Wars. The inter-war period saw the increasing use of road transport and the relative decline of rail transport. The many railway companies which had existed up to 1920 were amalgamated into four main groups. To help the railways, which were handicapped by a rigid system of fixing rates and fares, petrol was taxed and a system of licensing was introduced for road hauliers and for bus and coach operators.

6. Inter-war legislation. The two Acts of Parliament which laid the foundations for our present licensing system were the *Road Traffic Act*, 1930, and the *Road and Rail Traffic Act*, 1933. The first of these prohibited the carriage of passengers by road for hire or reward except under licence and the second did the same for the carriage of goods.

7. Post-war trends in transport. The railways' difficulties have continued into the post-war years. Their share of both freight and passengers carried has fallen, while that of road transport has increased. In road transport, the outstanding trends have been the growth of the use of the private car for passenger transport and the use of traders' own vehicles for the carriage of their goods.

8. Public ownership. The *Transport Act*, 1947, brought both the railways and public carriers in road transport under public ownership, leaving only vehicles used by traders for the carriage of their own goods un-nationalised. The 1947 Act set up a Transport Commission to administer all publicly owned transport, but a new scheme of organisation was introduced in 1959 and the various Boards now report direct to the Minister of Transport. In 1953, road transport was partly de-nationalised and the present position is that there is:

(*a*) A completely nationalised rail system.
(*b*) A nationalised road haulage organisation.
(*c*) Private firms of road hauliers.
(*d*) Vehicles owned by private traders and employed to carry the traders' own goods.

9. Current problems. In spite of a great deal of legislation and many changes in official policy, the major problems concerning inland transport in the United Kingdom remain unsolved. The more important of these are:

(*a*) The co-ordination of the various modes of transport, particularly road and rail freight transport.

(*b*) The maintenance of an adequate public passenger transport system in a society in which over half of all households have access to a car.

(*c*) The protection of the environment and the reduction of noise and other nuisance as road traffic and the size of heavy lorries increase.

(*d*) Compliance with the European Community rules regarding transport operations.

(e) The provision of finance for capital projects in the public sector, for the subsidisation of unprofitable but socially necessary services and for the maintenance of an adequate road network.

TRANSPORT POLICY

The problems outlined above have tended to become increasingly acute during recent years and increasingly, too, governments have attempted to intervene in order to achieve solutions by legislation and by the creation of new authorities.

10. The Transport Act, 1968. The principal objective of the *Transport Act* was to promote the integration of inland transport and in particular to achieve a sound balance between road and rail. It also contained provisions relating to social and financial problems arising from the rundown of the rail system and the increase of private motoring.

The *Transport Act*, 1968 established a *National Freight Corporation* (N.F.C.) and a *Freight Integration Council.* The N.F.C. incorporates the freight-liner and sundries services of the railways and the nationalised road haulage fleet. The Act also established a new licensing system and provided for a system of local *Passenger Transport Authorities*, these being charged with the duty of securing a properly efficient and integrated pattern of public transport in their areas.

11. The new licensing system. Under the new licensing system small goods vehicles of under 30 cwt (1524 kg) unladen weight were freed from control. This freedom applies to amost one million vehicles. Vehicles over that weight require an *operator's licence* which is given on a basis of the operator's fitness to run a transport fleet. Very heavy vehicles will be subject to "quantity licensing" as well as this "quality licensing." The effect of this provision is that a haulage contractor will require special authorisation to carry bulk goods over long distances. British Rail or the N.F.C. will be able to object to such an authorisation being given. The quantity licensing provisions have not yet been put into force.

12. Policy towards British Rail. During the whole of its existence British Rail has suffered repeated financial crises. Many attempts have been made to put the railways' finances on a more sound footing and the 1968 Act provided for a radical re-organisation, with British Rail's debt being written down from £1,500 million to £300 million. Even this was not effective. Further support was given by the *Railways Act*, 1974 and by 1975 the subsidy to the railways was running at £400 million a year. Clearly, some more radical approach than mere subsidisation is now required.

13. Developments in transport policy. The problems outlined in 9 were not solved by the *Transport Act*, 1968 and critics of that Act have pointed out that the new organisations and procedures imposed have added a bureaucratic structure that did not exist before. In 1976, the Government acknowledged the severity of the problems of co-ordinating the major modes of transport, of providing the necessary finance for capital outlays and of determining priorities. The position was set out in a consultation document (*Transport Policy*) in which it was stated that the Government did not believe that a new executive organisation to co-ordinate transport should be set up, but that a *National Transport Council* should be established on a representative basis. This body would review developments, would examine pricing proposals and would be available for the discussion of future government proposals. Whether a merely consultative and advisory body could contribute to the solution of real and urgent problems in a major sector of the economy must be a matter for discussion.

ROAD TRANSPORT

14. The road system. There are about 200,000 miles of roadway in Great Britain, of which just over 8,600 miles are trunk roads, over 80,000 miles are classified roads and the remainder, more than half of the total, are unclassified roads of merely local importance. Total expenditure on the roads averaged £1,600 million for the three-year period ending 1975–76, but the increasing volume of traffic makes even this sum too little to provide an adequate system. There are over 1,100 miles of motorway.

15. The growth of road transport. The use of road transport for the carriage of goods is shown by the following figures:

Year	*Ton-miles*
1960	30,000 million
1965	42,000 million
1970	51,000 million
1975	55,000 million (90 million tonne-km)

NOTE: A "ton-mile" is a composite unit representing one ton of goods carried for one mile. A three-ton load carried the 375 miles from London to Edinburgh would count as 1,125 ton-miles. Recent statistics employ the metric term *tonne-kilometre,* one tonne-kilometre being approximately equal to 0.6 ton-miles.

In 1975, there were over 13 million cars on the road and about 1.9 million commercial vehicles. The great increase in road passenger transport in recent years has been in private motoring rather than in the use of public service vehicles.

16. The road haulage industry. About half of the 55 thousand ton-miles of freight movements shown in the previous section for the year 1975 is represented by the carriage of goods in firms' own vehicles, often over comparatively short distances. The true road haulage industry consists of firms whose main business is the carriage of goods by road for profit. There are almost 40,000 public haulage operators in the business and many of these are still small firms operating less than five vehicles. Road haulage firms tend to specialise either in loads of a particular type, e.g. bulk liquids, or by length of haul. The nationalised part of the industry was organised in four limited companies which were owned by the Transport Holding Company. However this fleet of the Transport Holding Company was acquired by the National Freight Corporation as from 1st January, 1969. This road haulage fleet is the largest in the industry and is generally judged to be efficient and to provide a useful network of long-distance services, but it is opposed by the *Road Haulage Association,* to which many of the private contractors belong.

17. The organisation of road passenger transport. There are some 5,000 operators running bus or coach services and they can be grouped into five categories:

(*a*) Companies formerly owned by the Transport Holding Company and now controlled by the National Bus Company set up by the *Transport Act*.

(*b*) Large independent operators, between some of whom there are financial links and among whom there is little competition.

(*c*) Small independent companies.

(*d*) Municipal services.

(*e*) Services operated by the London Transport Executive.

The National Bus Company comprises thirty operating companies which provide both local and inter-city services throughout England and Wales. Privately owned companies account for less than 10% of bus services. The increase in car ownership during the 1970s resulted in a severe decline in the use of bus services and more and more routes have become uneconomic. At the same time, both fuel and labour costs have risen sharply, so that in 1975–76 it was necessary to subsidise the bus industry to the extent of £200 million.

18. Problems of the growth of road transport. The increased use of road transport poses very serious problems of:

(*a*) Public expenditure on the roads.

(*b*) The planning of towns to give access to town centres and parking space for vehicles without destroying the amenities of the area.

(*c*) Methods of reducing road casualties.

(*d*) Pollution from internal combustion engines.

(*e*) Congestion.

An indication of the seriousness of the congestion problem is given by the fact that car ownership in Europe increased threefold between 1962 and 1972 whereas road capacity increased by only 10%. Radical solutions to the related problems of congestion and pollution have been suggested, including the banning of cars from city centres and "road pricing" which involves metering the mileage driven on the more busy roads.

RAIL TRANSPORT

19. The railway system. The British railway system was the first to be constructed in the world and like many pioneering ventures it was excessively expensive. Its planning was piecemeal and many lines were duplicated. The system comprises about 40,000 miles of track on which 10,000 locomotives are operated. The railways own some 30,000 carriages, but many of these are out of use except at seasonal peaks. About a million wagons are in use. Every year about 200 million tonnes of freight are handled. much of it being coal, coke, minerals and other heavy goods.

20. Nationalisation. The railways were brought under public ownership in 1947. Lack of maintenance and failure to replace equipment in the war years left huge problems to be overcome by British Rail. Although the railways managed to make a working profit for the first few years after nationalisation, there was an *over-all* deficit, after interest payments etc., for every year except 1952. By 1960 the railways had lost altogether some £400 million. It was decided to write these losses off completely and also to relieve the railways of interest and redemption charges on another £800 million of their capital liabilities. This gave the railways a chance of recovering their position, but it was still necessary to carry on with the modernisation plans which had been started in 1955, to economise on manpower and cut down unprofitable services.

21. The Beeching Report. The Beeching Report outlined the steps to be taken if the greater part of the railways' deficit was to be eliminated by 1970. The intention was to use rail transport for those purposes for which it was best suited. One half of the routes in use were not even paying for the track and signalling costs, whereas the other half were covering the route costs six times over. The loss-makers, said the Report, were:

(*a*) In the freight field, wagon loads of general merchandise and short-distance sundries traffic.
(*b*) Rural passenger services.
(*c*) Suburban services. Even the London commuter services barely covered their costs.

Proposals made included:

(*a*) The discontinuance of many local services.
(*b*) The improvement of inter-city services.
(*c*) The rationalisation of coal and freight movements.
(*d*) Measures for modernisation and technical improvements.

Although the controversial closing of uneconomic lines was extremely unpopular at the time, the policy of reducing uneconomic services has continued, although at a much more gradual rate and where real social disadvantage would have occurred, provision has been made for the subsidisation and continuation of services under the *Transport Act*, 1968.

22. Current activities of British Rail. The years since the Beeching Report have seen a great reduction in railway manpower, with consequent saving in costs. In 1963, over 476,000 people were employed but by 1976 this figure had been reduced to 231,000. In line with the policy outlined in the previous section, inter-city services have been improved and high-speed passenger train (H.S.T.) services, travelling at speeds of up to 125 miles per hour, have been introduced in some areas. The still faster Advanced Passenger Train (A.P.T.) will offer even more rapid travel. The railways' advantage in freight services is restricted to long distance bulk traffic (*see* 26), but as this accounts for only about 20% of *all* freight movements by road or by rail, there is little chance of the railways improving their share of freight carriage. The remaining major aspect of the railways' work is in commuter passenger services, particularly in the south-east. None of the services mentioned above is profitable, although inter-city services come closest with only about 5% of their allocated costs not covered by earnings.

COMPARISON OF ROAD AND RAIL TRANSPORT

23. The characteristics of road transport. The following is a summary of the main characteristics of road transport.

(*a*) Road transport is a *flexible* means of transporting goods. There is no fixed track and so there is a much greater choice of routes.

(*b*) Having no fixed tracks or stops, *door-to-door* collection and delivery is possible.

(*c*) Road transport is suitable for *small consignments.*

(*d*) It is possible to make *intermediate stops.*

(*e*) A *return load* is needed unless lorries are to return empty.

(*f*) A comparatively small capital is sufficient to set up a road haulage business.

(*g*) Road transport is not very fast for long hauls, but this may be offset by the directness of the journey and by the lack of the need for trans-shipment.

24. Characteristics of rail transport. The main characteristics of rail transport are:

(*a*) The use of a fixed track means that the railways are *not very flexible* in operation.

(*b*) Routes run between *fixed terminals*, which again makes operations not very flexible and necessitates trans-shipment at the end of the rail journey.

(*c*) Railways tend to be good for the carriage of *large consignments over long distances.*

(*d*) Rail costs tend to be high for short hauls and for small consignments.

(*e*) Operating over fixed routes makes the railway dependent, to some extent, on the prosperity of the area through which it passes.

(*f*) *Capital costs* are heavy. This means that heavy fixed charges have to be allocated in some way to freight rates and fares.

(*g*) Single cross-country consignments require repeated trans-shipment and may be very slow in reaching their destinations.

25. Traffic density. The best load for the railways is a *full train load.* If several hundred passengers have to be shifted at one time from a particular point, they can be economically carried by train. If a dozen or so passengers appear at hourly intervals throughout the day, a train is a most unsuitable method of conveyance. The train, whether for passengers or freight, is a large capacity vehicle and requires full utilisation.

26. Comparison of costs. A study of costs reveals how each type of transport may best be used.

(*a*) Costs are likely to be lower by *rail* for:
- (*i*) Heavy flows of traffic.
- (*ii*) Direct routes.
- (*iii*) Long distances.
- (*iv*) Where there is direct access to the railway.
- (*v*) Goods of heavy bulk.
- (*vi*) Robust commodities.
- (*vii*) Situations where mechanical handling is possible.

(*b*) *Road* costs are likely to be lower for:
- (*i*) Light flows of traffic.
- (*ii*) Cross-country trips.
- (*iii*) Short journeys.
- (*iv*) Where there is not easy access to the railway.
- (*v*) Goods of small bulk.
- (*vi*) Fragile goods.
- (*vii*) Goods requiring personal handling.

Awareness of these factors was apparent in the Beeching Report which aimed at restricting the railways to the routes and loads which they could handle competitively. A more sympathetic approach to the problems of the railways was apparent in the licensing provisions of the *Transport Act*, 1968.

27. Co-ordination of transport services. The *Transport Act*, 1947 was drafted in the belief that a fully co-ordinated transport system would be possible in time. This ideal of using each form of transport for the purposes for which it is best suited was also a major motive underlying the *Transport Act*, 1968. Whether or not the Act was more successful than its predecessor, it is becoming increasingly apparent that some rationalisation of inland transport is necessary, and that this can only come about as the result of a series of compromises between social and economic objectives.

SEA TRANSPORT

28. The merchant fleet. Britain's merchant fleet still carries about 20% of the world's international sea-borne trade. About one-third of her present fleet consists of tankers. Tanker tonnage has doubled since pre-war days, but the tonnage of other classes of ships has fallen a little. Total tonnage at the beginning of 1975 was just over 30 million gross tons, excluding small vessels of 500 gross tons or less.

29. Ownership and management. Merchant shipping is run by private enterprise. There has been a strong tendency towards combination in the last forty years or so and today a large proportion of British shipping is controlled by a few large holding companies of which the most important are Cunard, Ellerman's, P. and O., Furness Withy and British and Commonwealth. The major oil companies control subsidiary companies which own and operate tankers. Large firms in other lines may also own subsidiaries which operate specialised ships. Refrigerated cargo ships are operated by a subsidiary of a meat-packing firm and the leading firm of banana growers and importers owns its own banana ships.

Owners of British ships must be persons or companies qualified to be so under the provisions of the *Merchant Shipping Act*, 1894. This provides that the registered owners must be British born or naturalised British subjects or companies registered in the United Kingdom or a British Dominion. The registered owner may or may not be the person registered as the manager. It is the ship manager who is legally responsible for compliance with shipping regulations. Some companies are formed especially for the purpose of managing rather than of owning ships. A shipping line may consist of vessels under several ownerships but run by a single managing company.

30. Registration. All British ships must be registered at the port of their owners' choice after a thorough survey. Particulars to be registered include a full description of the hull, the type of construction, the name of the builder and the tonnage of the ship. A numbered certificate is issued, referring to the registered ship and no other.

31. Lloyd's Register of Shipping. Lloyd's Register is concerned with the registration, classification and surveying of ships. It is run by a committee of management composed of shipowners, shipbuilders and marine underwriters and has no connection with the official registration described above. Lloyd's Register developed from records kept by underwriters and shipowners at Edward Lloyd's from the late seventeenth century onwards. At first the underwriters and shipowners kept separate registers, but in 1834 the two registers were merged into Lloyd's Register of Shipping. From the mid-nineteenth century onward, Lloyd's surveyors were inspecting ships and the Register was being marked to indicate the result of their inspections. The term "*A1* at Lloyds" has passed into ordinary speech.

32. The Chamber of Shipping of the United Kingdom. This is a representative organisation of shipowners. It is controlled by a council of representatives of British shipowners and is active in protecting and promoting shipping interests in parliament and elsewhere. It also promotes a great deal of useful research including work on cargo-handling, automation, corrosion prevention and other topics.

33. Liners. Liners follow regular routes, sail at set times and call at scheduled ports. While the largest liners carry only passengers and mails, many passenger liners carry cargo as well. Ships may also be specially built as cargo liners, often intended for specific cargoes and equipped to carry only a few passengers.

34. Problems of liner operation. Liners offer the advantages of regular sailings at fixed times, stable freight rates and fixed times of arrival at ports of call. They are usually speedy, small or large consignments of goods are accepted on most runs and standard contracts are offered. Regular sailings, full or empty, pose problems for the operator, however. A modern liner represents a considerable capital investment and a reasonable return can only be secured if the ship is used to capacity. This demands extensive advertising and publicity. One of the difficulties of operating a cargo liner is that the best freight jobs along the scheduled route may be taken by opportunist tramp operators, or that customers may be lured away by low freight rates elsewhere.

35. Shipping conferences. The problems of liner operation are partly solved by the establishment of liner conferences. The conferences are international organisations set up to control freight rates or fares in a particular area and over certain routes. Unless rates are kept at a reasonable level, the expenses of liner operation cannot be met. The conferences also try to establish firm links between the liner companies and the shippers who use their services, so that regular customers ship with the liner companies rather than with "outsiders" who might offer temporary advantages. One method of securing customer loyalty is by offering *deferred rebates*.

36. Tramp shipping. Tramps have no fixed times of sailing and are not operated on fixed routes. The tramp owner must be an opportunist, taking a profitable cargo wherever he can find it. A vessel may be chartered on a *voyage charter*, from one port to another, a *time charter*, for a set period, or a *demise* or *bare-boat charter* under which the charterer pays all the charges and maintains the ship just as if he were the owner.

A cargo liner may sometimes be switched to tramping if there is insufficient trade to justify liner work. A tramp voyage might last for up to nine months and be the subject of half-a-dozen charterparties (contracts) mostly negotiated while the vessel was at sea. Passages linking voyage charters might have to be made in ballast.

37. Freight rates. Tramp rates are determined by competition in the market. Rates depend on the length of the voyage, the possibility of a return cargo, the costs of operating the ship and, of course, on the demand for cargo space and the shipping available. At the time of writing the seaborne traffic in cereals is a dominant factor in the determination of freight rates. The Baltic Exchange is the world's most important shipping market, chartering normally being carried out through shipping brokers.

AIR TRANSPORT

38. Characteristics of air transport. The great advantage of air transport is speed. It is still a relatively expensive method of transport and is not suitable for bulk products or goods of low value density. International air traffic is growing at a faster rate than surface travel and is the most important means of international passenger transport.

39. Air freight. The advantages of air freight are speed of delivery and better conditions of carriage. Fast delivery to customers results in a smaller quantity of goods, and therefore of working capital, being tied up in transit. On short routes, air freight can actually be cheaper than surface transport, especially for goods requiring careful handling. About 10% of the exports of the United Kingdom are now sent by air.

40. Jet operation. The use of jet aircraft became common after 1958 when the Comet IV and Boeing 707 were introduced. Jet aircraft travel at over 550 miles per hour (885 km/hr). Time is saved, and travel is smooth, vibrationless and quiet. The quicker journey increases the productivity of the aircraft for both freight and passenger transport. The economics of jet operation have been greatly affected in recent years by two technical developments. These are the introduction of large wide-bodied ("jumbo") jet aircraft and the appearance of supersonic aircraft on commercial routes. Both of these developments have created new problems in devising fare structures.

41. The air corporations. Air transport was nationalised in 1946 by the *Civil Aviation Act.* This placed civil aviation in the hands of three state airlines: British Overseas Airways

Corporation, British European Airways and British South American Airways, although this last corporation was abolished in 1949 after a series of disasters. The two remaining corporations were eventually brought under the control of British Airways, a new organisation established by the *Civil Aviation Act*, 1972, and they were finally dissolved as separate entities in 1974. It was intended that the nationalised corporations should have a monopoly of scheduled services, but this position was gradually abandoned, the statutory monopoly finally disappearing in 1960.

42. The independent airlines. Although the independent airlines had a very precarious existence in the early post-war years, from 1950 onwards they found profitable work in air trooping, charter services, inclusive tours and vehicle ferry services. A fresh impetus was given to the independents by the *Civil Aviation (Licensing) Act*, 1960, which ended the nationalised air corporations' exclusive rights on scheduled services.

The development of the independent airlines has been marked by a series of mergers. Air Holdings Ltd., in which shipping interests had a major shareholding, operated British United Airways as the largest private airline, but this company, in turn, was taken over by Caledonian Airways in 1970. In the following year, as a consequence of this takeover, British Caledonian was formed and is now the leading private airline in the United Kingdom.

43. Civil Aviation (Licensing) Act, 1960. This Act introduced more stringent regulations to control air transport operations and established a new air service licensing procedure. Air carriers must apply to the *Air Transport Licensing Board*, set up by the Act, for air service licences. Applications are heard in public and objections may be made.

44. International regulation of air transport. It is generally recognised by air transport operators and by the governments concerned that free competition in international air transport is not practicable. Fares and freight rates are regulated by the traffic conferences of the *International Air Transport Association.*

THROUGH TRANSPORT AND CONTAINERISATION

45. Through transport. The ideal transport system would be a direct and uninterrupted flow of goods from the manufacturer to the final consumer. This may not be feasible, but it is possible to devise means of transport which involve a minimum of handling, loading, unloading and repacking. A system of flow- or through-transport is likely to involve *unit loads* prepared for transportation at the final stage of production, *palletisation*, to facilitate handling, and extensive mechanisation of handling.

46. Palletisation. A simple aid to the development of a system of through-transport is the pallet. Essentially, this is just a flat platform or deck supported by feet so that it can be handled by forklift trucks, although the term may refer to more complicated variants of the same idea. Used with fork-lift trucks on both docks and ships it is possible to load palletised cargo directly without the intervention of cranes, winches or manual handling.

47. Standardisation. The effective use of pallets and mechanical handling devices requires the acceptance of standard dimensions for loads and pallets. The extension of standardisation to containers (*see* below) and to air freight is effecting something of a revolution in transport. The full exploitation of the new methods requires not only standard dimensions, but standard fixtures, attachments and so on.

48. Containers. The biggest reductions in transport costs are likely to come with the full acceptance of standard containers as the routine method of transporting goods. A container is merely a large metal box with doors at one end. It is made in standard dimensions with an 8ft by 8ft cross-section and lengths of from 10ft to 40ft. According to the International Standards Organisation definition a freight container should be:

(*a*) Of a permanent nature and capable of repeated use.

(*b*) Specially designed for use by one or more modes of transport without intermediate reloading.

(*c*) Fitted with devices for ready handling.

(*d*) Designed for ease of filling and emptying.

Since containers can be carried by road to the docks and then transferred by advanced handling equipment directly to the ships, they have caused a complete change in work at the ports and much misgiving among dock-workers. They may be packed (or "stuffed") far from the ports and not unpacked until they reach their destination overseas. This means that special provisions must be made regarding documentation and customs clearance.

49. Container ships. The development of ships specially designed to carry containers is likely to have a considerable impact on shipping. A single container ship is able to carry over one thousand containers and can replace eight or nine conventional cargo ships.

PROGRESS TEST 23

1. What are the principal *general* problems confronting inland transport in the United Kingdom today? To what extent have recent policies contributed to their solution? **(1–13)**
2. Describe the pattern of ownership in road transport in Britain today. Discuss its merits and defects. **(8, 10–11, 15–17)**
3. Outline the main characteristics of rail transport. **(24, 25)**
4. What problems are likely to arise from the increased use of private road transport? **(9, 14, 15–18)**
5. What considerations would influence a manufacturer of domestic applicances in his choice of methods of transport for his product? Should his freedom of choice be curtailed or influenced in any way? **(4, 23–26)**
6. "The tramp owner must be an opportunist." Explain. **(36, 37)**
7. What are liner conferences? Is their existence justified? **(35)**
8. Describe the development of British air transport since 1946. **(38–44)**
9. What is meant by "through-transport" and what changes are required to bring about such a system? **(45–49)**

CHAPTER XXIV

INSURANCE

BASIC PRINCIPLES

1. Nature of insurance. Insurance is a pooling of risks. It provides a fund to which the many individuals who are subject to a certain risk may contribute and from which the few who actually suffer loss can be compensated. A seventeenth-century Act of Parliament defines insurance as a means whereby "the loss lighteth rather easily upon many than heavily upon few." This is the essence of the matter.

2. The contract of insurance. With the exception of those social benefits provided by National Insurance, insurance work is carried out by private individuals or organisations. Whatever is agreed between a person wishing to be insured against some risk and the organisation or individual giving the protection will be the subject of a contract. The parties to the contract are called the *insured* and the *insurers*. Before any contract is entered into, the person desiring insurance will have made an application called a *proposal*. The details of the contract of insurance will be set out in a *policy*. The payments made by the insured into the common fund are called *premiums*.

3. Insurable interest. Insurance cannot be given unless the insured has an interest in whatever is being insured, so that if the loss insured against happens, he will suffer financially. Obviously, if a person can gain by some accident or disaster which does not injure him personally, there is some incentive to bring the disaster about. Even in the absence of any evil intention, the lack of insurable interest reduces insurance to mere gambling. In the eighteenth century it was possible to insure the lives of strangers or of public men. This practice was made illegal by the *Life Insurance Act*, 1774 and the principle was extended to insurances on goods, ships and merchandise by the *Gaming Act*, 1845. The *Marine Insurance Act*, 1909, made it a criminal offence to effect marine insurance without insurable interest.

4. Good faith. A contract of insurance is a contract *of the utmost good faith* (*uberrimae fidei*). This means that each party to the contract must make full disclosure of all material facts, otherwise the contract may be completely void or, in less serious cases, voidable at the wish of the offended party. Since the proposer of a contract is usually the only person in a position to know all the facts, he has a very special duty to disclose any facts that he knows or ought to know.

5. Indemnity. With the exception of life assurance and personal accident insurance, most contracts of insurance are *contracts of indemnity*. The effect of this is to make it impossible for the insured to recover more than his actual loss if the event insured against happens. It should not be possible to make a profit from the occurrence of the event insured against; the effect of the contract should be to place the insured in the same position, financially, as before the event happened. If a car is "written off" as the result of an accident, the insurers will only pay out the value of the car at the time of loss, which may well be much less than the owner paid for it when it was new.

6. Subrogation. The insured is entitled to full indemnity, within the terms of the policy, but is not entitled to make a profit. If he has been fully indemnified by the insurers, it follows that the insurers are entitled to take advantage of any rights which the insured may have against other parties or to any residual sums which can be raised from salvage or in any other ways following from the loss. This is known as the principle of *subrogation*. If insured property is damaged by fire, the insurers, after paying out in full, will be entitled to sue any third party who caused the fire by his negligence and if any stock is salvaged, say from a warehouse fire, the insurers will be entitled to the proceeds from its sale. The standard fire policy requires the insured to lend his name to any action which the insurers may make against third parties.

7. Contribution. Where there is over-insurance because a loss is covered by policies effected with two or more insurers, the principle of indemnity still applies. In these circumstances, the insured will only be entitled to recover the full amount of his loss and if one insurer has paid out in full, he will be entitled to nothing more. The insurer who has paid out will be entitled to recover a proportion of the amount paid from the other insurers concerned.

8. Risks and premiums. Premiums charged must be related to the occurrence of claims in the class of insurance business in question. Where losses are heavy and frequent, premiums will be heavy; where the risks are less, premium rates will be less. Rates charged must be sufficient to cover the cost of claims, plus overheads and a profit sufficient to make the business worth while. It is necessary to classify the classes of business according to the risk involved, and the funds relating to the various classes of insurance should be separate and self-supporting.

9. Investments. Premiums are paid at the beginning of a contract of insurance, claims are made later, if at all. Premium income will therefore be available for investment in this period and the interest on investments may provide a substantial further income for the insurers. The long-term investments of UK insurance companies amounted to £18.3 thousand million in 1974, with some £5,300 million in other funds.

10. The main branches of insurance. Insurance in Britain is conventionally divided into four main branches: *Marine*, *Life*, *Fire* and *Accident*.

Alternative classifications are possible, but these correspond to the departments into which insurance companies divide their business. The range of risks experienced in modern life tend to become more complex and new types of insurance are devised to cover new risks. Thus aviation insurance has become important since the First World War and the risks covered by the accident branch have been extended to keep pace with developments in modern technology.

11. Insurance and assurance. The word "assurance" in modern British practice is confined to life assurance (*see* **17**).

In some marine insurance business the insurers are called the "assurers" and the policy-holder is referred to as "the assured." Although difficult to justify logically or historically the practice is quite definite.

INSURERS

12. The structure of the insurance market. Insurance business may be conducted by *mutual-benefit societies,* by *insurance companies* or by *Lloyd's underwriters.*

13. Mutual societies. The mutual principle goes back to the days when clubs were formed by groups of people with the intention of providing sums of money on the death or sickness of members. Relatively small periodic payments provided a fund from which members or their dependents could be paid. The mutual principle is still important in the life branch today and some of the biggest life offices are mutual societies, incorporated but having neither shareholders nor capital. Policyholders become members and share in the profits. Some mutual societies are limited by guarantee.

14. Companies. There are about five hundred British insurance companies, but the bulk of the business is conducted by about twenty large "composite" groups, each of which is able to conduct all classes of insurance business. The principal companies of most of these groups have histories that extend back for well over one hundred years. The trend since the beginning of this century has been towards larger groupings, recent amalgamations including that between the London Assurance and the Sun Alliance in 1965. There are a number of smaller, independent composite companies carrying out a range of insurance business, but it seems likely that some of these will be absorbed into the major groups in the near future.

Other companies may specialise to a greater or less extent, offering a range of services but often having the greater part of their business in one branch. Specialist companies offer cover for some particular risk such as television sets and aerials, goods in transit or plate glass.

15. Tariff and non-tariff companies. In fire insurance it is necessary to prevent rates from being forced down by competition to the point where funds are inadequate to meet losses. The majority of fire insurance companies are members of the Fire Offices Committee. By pooling their experience they are able to fix minimum rates of premium. A few of the larger companies and a number of the smaller ones, as well as the Lloyd's underwriters, operate on a non-tariff basis. In accident insurance, the tariff companies are members of the Accident Offices Association. British insurance companies have stood considerable losses on fire and accident business in recent years.

16. Lloyd's. Lloyd's is a centre where individuals, known as *underwriters*, accept insurance, transacting business on their own behalf and in competition with each other. Like many other City institutions, Lloyd's began as a coffee house, Edward Lloyd's in Tower Street. Being near the river, Lloyd's coffee house became a meeting place for ship-owners and merchants, many of whom offered insurance, several merchants each accepting or "underwriting" part of a risk. Gradually, the underwriters meeting at Lloyd's developed a corporate sense and by 1770 they had moved to new premises and were managing their own affairs.

Present-day underwriters must be elected *Underwriting Members of Lloyd's* and must conform to the strict standards laid down by the corporation of Lloyd's. The corporation owns the premises and provides services for the members. The committee also provides a world-wide system of Lloyd's agents. The public does not deal directly with Lloyd's underwriters but through one of the firms of Lloyd's brokers; Lloyd's brokers work on behalf of the proposer, endeavouring to find the most favourable terms possible. The underwriters, who number over five thousand, work in groups called *syndicates*. A risk may be placed among a number of syndicates, each of them accepting a proportion of the total. The underwriting room at Lloyd's is the centre of London's marine insurance market, although some syndicates specialise in various forms of non-marine business and insurance companies as well as Lloyd's underwriters undertake marine insurance.

INSURANCE AND THE INDIVIDUAL

17. Life assurance. This is probably the most important type of insurance for the individual. *Whole life* assurance provides for payment of a given sum on the death of the insured person. Other types of policy contain an element of investment as well as of life assurance. *Endowment policies* are paid out either on the death of the "life assured" or at the end of a stipulated period of time. Both types of policy may be either *with* or *without* profits. Recently, some companies have offered life assurance combined with unit trust purchases. For many elderly people, *annuities* are attractive, offering a fixed income in return for a capital sum. *Industrial life* assurance covers the same risks as ordinary life assurance, but is designed mainly for the protection of working-class policy holders, premiums being collected on a monthly or weekly basis.

18. Other policies. In addition to life assurance, individuals need to obtain protection for their property. The most usual policies are *householders' comprehensive* policies which give cover for both buildings and contents. Cover can be obtained for valuables outside the premises by means of *all risks* policies. *The Road Traffic Act*, 1960 makes it an offence to use a vehicle on the road without having in force an insurance policy in respect of injuries to third parties. Most motorists are not content with the minimum cover and the usual form of cover is the comprehensive policy.

INSURANCES EFFECTED BY A BUSINESS

19. The risks. The main risks in respect of which a business will require cover are those connected with its property and the risks of incurring legal liability.

20. Fire. This is probably the most obvious risk to a firm's property. Many businessmen calculate that a total loss is unlikely and reduce the premium paid by obtaining only partial cover. Fire policies may include a "condition of average" so that the insurers only bear a proportion of the loss suffered if full cover is not obtained. The reasoning is that the insurers have been bearing the whole of the risk, but the insured has only been paying a partial premium. Insurers will normally insist on a survey before accepting the insurance or deciding the terms.

21. Consequential losses. After a fire, a business may be out of action for some time, records may have been destroyed and orders may be lost. The business will therefore need cover against loss of profits. The premium paid will vary with the value of the property insured and with the "period of indemnity," some businesses being able to get back to normal in a comparatively short time whereas others might take a very long time indeed to return to normal trading.

22. Burglary insurance. Burglary and housebreaking involve actual breaking into premises and must be distinguished from larceny, which is mere stealing and is so common that it is not usually possible to insure against it. As with fire, the chances of a very large loss are often considered to be too slight to warrant full cover. Premiums vary with the security of the premises and the nature of the stock at risk. Burglary surveys help to minimise losses and ensure reasonable standards of protection.

23. Fidelity guarantee. In addition to the risk of loss from burglary by outsiders there is a risk of loss due to the dishonesty of employees. A fidelity guarantee policy provides that the insurer will make good such losses up to a given sum in exchange for a fairly small premium. Policies may be for single employees or for groups.

24. Cash. Protection can be obtained against loss of cash whether it is on the premises, in transit or even in the hands of employees. Premiums are calculated on the sums involved.

25. Goods in transit. Premiums for insurance of goods in transit depend on the nature of the journey, the goods concerned and the risks covered. Insurances are usually for all journeys for a period, rather than for a single consignment.

26. Employers' and public liability insurance. Employers' liability insurance gives cover against claims made by employees who have been awarded damages in respect of accidents caused by the employer's negligence. Public liability insurance gives similar protection against claims by members of the public. Products' liability insurance protects against injury following the use of a company's products.

27. Credit insurance. Trading on credit involves the risk of bad debts. Premiums for credit insurance are based on the turnover of the business, the standing of the firm's customers and the period of credit given. The Trade Indemnity Company specialises in credit risks. In order to ensure a degree of business prudence, only a proportion of the risk is covered. The political element in export credit risks is covered by the Export Credits Guarantee Department (*see* XXI, 3–4).

28. Other insurances. Risks connected with machinery, boilers, lifting apparatus and so on are covered by *engineering* insurance. A business will also have to take out suitable motor policies in respect of any vehicles which it uses. The services of the life branch may be used to provide pension schemes for employees.

PROGRESS TEST 24

1. Define "insurable interest." **(3)**
2. What is meant by the term "of the utmost good faith" in connection with a contract of insurance? What is its effect on (*a*) the insurer and (*b*) the insured? **(4)**
3. What is meant by a "contract of indemnity?" **(5)**
4. What is the relationship between risks and premiums? **(8)**
5. Write brief notes on "The basic principles of insurance." **(1–11)**
6. Outline the structure of the insurance market in Britain. **(12–16)**
7. What is "Lloyds"? **(16)**
8. Distinguish between whole life policies, endowment policies and annuities. **(17)**
9. What insurances might a prudent businessman effect in respect of a manufacturing business? **(19–28)**

APPENDIX I

EXAMINATION TECHNIQUE

Method. Most Commerce questions require an answer in *essay form.* To get good marks, not only must the information be there, in the essay, but it must be clearly expressed. To achieve a well-ordered essay:

(*a*) *Decide exactly what information* the question requires from you.

(*b*) If you find it helps, *list the points which you wish to include* in your answer.

(*c*) Having decided on the right approach to your question, *design your answer carefully.*

(*i*) Begin with an introduction, showing the line you intend to take,

(*ii*) start a fresh paragraph for each major point, and

(*iii*) sum up your answer in a short, concluding paragraph if you can.

It is not a bad idea to use a "key sentence" to begin each new paragraph. This key sentence should epitomise the subject matter dealt with in the paragraph and subsequent sentences can then elaborate the main idea and add any necessary detail.

Subject matter. The information which you use in answering questions in Commerce will come from these levels: (i) your systematic reading of text-books; (ii) from wider reading on commercial topics, and (iii) from your own observation. Do not be afraid to say what you mean and do not suppress facts because you are not absolutely sure that you are right. If you give an opinion, be sure that you back it up with reason and all the facts you can muster.

Examiners. Your examination answer is a practical exercise in communication, and the person that you are communicating with is the examiner.

The secret of good, clear written work is to be able to put oneself in the position of the person who will eventually read what has been written. If you are constantly aware of the need to make yourself clear to the examiner, you will avoid the turgid, untidy, incomprehensible answer that throws away marks because no one can ever know whether the student really understands the topic or not. Looking at things from the examiner's point of view may also encourage those whose handwriting is not particularly good to make a special effort to achieve legibility. Examiners are very busy people. They will have scores, or even hundreds, of papers to mark. With the best will in the world, they will find it difficult to do justice to a script which is barely legible.

Every year, hopeful candidates who cannot answer some particular question try to save the day by devising an answer to some similar question which they *can* handle but which is not actually on the examination paper. Since examiners are either working to a laid-down marking scheme or have agreed at an examiners' meeting how the questions should be answered, there is little hope of getting away with this. Read the questions carefully, decide what they mean, and answer the ones that you can do best. Examiners are also impervious to scribbled pleas for sympathy or dramatically broken-off sentences intended to show that in spite of the great fund of knowledge potentially available, there was not time actually to write down an adequate answer. If you are *really* short of time, it is much more effective to complete your answer in note form, even if these notes are very brief.

Timing your examination work. Timing is most important. If you have five questions to do in three hours and they all carry equal marks, it is folly to spend an hour and a half on a single question. You can only earn twenty marks on that question even if you write for the whole three hours. The extra time spent on it will have gained you perhaps two extra marks, but at what a sacrifice! All the other questions will have to be skimped and you will probably end the examination in a fine nervous sweat. Divide your time into equal portions for each question after having allowed a little extra time for reading through the paper and for checking it afterwards. Be prepared to be a little flexible, but don't over-run your time by more than, say, ten minutes even on your best question.

Revision. Try not to leave all your revision until the last week. Start revising early, give adequate revision time to *all* your subjects and try to arrive at the examination room right at your peak. Writing answers to old examination questions is good practice. Try to get hold of as many old papers as you can and check which questions you can answer easily. Answer them. Then get the missing information so that you can answer the other questions.

APPENDIX II

EXAMINATION QUESTIONS

Business Organisation

1. When the great advantages of incorporation are considered why is it that there are still so many partnerships? [R.S.A. II

2. How far does the organisation of a retail co-operative society differ from that of a joint-stock company? [L.C.C.I.

3. Explain the principle of limited liability and discuss the effect of its application in commercial activities. [C.I.I.

4. "Public undertakings are managed in a variety of ways." Discuss this statement. [R.S.A. II

5. Explain the distinction between a public limited company and a private limited company and show how each may obtain its share capital. [C.I.I.

6. For what purposes and by what means do firms form horizontal combinations? Examine the disadvantages of this form of combine. [R.S.A. II

7. Critically examine the methods of controlling monopolies operative in the United Kingdom. [L.C.C.I.

Stocks and Shares

8. Jobbers, brokers, bulls and bears are all to be found in the London Stock Exchange. What do they do? [R.S.A. III, F

9. There are over fifty firms who are members of the Issuing Houses Association. What do these firms do? [R.S.A. III, F

10. What is meant by a "non-par-value share"? Why do some people call for the introduction of such shares in British companies and what are the objections to these shares? [L.C.C.I.

Money and banking

11. Describe the functions of the London money and capital market and the institutions which make it up. [C.L.C.

12. What are the disadvantages of barter? [C.C.A.T.

13. State what is meant by "crossing a cheque" and give examples of crossings. What rules apply to bankers when dealing with crossed cheques? [R.S.A. II

14. What is a bill of exchange? How are bills of exchange used in discharging debts incurred in the course of commerce? [C.I.I.

15. What do you consider to be the primary functions of commercial banks in Britain and what part do they play in the conduct of British internal and external trade? [R.S.A. III, F

16. What does a banker mean by *liquidity*, and why is it important to him? [R.S.A. III, F

17. Explain and discuss the working of the credit transfer system. [C.I.I.

18. How is credit "created" by the joint-stock banks? [C.C.A.T.

19. In what ways are the banks prevented from creating unlimited amounts of credit? [R.S.A. III, F

20. What is meant by saying that the Bank of England is the bankers' bank? What is the effect of the relationship on the work of the Bank of England and that of the joint-stock and commercial banks? [R.S.A. II

21. During 1962 special deposits were reduced from 3% to zero. What does this mean and what significance would this have for the business man? [R.S.A. III, F

The home trade

22. What do you consider to be the most important trends in retail selling today? What advantages and disadvantages may they have for the retailer and the consumer? [R.S.A. III, M

23. Account for the continued existence of the small retail trader in the face of strong competition from the large multiple and co-operative stores. [C.I.I.

24. What is a supermarket? Discuss its place in our system of retail trading. [C.I.I.

25. Why do some manufacturers sell their goods by means of wholesalers while others sell direct to the public? [R.S.A. II

26. What services does a large general wholesaler render in the distribution of manufactured goods? [C.C.A.T.

27. It is sometimes said that the middleman is a parasite. Discuss this statement. [C.L.C.

28. Distinguish between credit sale and hire-purchase transactions and examine some of the advantages and disadvantages to the consumer of these methods of acquiring goods. [C.L.C.

29. Consider the arguments for and against resale price maintenance. [L.C.C.I.

International trade

30. What are the forces which give rise to international trade? Discuss the essential conditions for a large volume of international trade. [R.S.A. II

31. By what means does a British exporter secure orders from foreign merchants? What help can he obtain from the Government in his work? [R.S.A. II

32. Attempt a definition of the following terms and show how they are inter-related: (*a*) Balance of trade. (*b*) Invisible exports and imports. (*c*) Balance of payments. [R.S.A. II

33. A customer in Belfast has ordered a quantity of cloth from a wholesaler in Manchester. What are the main documents which the wholesaler will have to use in connection with this transaction? [L.C.C.I.

34. Write an essay on the measures adopted by the Government in order to assist British exporters. [L.C.C.I.

35. Describe the principal functions of London commodity markets. To what extent have these markets useful commercial functions? [C.L.C., H.N.C.

36. Explain the difference between the "balance of trade" and the "balance of payments" and discuss the sigfincance of each. [C.I.I.

Advertising, transport and insurance

37. What are the functions of advertising? Do advertising costs increase the price of consumer goods? [C.I.I.

38. What is a consumer survey? State as concisely as you can:

(*a*) How such a survey may be made.
(*b*) The sort of information it is designed to provide.
(*c*) The use to which that information might be put.

[R.S.A. III, M

39. Your product has enjoyed excellent sales but is now declining. What data would you require in order to assess the position before taking steps to remedy matters? Give a check list of the main kinds of information you would need.

[R.S.A. III, M

40. What steps should a trader take when entering a new market? [C.I.I.

41. Give, with reasons, your opinion as to how far traders

should be free to choose whichever form of transport they may prefer for their goods, in Britain. [C.L.C.

42. Compare and contrast the competitive positions of (*a*) the railways, and (*b*) road hauliers, in connection with short- and long-distance carriage of goods. [L.C.C.I.

43. Discuss the factors that determine the choice of method of transport for goods of heavy bulk. [C.I.I.

44. Why do traders and manufacturers sometimes operate their own fleets of vehicles? [C.I.I.

45. Describe the services provided by coasters, tramps, tankers, cargo liners and liners. How do shippers arrange for the carriage of their exports or imports and how are freight charges determined? [R.S.A. II

46. Explain and illustrate the principles underlying contracts of insurance. [C.L.C., H.N.D.

47. Insurance against losses at sea is generally effected at "Lloyd's." Describe "Lloyd's" and outline the procedure for taking out a policy against the loss of a ship and its cargo. [R.S.A. II

Miscellaneous

48. Explain the forces that determine the price of a commodity. [C.I.I.

49. Write short notes on *three* of the following:

(*a*) Bill broker.
(*b*) Commission agent.
(*c*) Shipping agent.
(*d*) Stockbroker. [C.I.I.

50. Explain the relationship between industry and commerce and discuss the role of commerce in the modern world. [C.I.I.

51. Some types of business carry particularly large overheads. How does this influence their pricing policies? [L.C.C.I.

52. Write short notes on the following:

(*a*) A bank statement.
(*b*) N.E.D.C.
(*c*) A bill of lading.
(*d*) A C.I.F. price.
(*e*) A debenture. [C.L.C.

53. What do you understand by (*a*) "extractive industries" and (*b*) "direct services?" [C.C.A.T.

54. What are the main differences between a produce exchange and a stock company? [R.S.A. III, F

INDEX